Tropics Bound

Tropics Bound

Elizabeth's Seadogs on the Spanish Main

JAMES SEAY DEAN

To my sons, Christopher and Alexander

For a man to have lived he has to have planted a tree, raised a son, and built a boat
Portuguese proverb

First published 2010

The History Press
The Mill, Brimscombe Port
Stroud, Gloucestershire, GL5 2QG
www.thehistorypress.co.uk

British Library Cataloguing in Publication Data.
A catalogue record for this book is available from the British Library.

ISBN 978 0 7524 5096 4

Typesetting and origination by The History Press
Printed in Great Britain
Manufacturing managed by Jellyfish Print Solutions Ltd

CONTENTS

Sea-discoverers to new worlds have gone
John Donne, 'The Good Morrow', published 1633

—— ❧ ——

O my America! My new-found land
John Donne, 'To His Mistress Going to Bed', published 1633

—— ❧ ——

He that will sail without danger must never come upon the main sea
Seventeenth-century proverb

PREFACE

Tropics Bound recounts the largely forgotten English trade voyages to Latin America in the sixteenth and early seventeenth centuries, from the reign of Henry VIII to that of Charles I. Those voyages, nearly 100 of them – at least, those that were recorded – were made from about 1520 to 1620. The words of the Elizabethan seamen who sailed on those voyages provide vivid accounts of storms, leaky ships, broken masts, foul water and rotten meat, malaria and dysentery, Spanish gunfire, exotic fruits, Edenic forests and meadows, cargoes of hides, sugar and ginger, and sometimes pearls, silver and gold. They are tales told from the deck, from both the height of the quarterdeck and forward before the mast.

This is a seaman's book that chronicles 100 years of English voyages to the American tropics lying between Capricorn and Cancer. It pieces together what historians from Hakluyt to the present usually leave out: the sea passages themselves. It tells how critical the seizing of a Portuguese or Spanish pilot and his charts could be, and how essential it was to learn the currents, magnetic variation and the ways of hurricanes in the Caribbean. Beyond the ocean passages, this book limits time ashore to how far a ship's boat could navigate upriver with fresh water and enough powder and shot, or how far men could march for a few days through mangrove swamps on ship's biscuit, salt pork and tropical fruits. It documents how trading was often done at gunpoint or on a lonely beach at midnight. The book draws on sources from English and Spanish archives and includes mariners' journals, Admiralty depositions, letters and official reports. It includes details from the sailors themselves as they challenged Portuguese and Spanish rule in the name of God, England and Profit.

This account deals with what is important at sea. Sailors then, as now, wanted a sound, sea-kindly ship, well-provisioned with supplies, food and water, an experienced crew and captain, an able navigator, a profitable cargo, a healthy ship and a swift passage out and back. *Tropics Bound* is principally nautical history, not political history. It is a book that Captain John Smith or Henry Mainwaring would recognise; the sort of book in which the experience of Hawkyns, Ralegh and Drake is to be found. It deals with the practicalities of sixteenth-century voyaging to the tropics, of sailing there and back safely and profitably. At sea and on foreign shores, the politics of Whitehall and Seville were distant matters that had to give way to hurricanes, mosquitoes, enemy broadsides and dragging anchors.

These pages chart the Elizabethans' efforts to establish an England in the tropics, as told in the words of her seadogs. Research for this book benefited from a year as Visiting Fellow at Harris Manchester College, Oxford (2005–06) and earlier research fellowships at Exeter University and the University of East Anglia (2000–01). Behind the words are the volumes and manuscripts of English and American libraries: the Bodleian Library, Oxford; the British Library, London; The National Archives, Kew; the Wellcome Institute Library, London; the Library of the National Maritime Museum, Greenwich; the Chester Nimitz Library at the United States Naval Academy, Annapolis; the John Carter Brown Library, Providence; the Folger Shakespeare Library, and the Library of Congress, Washington.

Too many of the British and American popular history accounts and often even major museum exhibitions skip over those hundred years and argue the assumption of success forward from Jamestown in 1607 and Plymouth in 1620 – a Virgilian fallacy of manifest destiny. A few scholars know otherwise, those such as Sir Julian S. Corbett, Louis B. Wright, K.R. Andrews, I.A. Wright, Samuel Eliot Morison, D.B. Quinn, A.N. Ryan, James A. Williamson and J.H. Parry, and more recently, David Loades and N.A.M. Rodger. These historians paint with a broad brush in the context of the greater English colonial and naval expansion. A finer brush is that of the Hakluyt Society, which for many years has been publishing scores of texts of the accounts to the tropics, editions such as those of I.A. Wright, and continued in those of Kenneth R. Andrews and Joyce Lorimer. No one, however, has brought that detail to bear on the larger question of England's drive for a sun-drenched land of hope and glory.

Like the historians, biographers of the Elizabethan seadogs have painted detailed portraits of the main figures: the three generations of Hawkyns' through James A. Williamson and Harry Kelsey; Ralegh, by A.L. Rowse, Raleigh Trevelyan and Stephen Coote; Drake, by Harry Kelsey and John Sugden; Frobisher, by James McDermott; and Cumberland, by Richard T. Spence. Essential nautical considerations have been researched by D.W. Waters (navigation), Arthur Nelson and Ian Friel (naval ships, men and organisation), and J.J. Keevil (naval medicine).

Yet despite these excellent efforts, no one has written a maritime history seen through sailors' eyes that draws together these aspects of a century of early English voyages to the tropical Americas, and it is a story worth telling – a sea story of adventure, hardship and character; of a paradise lost and regained.

The Prudent Mariner

The reader of these Elizabethan voyages needs some local knowledge to pilot the waters safely. Tudor, Stuart and Continental texts have been silently modernised and made consistent for the sake of the reader, though the syntax, vocabulary and punctuation of the originals are largely kept. Scholars will find that the notes and bibliography can take them to original sources. In the interest of clarity and where several versions are treated together, notes are at times flagged at the start of a passage. Facts often differ according to the source. The Spanish, the Portuguese, the English and the French often see things in different ways. Generally, the Spanish account, written ashore and with more time, is more accurate and detailed than the English one, written in haste, at sea. Editor Hakluyt's telling is pressed by his own time and place, as in being most circumspect about Drake's circumnavigation, since England and Spain were at war when he was publishing his *Navigations*, first in 1589, then in 1598–1600. Similarly, Purchas' *Pilgrimes*, when published in 1625, appeared at the time England was beginning to expand its colonies into the Caribbean. In writing this book the author has chosen what he judges the most probable version of events. And, like any good navigator, the author finds course corrections welcome and essential, especially as new facts in this period come to light.

Then there is the matter of hours, days and years. A seaman measures time traditionally from noon to noon, not as the landsman, whose civil time begins the day at midnight. In this book the landsman's time is generally followed. Calendar dates from the English documents are given in Old Style (the Julian Calendar), and Spanish and Portuguese ones generally in New Style (Gregorian), which in this period moves Spanish dates ten days on from the English. The English did not adopt the NS calendar until 1752, the year it also made 1 January the start of the new year. Until then both 1 January and 25 March (Lady Day, the Feast of the Annunciation of the Blessed Virgin, a date close to the vernal equinox on 20 or 21 March) were variously observed as the year's beginning.

Measurements also differ in this period. Latitude (height) was commonly taken, longitude not so. To measure latitude first the astrolabe, then the jack-staff and back-staff were used. Minutes and seconds of latitude were of course then divided by sixty. Tons (as in the size of a ship) derived from the number of barrels (tuns) that could be carried in the hold. Different countries calculated tonnage differently. Distances were measured in leagues both at sea and on land. (One league is 3 nautical miles; 3.18M, nautical miles, are approximately one minute of latitude.) At sea, distance and heading were recorded on a traverse board, hence so many boards sailed. Barometric pressure was not yet measured (Toricelli's discoveries were in the 1640s). Beaufort's scheme of wind forces came in the nineteenth century. Depths were measured in fathoms by a sounding lead. (One fathom equals 6ft.) Though tide tables were well known in European waters, in the Caribbean there were none (a critical fact for Drake, Richard Hawkyns and Cumberland, even though the tidal range was not as great as in parts of England).

Ship types differ in this period from now. Brigantines, frigates, pinnaces, flyboats, galleys, shallops, galleons, caravels, carracks – these and more were something else to the Elizabethan sailor and were different still to the Spanish sailor. Whatever the country, piloting, navigational and sailing terms are now often obsolete (these are usually explained contextually). If not, or if the reader wants more, then he or she could consult the *OED* or the *Oxford Companion to Ships & the Sea*, Rogers' *Origins of Sea Terms*, Webb and Manton's *Yachtsman's Ten Language Dictionary*, or for often obsolete terms, Admiral Smyth's *Sailor's Word Book*. Ranks within fleets differ too. Some of the same titles are used on land as well as at sea. In this period the English call both the naval commander and his vessel the admiral, next in command (and vessel) the vice-admiral, then the rear admiral. Here, for clarity, Spanish ranks have been rendered the English way.

The matter of names is worth a mention. Ralegh was commonly the spelling for the name, though Raleigh, Raley and Gualterral, as the Spanish heard it, are variants. Similarly, Drake appears in Spanish as *el Draque*. Place names generally follow their present form, though names, such as 'Nueva España', have been preferred over New Spain or México. The 'Spanish Main', however, may also be called 'Tierra Firme'.

In the sixteenth and early seventeenth centuries the same vessel may be listed as having different tonnages. In this period measurement of tonnage varied from location, from England to Spain and Portugal (tons differed); the decade noted (as ships grew leaner their cargo capacity in tons decreased); and the purpose of the measurement (e.g. to inflate an investor's stake in a voyage). Originally a ship's burden indicated how many tuns (barrels) of wine she could carry. Later in the period, tonnage in England was calculated by multiplying length (in feet) by maximum beam, by the depth of the hold below the main deck, that sum divided by 100. The result was her tonnage, or tons burden (used for both merchant and warships). Such was Matthew Barker's Builder's Measurement (BM), the standard used from 1582 until 1652. This calculation allowed tons burden or net tonnage (cargo capacity) to be distinguished from gross tonnage (total internal volume of the vessel). Later still, displacement tonnage was applied to warships – the actual weight of ship, crew, stores, fuel, water that displaced that weight (volume) of the sea by the vessel. Merchant ships measured deadweight tonnage – the weight added to the ship (cargo, etc.) to bring her down to her waterline mark.

ACKNOWLEDGEMENTS

Tropics Bound first began years ago with the encouragement of Louis B. Wright, Director of the Folger Shakespeare Library, Washington. Since then, it has benefited from the judgement of the late Malcolm Robinson, Royal Navy, Brixham, Devon; Professor Barry Gough, Victoria, British Columbia; Professor Michael Duffy, Exeter University; and Dr James Casey, University of East Anglia; and the support of Dr Ralph Waller, Principal of Harris Manchester College, Oxford. There were summers with National Endowment for the Humanities fellowships at the John Carter Brown Library, Providence, Rhode Island; at Mystic Seaport, Mystic, Connecticut, and elsewhere; and many hours over the years at the Chester Nimitz Library, the Naval Academy, Annapolis, Maryland; the National Maritime Museum, Greenwich; the Bodleian Library, Oxford; the British Library and the Wellcome libraries, London. Shipwrights from Bristol working on Cabot's *Matthew* have had their say. US Naval Academy instructor Aubrey Smith taught me celestial navigation. Many sailing ship captains under whom I have served have shown me the way of a ship, including the late Ulrich Pruesse, Roger Ghys (co-author with me of another book) and captain of the *Mercator*, the Belgian training vessel, Captain James McDonald, US Coast Guard; and finally the late Captain Sloan Wilson, USCG and Captain Serge Yonov, US Navy. Nearly fifteen years of sailing the Caribbean and some eighteen years of summers and several years in Brazil (in part as a Fulbright Fellow) have brought a tropical perspective.

Especially valuable have been my editors, Camilla Turner in Victoria, British Columbia, and Simon Hamlet and others, most notably Christine McMorris and Abigail Wood, at The History Press, Stroud, measuring this text from trough to crest, to gauge what will make a book both pithy and pleasant for the reader. *Sailing*'s editor Wm F. Schanen, production manager Jane Farnham, graphic designers Stephanie Foelker and Brook Berth, and features editor Tim Gregoire, as well as John Lawson, former editor of *Anglia Afloat*, have brought the present beauty of sail to often dry hard tack. At the University of Wisconsin-Parkside, Dean of Arts & Sciences Donald Cress and photo/graphics manager Donald Lintner provided help. Librarian Sue Halloran, at Harris Manchester College, Oxford, showed me how to navigate the libraries of academe. Luso-Brazilian scholar, the late Professor Alexandrino Severino Vanderbilt, provided Luso-Brazilian matter. By sea and by land others have in their way seen this book through: in England are Sheila Robinson, Ian Gordon, Robin Wilshaw, Gerald Seymour and Clare Ford-Wille. In America, Maria Angélica Guimarães Lopes years ago heard the first thought. My first mate, Mary Zielke, who knows the feel of the Atlantic swell, has seen it at its end. Credit them and others for any felicities, the author for errors. He welcomes any corrections to the log, for as Plutarch (and the Hanseatic League) believed, *navigare necesse est, vivere non est necesse* (to sail is necessary, to live is not necessary).

TIMELINE

1516–17 **Sebastian Cabot** and **William Pert** sail to Hispaniola. These first English ships in the Caribbean are fired on by Spanish.

1530 **William Hawkyns the Elder** sails to Guinea and Brazil, trading ivory, pepper and brazilwood for English goods.

1531 **William Hawkyns** sails again to trade in Brazil, leaves Englishman in exchange for a Brazilian chief, who is presented to the English court at Whitehall and dines with Henry VIII.

1532 **William Hawkyns** makes third voyage to Brazil. Brazilian chief dies at sea. Profitable cargo in brazilwood. Sends other ships to Brazil in later years. Son **John Hawkyns** born 1532, and his relative, **Francis Drake**, born 1540. Southampton merchants expand Brazil trade.

1558 **Elizabeth Tudor**, on death of half-sister Mary, ascends English throne, returns England to Protestant faith. Their father, Henry VIII, had died in 1547, leaving the throne under a protectorate to Edward VI. On his death in 1553, the Crown had passed briefly to Lady Jane Grey, then to Catholic Mary Tudor, 1553–58. **Walter Ralegh** born *c.* 1552.

1562–63 **John Hawkyns** makes his first transatlantic voyage. Calls at Guinea, takes on slaves, 'black gold', then sells them and English goods to Spanish colonists in the Caribbean despite official Spanish prohibitions.

1564–65 **John Hawkyns** makes a second profitable slaving voyage to the Caribbean, similar to his first but now with royal support. Despite official embargoes, gets orders from Spanish colonists for more slaves and English goods.

1567–68 **John Hawkyns** and **Francis Drake** make a third slaving voyage to the Caribbean in six vessels, with royal support. Official Spanish resistance stiffens. Caught in storm, fleet seeks refuge in Nueva España's port of San Juan de Ulúa, loses four of six ships to the

Spanish: first important English-Spanish naval engagement in the Americas. Numerous voyages of reprisal follow.

1570 **Francis Drake** returns to Caribbean. 'El Draque' plunders Spanish settlements in voyages during 1571, 1572–73.

1577–80 **Francis Drake** transits the Strait of Magellan, raids Spain's Pacific ports, captures the *Cacafuego's* silver and gold, proclaims Nova Albion as English, seeks Northwest Passage, and returns to England by circumnavigating the globe westward, the second in history after Magellan's ship. Voyage yields great profit. Queen Elizabeth I knights Drake.

1582 **Richard Hakluyt** publishes *Divers Voyages*, rebukes the English for allowing the Spanish and Portuguese to colonise the Americas exclusively, and proposes an English settlement in Florida. In 1584, makes appeal to Crown for colonisation in *Discourse of Western Planting*.

1584 **Humphrey Gilbert** sails under first colonial letters patent to found a colony in the Americas. On return voyage, Gilbert in the *Squirrel* is lost at sea. Elizabeth I knights Ralegh and transfers Gilbert's patent to him.

1585 **Drake** commands royal fleet of more than two dozen ships and eight pinnaces to West Indies, sacks Puerto Rico, Santo Domingo and other ports. A prosperous voyage. **Ralegh** establishes English colony at Roanoke, Virginia – the doomed 'Lost Colony'.

1586 **George Clifford, 3rd Earl of Cumberland**, sails on the first of his twelve voyages, the first of three to the West Indies and South America.

1586–88 **Thomas Cavendish** circumnavigates the globe, third to do so after Magellan's voyage and Drake's. Raiding and piracy yield good profit.

1588 **Spanish Armada**, the ill-fated 'Enterprise of England', attempts invasion of England. Repulsed by English fleet led by Howard, Hawkyns, Drake, Grenville and others. Storm hits Spanish in North Sea. Hawkyns knighted.

1589 **Richard Hakluyt** publishes *Principall Navigations, Voiages and Discoveries of the English Nation*, first edition of England's maritime prose epic.

1591 Privateers, more than eleven in a year, prey on Spanish shipping in the West Indies. **Christopher Newport** leads first of nine profitable privateering voyages to the Caribbean.

1593 **Sir Richard Hawkyns**, son of Sir John Hawkyns, transits Strait of Magellan and sails into the Pacific, the Mar del Sur. His *Daintie* fights hard but is outgunned by Spanish fleet. After years in captivity, he is ransomed, 1609.

1594 **James Lancaster** sails to Brazil, fights Portuguese in Bahia, engages in 'trade at gunpoint'. In 1601 sails on 'nutmeg voyage' to the Spice Islands, fights the Dutch, returns with substantial profit. **Sir Robert Dudley**, courtier and later military engineer, sails for the Spanish Main, faces stiff opposition.

1595   **Sir Walter Ralegh** sails on his first transatlantic voyage to Orinoco River in Guiana, hoping the rumoured El Dorado will return him to Elizabeth's favour. Ralegh is the first Englishman to penetrate South American mainland and plant a colony, ten years after his failed colony in Virginia (Roanoke) and twelve years before Jamestown, second permanent North American settlement by English, 1607, after St John's, Newfoundland, in 1583. Sends subsequent expeditions to Guiana. Ralegh's Guiana is the first of more than a dozen English colonies on the South American main over next twenty years. Years 1595–96 the most important years for England in the tropical Americas.

1595–96   **Sir John Hawkyns** and **Sir Francis Drake**, co-commanders under Elizabeth I, sail in armada of twenty-seven ships, six of which are hers. Before attacking San Juan, Hawkyns falls ill, dies and is buried at sea. Drake takes command and is repulsed at San Juan. He sails for Nombre de Dios, fails to seize gold and silver. Fever spreads through fleet. In middle of night, Drake dons battle armour, becomes delirious and dies of the bloody flux (probably dysentery). Buried at sea in lead coffin off Portobelo. **Sir Thomas Baskerville** takes command. Fleet limps home, her greatest commanders, Hawkyns and Drake, lost to disease. Voyage a disaster.

1597   **Cumberland** makes the last of his twelve voyages (three to the Caribbean). Sacks San Juan, Puerto Rico. His chaplain on board, Dr Layfield, describes detailed symptoms fitting those that had killed Hawkyns and Drake.

1598–1600   **Hakluyt** publishes the second edition in three volumes of *The Principal Navigations, Voyages, Traffiques & Discoveries of the English Nation*. Affirms English maritime zeal, hardship, success in voyages worldwide. Draws attention to the Caribbean as England's as-yet-unfulfilled destiny.

1601–06   **David Middleton**, **William Parker** and many others sail to Spanish Main, Caribbean and Florida, and take profitable cargoes. **Charles Leigh** furthers Ralegh's Guiana. **William Turner** sails to Guiana, praises fertility of Caribbean islands. **John Wilson** reports sickness and death spreading in Guiana, while mariner/colonists increase in number on South American mainland and islands of the West Indies.

1603   **Queen Elizabeth** dies, **James I (James VI of Scotland)** accedes to English throne. Within four months, Ralegh is convicted of treason on dubious evidence and condemned to the Tower of London, remaining there for next fourteen years.

1604   Treaty of London signed, bringing official end to Anglo-Spanish War that began in 1585.

1607   Jamestown established in Chesapeake. Swampy site on James River breeds disease and dissention. Colony flounders, many die.

1608–11   **Robert Harcourt** sails to Guiana and Amazon. Prosperous colony, harmony with Indians.

1617–18   **Ralegh** released on parole from Tower in 1617 to sail for Guiana and bring back gold. Further proviso is not to antagonise Spanish. Contracts bloody flux, stays on board. Sends **Lawrence Keymis** ashore as commander. Ralegh's firebrand first-born, Wat, attacks Spanish at the San Thomé settlement on the Orinoco, is killed. Keymis commits suicide. On return to England, Ralegh, last of Elizabeth's great seadogs, is beheaded at the Tower, autumn 1618.

1620   Plimouth plantation, a religious undertaking by Protestant dissidents, founded in Massachusetts. After tenuous start, this colony becomes third permanent English colony in North America.

1623–38   Tropical English colonies established in West Indies, Gulf of México, Central and South America: at Somers Isles, on Bermuda, back in 1615 (outside tropical Americas); at Saint Christopher's (St Kitts), 1623; Barbados, 1627; Henrietta (off Colombia), 1627; Antigua, Barbuda and Redonda, 1632; Suriname, 1633; St Lucia, 1638; Eleuthera, 1647 or 1648; and later, Belize, Trinidad, St Vincent, Jamaica, the Virgin Islands, Dominica and others. James I dies in 1625; his son Charles I accedes throne. Samuel Purchas publishes *Purchas His Pilgrimes*, 1625, a sequel to Hakluyt's work. In Treaty of Paris, 1763, Louis XV cedes Canada and more to England in exchange for the French islands of Guadeloupe, Martinique and a few others rich in sugar.

INTRODUCTION

*W*arm waters, palm trees and gold drew Elizabethan sailors to the American tropics. For nearly a century before the nascent English colonies of St John's, Newfoundland (under Humphrey Gilbert's 1583 patent), Ralegh's lost Roanoke on the North Carolina coast (1585), Jamestown, Virginia (1607) and Plymouth, Massachusetts (1620), English mariners had been sailing to the Caribbean and to the shores of Central and South America to trade, to make war on the Spanish, and to colonise an England there. This book is a chronicle history (by date) of those sixteenth-century voyages. It is a salt-encrusted tale told by those early seamen.

The earliest voyages date from 1516–17, when the first English ship reached the West Indies and immediately faced Spanish gunfire. This chronicle extends to 1618, when Ralegh's *Destiny* returned to Guiana for gold and country, only for him to learn that his impetuous son Wat had been cut down by Spanish musket fire and his own hopes for a royal pardon were also cut off. Ralegh's beheading in 1618 ended the line of Elizabethan seadogs; one that had included two generations of the Ralegh family, three of the Hawkyns', three of the Drakes', Martin Frobisher and George Clifford, the Earl of Cumberland.

When, in autumn 1618, Ralegh laid his head on the block to be executed for treason, England's hope for a South American tropical empire also died. His paradise was lost. For 100 years the steamy dream of profit and pleasure had driven scores of ships westward to that warm band of the Americas, latitude 30° N to 30° S, long before permanent settlement in North America and English colonies in the Caribbean islands. That century from 1516 to 1618 was critical to later success. More than fourscore voyages made in those years produced a new world of seafaring history: trade, freedom, warfare, Nova Albion, palm trees and white sands, fetid swamps, Arawak remedies, fever, shipwreck, gold, tobacco, greed, Spanish broadsides, starvation, God and profit, England and St George.

All these experiences, prosperous or disastrous, prepared the English colonists for their eventual settlement in the early seventeenth century in the West Indies and along the eastern North American mainland.

What was this tropical America? The waters include those of the northern coast of South America, the Caribbean Sea and the Gulf of México, collectively known then as the Ocean Sea (Mar Oceano), the Atlantic (Mar del Norte), or simply the Northern Sea. Tropical America further includes the coast of South America south to around Rio de la Plata. The Pacific was then known as the Southern Sea or the Mar del Sur, southern because it seemed to lie to the south of Panamá. The lands of the tropical Americas include Florida, the Caribbean islands, Central America, the northern and eastern coastlines of South America, and Baja California. The Strait of Magellan and Tierra del Fuego figure as well. Though hardly tropical at latitude 52° S, that area was strategically important as part of England's dream for an empire in South America. Similarly, California at latitude 35° N to 40° N, claimed by Drake as Nova Albion for England while he was exploring for the Northwest Passage, was part of that dream.

What of commercial conquest? If Portugal had posted factors in its outposts in India, why could England not do so in the tropical Americas? Commerce sent both countries to sea. For a marginal country without adequate resources in money and manpower, it was a cheap means to profit. Supporting England's armies against France, then against Spain in Holland, had seriously drained the royal treasury, but with northern Europe's financial centre shifting to London in the 1550s, joint stock companies formed in the City could begin to undertake costly foreign enterprise. A few English merchants established themselves in Nueva España (the land and coasts of México) and in Brazil, but they typically had married into the Iberian cultures. Such arrangements were rare. Most companies wanted the vertical structure of ownership of land, production and transportation from raw to finished product. The vital links to profit were the ships and the men who sailed them. Despite coming late to tropical America to challenge the Spanish and Portuguese presumption of exclusive rights to the New World, the seafarers show in their words their determination to make at least some portion of the Caribbean English-speaking.

That century of voyages to the tropics of the Americas was England's first sustained transatlantic effort. The Tudor navies of Henry VII and much of Henry VIII's had stayed close to England or, at best, had engaged in European coastal trading ranging from Portugal to North Sea ports. But beginning in the second decade of the sixteenth century, merchant ships began to set their main course for tropical latitudes between 30° N and 30° S, and by the start of the seventeenth century, these ships carried back the first profitable cargoes from England's South American colonies along the banks of the Amazon and Orinoco rivers. While Jamestown was struggling to survive and Plymouth was still in the future, these tropical colonies were profitably exporting, if on a small scale, various woods, dyes, linen and tobacco.

English voyages to the American tropics chart the Elizabethans' illusions and later disillusion with establishing a presence there. Why did the dream of a tropical England along the Spanish Main die? The obvious answer is the dominance of Spain in the sixteenth century. She took over Portugal in 1580 and attempted the same with England in 1588. Relatively weak, England had to pick her conquests carefully. The highest priority was defence. Overseas ventures came a distant second. Why then set out on an uncertain sea? Three reasons: to reap a profit, to attack the Spanish (best done from a naval base) and to colonise.

The sailing route from Europe to the tropics was relatively easy – much easier, for instance, than attempting a north-east passage to Muscovy, as Stephen Borough had painfully learned in the 1550s. The tropical run was a much gentler path to riches. North Atlantic trade winds allowed ships to run south to the Canaries or the Cabo Verdes, then westward to the Caribbean or down to Brazil on a broad reach, which was a point of sail favoured by the vessels of the day. On the return passage, the Gulf Stream and the prevailing westerlies squeezed between the barometric pressure systems known as the Icelandic Low and the Azores High and, squirting through, carried ships homeward on yet another reach or run. The alternative was a direct course to North America via the higher latitudes, which meant beating into currents, wind, fog and occasionally ice. Beating to windward was the wrong way. Furthermore, a tropical passage meant good weather, as long as the captain kept an eye out for the Caribbean hurricane season from July to October.

Throughout the period 1520 to 1620, the Spanish and Portuguese authorities were hostile to any outsiders sailing into their New World ports, especially armed merchant ships, as nearly all were. Ralegh spoke for the merchant seamen when he said the nation that controls the seas controls trade, and that trade controls the world. But the American tropics were not England's domain in the sixteenth century, for the Spanish and Portuguese had command of those seas and of commerce. This century saw all that begin to change. Pax Britannia, ruling the waves and sailing the world's trade routes was to come later. Elizabeth's seadogs came first.

one

⸺❧⸺

BRAVE NEW WORLD, 1516–68

Whosoever commands the sea commands the trade; whosoever commands the trade of the world commands the riches of the world, and consequently the world itself.
                                    Sir Walter Ralegh, *History of the World*, 1614

he first English mariners reached the Caribbean in 1516, greeted by fiery Spanish cannon.[1] As the English ship bore into the harbour at Santo Domingo, Governor Francis de Tapia writes that he 'caused a tire of ordnance to be shot from the castle at the ship, for she bare in directly with the haven. When the Englishman saw this, they withdrew themselves out, and those that were in the shipboat, got themselves with all speed on shipboard.' The English sailed on to St John,

> and entering into the port of S. Germaine, the English men parled with those of the town, requiring victuals and things needful to furnish their ship, and complained of the inhabitants of the city of S. Domingo, saying that they came not to do any harm, but to trade and traffic for their money and merchandise. In this place they had certain victuals, and for recompense they gave and paid them with certain vessel of wrought tin and other things. And afterward they departed toward Europe.

The events are first recorded by a Spaniard, Gonsalvo de Oviedo, translated to Italian, then into English. Thus Richard Hakluyt, assiduous translator, editor and cleric, presents this first account of the English in the American tropics in his monumental *Principall Navigations, Voiages and Discoveries of the English Nation*, 1589, and its retitled sequel, *Principal Navigations*, 1598–1600. Who were these first Englishmen in the West Indies? Hakluyt reports that an English fleet commanded by Sir Thomas Pert and Sebastian Cabot had been sent by Henry VIII on a voyage of discovery to Brazil, Hispaniola and Puerto Rico. 'Fleet' or 'vessel' may, in translation, be one and the same and may be what Oviedo describes. Hakluyt roundly criticises Pert's 'cowardice and want of stomach' as well as his 'faint heart' for failing to bring back the 'infinite riches' of Perú to the Tower of London.[2] Hakluyt's successor, cleric Samuel Purchas, wrote in 1625 that Henry VIII had sent Sir Thomas Pert and Sebastian Cabot to sea with a fleet destined for the West Indies, and suggests the English ship that appeared at Hispaniola and other Caribbean islands the same year could have been part of Henry's fleet.[3]

For the next 100 years, the thrust and parry of this first English–Spanish encounter was to be repeated over and over again along the Spanish Main and throughout the Caribbean, compounding this story of trade, pillage and plunder, all for profit. As England hotly fought Spain in America's tropical waters, these battles were, above all, for wealth.

The issue was initially 'traffique', the word Hakluyt emblazons on the title page of his second edition. The emphasis, especially in the first two decades of the century, is on trade, not politics or religion. Henry VIII's break from Rome came only in 1534 and his subsequent excommunication in 1538. Before Columbus' discovery in 1492, England and Spain had signed the Treaty of Medina del Campo in 1489, recognising unfettered trade between the two countries. The discovery of the Americas changed all that. The Spanish Pope Alexander VI's Treaty of Tordesillas (1494), signed by João II of Portugal and Ferdinando II of Aragón, defined the newly discovered lands as either Portuguese or Spanish. Other countries were excluded. Thus to the Spanish, foreign voyages to the Americas, including those of England, violated the terms of that document.

That pivotal treaty gave to Portugal all lands east of a meridian 370 leagues west of the centre of the Cape Verde Islands, off the African coast in the Atlantic, and gave to Spain all lands west of that line. To settle João II's objection that Portuguese discoveries would not be recognised, especially Cabral's discovery of Brazil in 1500, Pope Julius II issued the papal bull *Ea quae* (1506), which moved the original meridian further westward. Two decades later, Portugal and Spain were again at odds, this time over the Oriental spice trade, specifically cloves from the Moluccas. The Portuguese paid the Spanish some 350,000 ducats and the two powers signed the Treaty of Saragossa (1529), which set the anti-meridian at 297½ leagues east of the Moluccas, making the spice trade a Portuguese affair.

To the English, even before England's break with Rome, all these treaties were a matter of popish presumption. Why should England herself not have the right to trade freely? If she could trade with Portugal and Spain in Europe, why not in Africa or the Indies? Furthermore, a paper treaty or a few stone pillars along Africa's coastline did not confer exclusive trading rights or sovereignty over these non-European areas. Only substantial occupation, exploitation and governance could do that.

Brazilian King Dines at Whitehall

In 1530, fourteen years after that first voyage to the West Indies, William Hawkyns the Elder set sail from Plymouth in his 250-ton *Paul* on the first of at least three voyages to Brazil. It was this William Hawkyns, senior member of the famous family of West Country merchant-shipowners, who started the profitable triangular trade route of England–Africa–America and round again to England. A contemporary of Henry VIII, Hawkyns (*c.* 1490/1500–1554), shared his king's belief that stalwart ships and profitable cargoes made for a strong country. His two sons, William (*c.* 1519–89) and John (*c.* 1532/33–95), eventually carried on and expanded the family business of merchant shipping. John, besides engaging in trade, also took on responsibilities as treasurer and later comptroller of the Royal Navy, gaining a knighthood in fighting the Spanish Armada. The second William Hawkyns also had a son, William (the third, *c.* 1560–1613), and John Hawkyns a son, Richard (1560–1622). Both John and his son Richard were knighted by the Crown. More than any other sixteenth-century family, these three generations of Hawkyns dominated Elizabethan maritime enterprise.[4]

All of the elder William Hawkyns' voyages – those of 1530, 1531, 1532 and probably others – were undertaken for trade, not plunder, and not dominion.[5] He sailed to Guinea on the west coast of Africa where he trafficked with the people there for elephants' teeth and other commodities and then sold these in Brazil, where 'he used there such discretion and behaved himself so wisely with those savage people that he grew into great familiarity and friendship with them'.

On his second voyage he brought back to England a Brazilian 'king', leaving behind in exchange one of his crew, a Plymouth man named Martin Cockeram. The Brazilian king, or chief, was presented to Henry VIII:

> lying as then at Whitehall: At the sight of whom the King and all the nobility did not a little marvel, and not without cause: For in his cheeks were holes made according to their savage manner, and therein small bones were planted, standing an inch out from the said holes, which in his own country was reputed for a great bravery. He had also another hole in his nether lip, wherein was set a precious stone about the bigness of a pease [a pea or lentil]. All his apparel, behaviour, and gesture, were very strange to the beholders.

This exotic spectacle in 1531 anticipated Martin Frobisher's return from the Arctic in 1576 with a captive Inuk, who was pleased to demonstrate his skill with his kayak in the River Avon before the amazed mayor and citizens of Bristol.[6] Such spectacles fired the English with a sea fever designed to fuel further investment in the Americas.

The Brazilian king stayed in England for nearly a year before Hawkyns set out with him back towards Brazil, but unfortunately, 'by change of air and alteration of diet, the said Savage king died at sea'. Hawkyns persuaded the Brazilians that his account was honest, and so they returned Martin Cockeram. Resuming his business in Brazil, Hawkyns saw his vessel 'freighted, and furnished with the commodities of the country', then weighed anchor and returned to England.

William Hawkyns the Elder apparently made other voyages. In a letter dated 1536 to the Lord Chancellor Thomas Cromwell, in which he asks for aid from the Crown, the style helps flesh out the man.[7] Hawkyns writes that at various times he had successfully ventured his ship and goods to bring back commodities from unknown countries. He explains that only because one of his pilots had lately 'miscarried by the way' is he now asking Cromwell to commend his request to the king:

> to have of His Grace's love four pieces of brass ordnance and a last of powder, upon such good sureties to restore the same at a day. And furthermore, that it may please His Grace, upon the surety of an hundred pound lands, to lend me £2,000 for the space of seven years towards the setting forth of three or four ships. And I doubt me not but in the meantime to do such feats of merchandise that it shall be to the King's great advantage in His Grace's custom.
> [Signed] Your most bounden orator, William Hawkyns of Plymouth.

Here was West Country enterprise, if verbose.

Records do not show that the Crown paid Hawkyns. The *Paul* apparently made another Africa–Brazil voyage, since Plymouth Customs Register shows that in October 1540 the ship returned to Plymouth with 'one hundredweight of elephants' teeth' and '92 tons of Brasil Wood'.[8] We have no knowledge of further voyages to Brazil by William Hawkyns.

An Englishman in México

Politics in Europe was changing shipping in the 1540s. The Anglo-French War (1543–46) brought English ships back to home waters. Overseas commerce gave way to privateering in the Channel. Profit could be found closer at hand, without the hazards of the long sea voyages. In 1554 Queen Mary married the Spanish royal, Philip, and two years later Philip became King of Spain.

During the shifting winds of succession in politics and religion, from the death of Henry VIII in 1547 to the accession of Elizabeth eleven years later, how fared these English mariners, the seadogs? When Elizabeth took the throne in 1558, John Hawkyns was about 26 and, though still a burgess and merchant of Plymouth, he moved to London that year. Francis Drake was then about 18 and Walter Ralegh a boy of about 5. These West Countrymen – Sir John Hawkyns, Sir Francis Drake and Sir Walter Ralegh – are the principals in this drama. There were others too who figure in the great account on the watery stage, including George Clifford, 3rd Earl of Cumberland, and ciphers such as Job Hortop.

In 1555 Catholic Mary had been on the English throne for two years and was to reign for another three. The English merchant Robert Tomson, from Andover, Hampshire, sailed in 1555 from Bristol on a three-year voyage, first to Spain and then to the American tropics.[9] Tomson's detailed account, printed decades later, shares several features of the episodic Elizabethan romances popular in the 1580s and 1590s: short on character but long on coincidence, fact and action. His fastidious notes cover the trade goods and their cost, the currencies in use, and commentary on the food, housing, work and religions of the Indians and the New World Spanish.

Tomson had left Bristol on his 'travail' with other local merchants in March 1555 in the 'good ship' *Barke Yong*. He stopped at Lisbon before continuing to Cádiz and on to Seville, where he sought out the house of an English merchant, John Field and his family, resident there a long time. Tomson lived with the Fields for a year, 'the one to learn the Castilian tongue, the other to see the orders of the country, and the customs of the people'.

Field, his family and Tomson embarked from Sanlúcar aboard a caravel owned by another Englishman, John Sweeting, whose daughter-in-law was Spanish. The captain of the caravel was Sweeting's son-in-law, Leonard Chilton. Still another English merchant was in their company: Ralph Sarre from Exeter. The caravel sailed to the Canaries, where ship and passengers waited eight months to join the Spanish fleet bound for Nueva España (México). The fleet of eight set out from the Canaries for the Indies in October. After a short thirty-two-day passage it made landfall on Hispaniola and entered the port of Santo Domingo, where they stayed sixteen days watering and reprovisioning.

Tomson and the Fields left Santo Domingo in early January 1556 for Nueva España. Twenty-four days out and 15 leagues from San Juan de Ulúa, the small but important port from which México shipped her treasures back to Spain, the fleet was struck by a tropical cyclone or hurricane. Tomson describes the event: 'There rose a storm of northerly winds, which came off from Terra Florida, which caused us to cast about into the sea again, for fear lest that night we should be cast upon the shore before day did break, and so put ourselves in danger of casting away.'

The wind and sea grew so foul and strong, he reports, that within two hours from the onset of the storm, their eight ships had been so dispersed they could no longer see one another. 'One of the ships of our company being of the burden of 500 ton called the *Hulk of Carion*, would not cast about to sea as we did, but went that night with the land, thinking in the morning to purchase the port of S. John de Ulúa, but missing the port went with the shore and was cast away.' Seventy-five men, women and children drowned. Sixty-four were saved.

The storm raged on for ten days 'with great might, boisterous winds, fogs and rain'. The vessel that the Fields and Tomson were on, 'being old and weak was so tossed, that she opened at the stern a fathom under water, and the best remedy we had was to stop it with beds and pilobiers [pillows?], and for fear of sinking we threw and lightened into the sea all the goods we had or could come by: But that would not serve'.

They cut away the mainmast and threw all their ordnance into the sea,

saving one piece, which early in a morning when we thought we should have sunk, we shot off, and as pleased God there was one of the ships of our company near unto us, which we saw not by means of the great fog, which hearing the sound of the piece, and understanding some of the company to be in great extremity, began to make towards us, and when they came within hearing of us, we desired them for the love of God to help to save us, for that we were all like to perish. They willed us to hoist our foresail, as much as we could and make towards them, for they would do their best to save us, and so we did. And we had no sooner hoisted our foresail, but there came a gale of wind and a piece of a sea, stroke in the foresail, and carried sail and mast all overboard, so that then we thought there was no hope of life.

In dire peril they prepared themselves for death:

And then we began to embrace one another, every man his friend, every wife her husband, and the children their fathers and mothers, committing our souls to Almighty God, thinking never to escape alive: Yet it pleased God in time of most need when all hope was past, to aid us with his helping hand, and caused the wind a little to cease, so that within two hours after, the other ship was able to come aboard us, and took into her with her boatman, woman and child, naked without hose or shoe upon many of our feet. I do remember that the last person that came out of the ship into the boat, was a woman black Moor, who leaping out of the ship into the boat with a young sucking child in her arms, leapt too short and fell into the sea, and was a good while under the water before the boat could come to rescue her, and with the spreading of her clothes rose above water again, and was caught by the coat and pulled into the boat having still her child under her arm, both of them half drowned, and yet her natural love towards her child would not let her let the child go. And when she came aboard the boat she held her child so fast under her arm still, that two men were scant able to get it out.

The crew, Tomson, the Fields and the other passengers abandoned the English caravel and her cargo, worth, writes Tomson, 4,000 ducats. On 16 April 1556, three days later, the fleet reached San Juan de Ulúa.

Tomson, a practical Protestant, writes that during the storm, in the night:

> there came upon the top of our main yard and main mast, a certain little light, much like unto the light of a little candle, which the Spaniards called the *Cuerpo santo*, and said it was S. Elmo, whom they take to be the advocate of sailors. At which sight the Spaniards fell down upon their knees and worshipped it, praying God and S. Elmo to cease the torment, and save them from the peril that they were in, with promising him that at their coming on land, they would repair unto his chapel, and there cause masses to be said, and other ceremonies to be done. The friars cast relics into the sea, to cause the sea to be still, and likewise said Gospels, with other crossings and ceremonies upon the sea to make the storm to cease, which (as they said) did much good to weaken the fury of the storm. But I could not perceive it, nor gave no credit to it, till it pleased God to send us the remedy and delivered us from the rage of the same, His Name be praised therefore.
>
> This light continued aboard our ship about three hours, flying from mast to mast, and from top to top: And sometime it would be in two or three places at once. I informed my self of learned men afterward what that light should be, and they said, that it was but a congelation of the wind and vapours of the sea congealed with the extremity of the weather, which flying in the wind, many times does chance to hit on the masts and shrouds of the ships that are at sea in foul weather. And in truth I do take it to be so: For that I have seen the like in other ships at sea, and in sundry ships at once. By this men may see how the Papists are given to believe and worship such vain things and toys, as God, to whom all honour does appertain, and in their need and necessities do let to call upon the living God, who is the giver of all good things.

Tomson's description is possibly the first English account of St Elmo's fire. That storm in April 1556 prefigures in an eerie way the one John Hawkyns was to encounter twelve years later: the same waters, off the same port, but in September, during hurricane season.

On arrival, crew and passengers were 'very naked and distressed of apparel, and all other things'. Field was met by an old Spanish acquaintance, Gonçalo Ruiz de Cordova, 'a very rich man'. But riches did not prevent the travellers from contracting an ague. Four of the eight in Field's party died. Tomson survived. He then recounts that being English and therefore presumed to be a 'Lutheran heretique' (though England, under Mary, in 1556 was Catholic), he was apprehended by authorities and transported back to Seville, where he lay in prison for three years.

Upon his release his fortunes improved dramatically – indeed, providentially. A Spaniard years before had gone to the Indies, writes Tomson, where he 'had got great sums of gold and silver, and with one only daughter shipped himself for to come for Spain, and by the way chanced to die, and gave all that he had unto his only daughter, whose name was Marie de la Barrera'. By good fortune, she and Tomson met in Seville:

> It was my chance to marry with her. The marriage was worth to me 2,500 pounds in bars of gold and silver, besides jewels of great price. This I thought good to speak of, to show the goodness of God to all them that put their trust in him, that I being brought out of the Indies, in such great misery and infamy to the world, should be provided at God's hand in one moment, of more than in all my life before I could attain unto by my own labour.

Such Godly fortune indeed.

Tomson describes San Juan de Ulúa in the 1550s:

> The port of S. John de Ulúa is a very little island low by the water side, the broadest or longest part thereof not above a bow shot over, and stands within two furlongs of the firm land. In my time there was but one house, and a little chapel to say mass in, in all the island: The side to the landwards is made by man's hands, with free-stone and gravel, and is four fathom deep down right, wherefore the great ships that come in there do ride so near the shore of the island, that you may come and go aland upon their beak noses. They use to put great chains of iron in at their hawsers, and an anchor to the landward, and all little enough to moor well their ships for fear of the northerly winds, which come off the coast of Florida, that sometimes have carried ships, and houses, and all away to the shore. The king was wont to have twenty great mighty Negroes, who did serve for nothing else, but only to repair the said island, where the foul weather doth hurt it. The nearby country is 'very plain ground'. A mile inland the woods are filled with red deer, which the sailors kill for food.

Nearby was the pestilent town of Vera Cruz. Tomson writes:

> In my time many of the mariners and officers of the ships did die with those diseases, there accustomed, and especially those that were not used to the country, nor knew the danger thereof, but would commonly go in the sun in the heat of the day, and did eat fruit of the country with much disorder, and especially gave themselves to women's company at their first coming: whereupon they were cast into a burning ague [gonorrhoea, not malaria], of the which few escape.

Slaving Voyages to the Caribbean

With John Hawkyns' three slaving voyages to the Caribbean, made in 1562–63, 1564–65 and 1567–68, trade came to be conducted at gunpoint. No longer could

English merchants book passage in English hulls sailing with Spanish *flotas* to the Americas to conduct traffique. On 17 November 1558, with the accession of Elizabeth to the throne, England returned to the Protestant faith, and Spanish resistance stiffened to English trade in the tropics. At the start of his 1562–63 voyage, Hawkyns may initially have believed that England could trade legitimately with Spain. He had proposed to the Spanish Crown, for example, that he could provide escort vessels to protect the Spanish *flotas* from attacks by French corsairs, an offer not surprisingly ignored. After his third voyage in 1568 it became clear that eventually there would be war with Spain.

In 1562 John Hawkyns was about 30 and, as J. A. Williamson sketches him, was

> genial, wary and alert, a good mixer, a man with a charm of manner who made friends, with common sense and give-and-take the basis of his dealings; and in the background he kept things of which he did not talk, the hidden springs of his actions. He liked good clothes, too, the fine material and brilliant colouring which then cost so much, and the golden chains and buttons that a man of spirit loved to flaunt. He was once, to his own undoing, mistaken for Sir Christopher Hatton, the greatest dandy of the court. All these are the externals of a character bred in the home of one of the principal sea captains in the west parts of England.

It was in 1588, while fighting the Spanish Armada, that John Hawkyns gained his knighthood and coat of arms, the latter's crest emblazoned with a demi-Moor bound in a cord. Selling slaves had indeed proved lucrative, but behind the velvet manners and silken profits, as Williamson observes, there was a

> sea-captain, skilled to conduct a difficult voyage, and also a shipmaster conversant with every detail of the handling and running of a ship. It is clear that he had ships and squadrons in the hollow of his hand. In crisis of storm or battle, this mastery made him the leader that all looked to ... In difficult land employments he was sometimes querulous and pessimistic. Amid the perennial difficulties and anxieties of the sea he was cheery and radiant of well-being.[10]

As treasurer of the navy, John Hawkyns introduced fast race-built ships with a new beam-to-length ratio of 3:1 and a stripped-down superstructure, their hulls sheathed in elm sealed with pitch and hair to deter the teredo worm, their topmasts fashioned to be lowered and stowed in heavy weather, and their sails cut flatter to allow sailing closer to the wind. These were practical innovations, considerations that mattered much at sea. His brother William was quite content to look after family business interests from behind a desk ashore in Plymouth, but John was more at home standing on a quarterdeck. He was cautious and diplomatic, a shrewd merchant mariner whose aim was to turn a profit at minimum risk.

He was also one who, when necessary, would take up arms against the sea of Spanish bureaucracy. Queen Mary, married to Philip II, had prohibited any African trade during her rule from 1553 to 1558.When the Portuguese royal line died out in 1580, Philip added the Portuguese crown to his Spanish one in a merger that instantly doubled his naval power.Yet despite overwhelming odds, the English continued to challenge the protectionist and xenophobic terms of the Treaty of Tordesillas and subsequent treaties, particularly as they applied to the new Spanish and Portuguese territories in the Americas.To the English, the arrangement was not fair.

Williamson explains that to help matters, in 1559 French and Spanish negotiators had agreed to 'lines of amity' at the Peace of Cateau (or Château) Cambrésis. These lines were the latitude of the Tropic of Cancer (latitude 23° 26' 22" N) and the longitude of the then prime meridian, which the negotiators set through El Hierro (Ferro) in the Canary Islands (longitude 17° 39' 46" W).The treaty was to be binding north and east of the two lines, and to the south and west; any breach was to be ignored. In reality there was no peace beyond the line.[11]

Responding to persistent attacks on treasure fleets returning from the Americas, and acting on the advice of Admiral Pedro Menéndez de Avilés, Philip II in 1566 formalised the existing transatlantic convoy system of the *flotas de Indias*. In the South Sea, Pacific Ocean, a similar system, the *galeón de Manila*, already protected Spanish ships on their scheduled runs between Manila and Acapulco.

The *flotas de Indias* were put under the direction of the Casa de Contratación, the House of Trade.Two annual *flotas* sailed from Spain. One sailed to Nueva España, into the Caribbean port of San Juan de Ulúa, where colonists received European goods and exported Aztec gold and silver in the *galeones*. The other delivered cargoes to Tierra Firme, into the port of Nombre de Dios in Panamá, from where other *galeones* took aboard gold and silver from Perú for export to Spain.The two return fleets assembled at La Havana for the return passage to Spain.The *flotas* kept a regular schedule, ever mindful of the hurricane season from July to October. Each fleet was initially accompanied by a single galleon of thirty-six guns, but later two galleons were assigned to protect the fleet from attack.

When John Hawkyns sailed with just a handful of vessels to the Caribbean in the 1560s, he was hoping to break into Spain's monopoly on commerce in the West Indies and along the Spanish Main. His intention at first, following his father's example, was to engage in legitimate trade with the Spanish. For that initial voyage in 1562–63, his outlay was modest.[12] He could have underwritten the entire cost himself, but by soliciting subscriptions from key people in London, he may well have been anticipating their support in future enterprises.Though the Portuguese *carreiras da Índia* had earlier established commerce between Lisbon and Goa and a profitable slave trade between Africa and Brazil, John Hawkyns was the first Englishman to augment his cargoes of manufactured goods, gold and ivory with African slaves – deemed 'black ivory' or 'black gold' – to work in the sugar fields of the Americas and the Caribbean.

For that first voyage, Hawkyns outfitted three vessels and possibly a fourth. Two were his own: the *Salomon*, 120 tons, commanded by himself; and the *Swallow*, 100 tons, commanded by Thomas Hampton, another Plymouth merchant. The bark *Jonas*, 40 tons, may also have been a Hawkyns vessel. The three totalled just 260 tons. The crew of fewer than 100 was drawn largely from Plymouth. It is likely that Hawkyns' second cousin, Francis Drake, then in his early twenties, signed on as an ordinary seaman but returned home from West Africa on an unnamed vessel.[13]

This first voyage in 1562, though a Plymouth-based enterprise on a small scale, nevertheless had Crown support. A joint royal and commercial venture such as this one generally drew up an indenture to show the obligations of the parties involved – in this case, the queen and merchants. The queen, at her cost, was to have the ship ready by a particular date, fully rigged and equipped with ordnance, munitions and boats, and was liable for any adventure or loss the vessel might encounter. Merchants, here at their own risk, were to victual the vessels, lade £5,000 of goods, provide seamen, pilots and gunners, and bear the cost of maintenance.

The fleet set sail from Plymouth in October 1562. It called at Tenerife, where John Hawkyns took on a Spanish pilot. In Sierra Leone he seized Portuguese ships and goods and took aboard some 300 slaves (the Portuguese claimed 900, the Spanish 400). Instead of sailing for Brazil, which had been his father's practice, Hawkyns set course for Hispaniola in the Caribbean.

Trade and trade winds figured in his decision. In the 1560s what is now Brazil was then two parts, called Maranhão in the north-east and Brazil in the south. Winds and currents fork westward or southward on reaching the coast at Cabo São Roque. In choosing not to follow his father's route south to Portuguese Brazil, but to sail for the Spanish Main and the Caribbean, Hawkyns was following the easier triangular sailing route that employs the trade winds: Europe–Canaries–Caribbean–Europe. Such a route offered more commercial opportunities, but it also directly challenged Spain's official prohibition against her colonials trading with foreigners by offering a commodity these colonists needed – slaves. Any legal scruples gave way to profit and practicality.

On this first voyage Hawkyns worked out a system that allowed him to trade with the Spanish in the West Indies. Dealing beyond the pale of Spanish law, he either paid large bribes or sold his slaves and merchandise for less, while still making a profit. In exchange for slaves, he took on gold, silver, pearls, hides and sugar. This trading was done outside the watch of the official eye of the Crown, in small seaports such as Hispaniola's La Isabela, Puerto de Plata and Monte Christi. With future business in mind, he would leave each port taking a testimonial of his good behaviour from the local Spanish officials.

Since the hides and sugar on this first voyage exceeded the 260 tons Hawkyns could carry in his vessels, he chartered two Spanish caravels in Hispaniola to carry the extra goods home. He loaded about 500 hides and two chests of sugar in the caravels. One of them, the *Sancto Amarco*, sailed for Lisbon. Once there, she and her goods were seized by the authorities. The other vessel sailed to Sanlúcar, the port for Seville, and that vessel and her goods were also impounded. Hawkyns' own ships left the West Indies and returned to Plymouth in August or September 1563. Despite the seizure of the two chartered ships and their cargoes, which were not especially valuable, the enterprise was a financial success. Hawkyns had conducted the voyage as a canny trader, operating effectively despite the Spanish monopoly. After expenses were met Elizabeth got a good return. Her portion, payable to the treasurer of the navy, was a sixth of the profit, or £1,000.[14] She and others in London were keen to invest in a second voyage.

After this first foray into the Caribbean market, however, the Spanish were alarmed at Hawkyns' plans for further voyages, and the *Audiencia* (Court of Justice) in Santo Domingo ordered the authorities to seize any English ships and their cargoes. It feared that Hispaniola would become an English colony unless such trading was stopped.

Cross of St George, Slaves, Bullion, Pearls

Two of Hawkyns' investors for his second voyage included his father-in-law Benjamin Gonson, treasurer of the navy, and William Winter, surveyor of the navy and master of the ordnance. To these Hawkyns added Sir William Garrard, Sir William Chester and Edward Castlyn, representing the City. Sir William Cecil, Lord Robert Dudley, 1st Earl of Leicester, and Lord Edward Clinton, the Lord High Admiral, among others, brought aboard Crown interests. For her part Elizabeth supplied one of her royal ships, the venerable 700-ton carrack *Jesus of Lubeck*. Her tonnage alone was two and half times that of Hawkyns' entire first fleet. At setting the *Jesus of Lubeck*'s value at £2,000, the queen had grossly over-valued her stake in the enterprise. Still, 700 tons of carrack was palpable proof of royal support.

The *Jesus of Lubeck* was a large Baltic trader bought in 1545 from the Hanseatic League as a relatively new ship by Henry VIII. Henry had been much taken by large ships, as evidenced by his pride, the warship *Great Harry*, but in the eleven years between his death and the accession of Elizabeth, the upkeep of the *Jesus* had been neglected. Furthermore, she had been built of green wood, a practice long used in ship construction, like during the 1490s with the building of Sebastian Cabot's caravel *Matthew*. By 1564 the *Jesus* was nearly twenty years old and not sound. She had already been granted a reprieve from being sent to the breakers. She was a stable, beamy vessel that maximised space over speed and strength,

well suited to trading in cold northern European waters but ill-suited to the hot
climate of the Caribbean. As sun and heat dried out planking, northern European
vessels in tropical waters required constant attention to the re-caulking of deck
and hull seams, and the coopers were kept busy keeping water casks intact.

A drawing of the *Jesus of Lubeck*[15] shows she had a high forecastle and poop,
good for defence, but the design added considerable windage that was a liability
in the lighter winds in the Caribbean. She was not weatherly. The high superstructure was offset by a comparatively deep draft – a problem in shoal waters.
She had four masts. On the fore and mainmasts she carried a course and topsail,
and on the mizzen and bonaventure mizzen a single lateen sail each. Her old-
fashioned high transom and centre-hung rudder mounted outboard on the flat
transom were typical of vessels of the 1540s.

Another consideration was her artillery. Her freeboard and beam allowed her
to carry some heavier ordnance above the waterline (four main cannon to starboard, four to port), with smaller guns on the upper decks. The *Jesus* also carried
eight cannon in her stern of smaller bore than her eight main guns. Two of those
were just above the waterline on either side of the rudder. Here lay a major
design fault. A high and flat transom weakened by eight gun ports meant that the
stern planking could, and certainly would, work in a heavy seaway. Such a transom was also not strong enough to withstand the stresses from the recoil when
her stern cannon fired. Precisely the same problem – the seams of the transom's
planking opening enough to allow a man's wrist through and for fish to swim
in and out – had afflicted Robert Tomson's vessel in 1555. Though she was the
admiral and flying the royal standard, the queen's venerable carrack was eventually to prove a liability.

The three other ships in this second voyage belonged to the Hawkyns family.
The *Salomon*, 130 tons, had sailed in Hawkyns' 1562 voyage. The *Tiger*, 50 tons,
was a small but heavily armed privateer that had already shown her worth in the
Channel. The third vessel was the *Swallow*, 30 tons (not the *Swallow* that sailed in
the first voyage). At over 910 tons, this fleet was more than three times larger than
his first one. The crew numbered 150 men and again included Francis Drake, as
ordinary seaman, on his first transatlantic passage.

Elizabeth issued Hawkyns his sailing instructions. He was to regard the fleet as
hers and he was to offer help to King Philip against French corsairs plaguing the
Spanish in the Caribbean. Hawkyns, as the queen's officer, was to sail under both
the Cross of St George and Elizabeth's royal standard. Clearly, this second voyage
carried political as well as commercial freight. Hawkyns thus owed two sorts of
duty, that to his queen and that to the customs officers.

The fleet of four vessels sailed from Plymouth on 18 October 1564, bound first
for Lower Guinea, as before. The wind was prosperous, but the start saw a bad
omen. John Sparke, a literate writer later twice Mayor of Plymouth, provides details:
'At which departing, in cutting the foresail, a marvellous misfortune happened to

one of the officers in the ship, who by the pulley of the sheet was slain out of hand, being a sorrowful beginning to them all.'[16] A late October storm drove Hawkyns into Ferrol, Galicia, for five days until the weather cleared.

At Sierra Leone Hawkyns took on ivory, gold and around 600 slaves. His four vessels weighed anchor on 29 January 1565 and set sail from Africa on a broad reach towards the West Indies.[17]

For over two weeks Hawkyns found himself becalmed in the doldrums,

> having now and then contrary winds, and some tornadoes, amongst the same calm, which happened to us very ill, being but reasonably watered, for so great a company of Negroes, and our selves, which pinched us all, and that which was worst, put us in such fear that many never thought to have reached to the Indies, without great death of Negroes, and of themselves: but the Almighty God, who never suffers his elect to perish, sent us the sixteenth of February, the ordinary breeze, which is the [north-east] wind, which never left us, till we came to an island of the Cannibals, called Dominica, where we arrived the ninth of March, upon a Saturday.

Landfall was a desolate beach with no freshwater springs but only puddles of rainwater, 'whereof we filled for our Negroes'. It had been a most troublesome forty-day passage. Being becalmed for more than two weeks made water and food (mainly beans) a major concern for the crew and slaves.[18] From Dominica he sailed SSW on a beam reach to La Margarita, the island off the Spanish Main famous for its pearls, then made for the headland of Cabo de la Vela, arriving there on 16 March. The Spanish viceroy in Santo Domingo had published orders that 'no man should traffic with us, but should resist us with all the force they could'. Hawkyns sailed on, and by 3 April reached Borburata on the Spanish Main.

Rowing ashore, John Hawkyns declared to the Spanish that he was English and that he 'came thither to trade with them'. They dutifully replied that the king had forbidden them to traffic with any foreign nation and warned him to depart. Hawkyns in turn stated that 'his necessity was such, as he might not so do: For being in one of the Queen's Armadas of England and having many soldiers in them, he had need both of some refreshing for them, and of victuals, and of money also, without the which he could not depart.' He declared that he would deal honestly with them, 'unless he were too rigorously dealt withall, which he hoped not to find at their hands, in that it should as well redound to their profit as his own, and also he thought they might do it without danger, because their princes were in amity one with another, and for our parts we had free traffic in Spain and Flanders, which are in his dominions, and therefore he knew no reason why he should not have the like in all his dominions'. Over and over again in his voyages to the Caribbean Hawkyns employed these reasons, at first with success but not so later on. For their part, the Spanish colonists wanted Hawkyns' slaves but feared punishment from the Crown.

The Spanish colonists 'made answer, that it lay not in them to give any licence, for that they had a governor to whom the government of those parts was committed, but if they would stay ten days, they would send to their governor who was threescore leagues off, and would return answer within the space appointed, of his mind'. Hawkyns did not wait for the governor's answer but sold off his slaves to the colonists, albeit at a cheaper price. That price was offset by a 7.5 per cent duty to the Crown instead of the official rate of 30 per cent. He still made a profit and, moreover, was paid in silver, not hides.

Onward he sailed to Curaçao but found no safe place to anchor there, despite the fine harbour on the south coast of the island:

> We had sour sauce, for by reason of our riding so open at sea, what with blasts whereby our anchors being aground, three at once came home, and also with contrary winds blowing, whereby for fear of the shore we were fain to haul off to have anchor-hold, sometimes a whole day and a night we turned up and down; and this happened not once, but half a dozen times in the space of our being there.

The *Jesus of Lubeck* and the other three ships ran westward past the island of Aruba to Río de la Hacha on the Spanish Main, where Hawkyns sold the rest of his cargo of wine, flour, biscuit, cloth, linens, clothing and 300 slaves in exchange for more Spanish gold and silver. He did not get payment for a debt owed him from Borburata but he did take orders at Río de la Hacha for more slaves and goods to be provided on his next voyage out, and obtained a letter from the Spanish treasurer attesting to his fair dealings.

His traffiques finished, Hawkyns spent some time surveying the coast and islands, and making charts of the area for his return. The *Jesus of Lubeck* set sail with the others on 31 May, their course north-east for Hispaniola. The passage north across the Caribbean was swift, but the landfall was not the one Hawkyns expected. These waters were new to him and the Caribbean Current had set him westward, missing first Hispaniola and then Jamaica. Hawkyns' ships, especially the *Jesus*, could not beat efficiently to weather, and his pilot did not know these waters well enough. Hawkyns was greatly disappointed to lose his chance to buy more hides, for there was room below in the ships' holds for more. The fleet rounded Cabo San António at the west end of Cuba and sailed along Cuba's north coast. Homeward bound, he called at Newfoundland, where he provisioned with fresh cod before making the Atlantic crossing.

Sparke, 'who went upon the same voyage, and wrote the same', concludes his tale: 'With a good large wind the twentieth of September we came to Padstow in Cornwall, God be thanked, in safety, with the loss of twenty persons in all the voyage, and with great profit to the venturers of the said voyage, and also to the whole realm, in bringing home both gold, silver, pearls and other jewels great store.' It had been a profitable eleven-month voyage, with only twenty of the original 150 men lost. Back in England, after her year under the hot tropical sun, the *Jesus of Lubeck* needed essential repairs costing £500, a quarter of her assessed value, before she could be sailed the following spring from Padstow up the English Channel and the Thames to Chatham.

On reaching Cornwall, though, Hawkyns left his ships and returned by land to London in the autumn of 1565. There he was invited to dinner by Don Guzmán de Silva, the Spanish ambassador. Silva enquired after the details of Hawkyns' most recent venture[19] and was to report to King Philip that Hawkyns' second voyage had yielded an enviable 60 per cent return.[20] More pointedly, the ambassador wanted a chance to fathom the character of this most troublesome Englishman. After their evening together he wrote back to Spain that the matter of Hawkyns 'needs decisive action'. He concluded by saying that 'it may be best to dissemble so as to capture and castigate him on the next voyage'. Early in 1566, Hawkyns again dined with Silva and had still other meetings with him. Hawkyns showed the ambassador his licences to prove he was an honest merchant and said he would not go to the Caribbean without the king's permission. Silva was not convinced. He advised his king 'to get this man out of the country, so that he may not teach others, for [the English] have good ships and are greedy folk with more liberty than is good for them'. Hawkyns then suggested to Silva, perhaps again to show he was an honest broker or perhaps on a quiet order from the queen, that he could serve the king of Spain by attacking the Turks in the Mediterranean. Months rolled by with no reply from Philip. None would ever come.

Before the year was out, Hawkyns despatched another fleet of four vessels to the Caribbean on 9 November 1566, for which he posted a £500 bond assuring the Crown that he would not go to the Caribbean or send his ships there. The sum was relatively small, and he knew it could well be offset by a profitable voyage. Hawkyns himself did not go but sent a relative, John Lovell, to lead the four ships, two of about 140 tons each, another of 80 tons and one of 40 tons; in sum, 400 tons of shipping. Francis Drake sailed with Lovell, again as ordinary seaman.

Lovell had local knowledge of the Caribbean but lacked Hawkyns' business acumen. His arrogance raised the hackles of the Spanish officials, and his ineptitude at selling slaves quietly made his voyage a loss, as the investors found when the cargo had been tallied on his return in September 1567. Thanks to John Lovell, official Spanish opposition to the English had hardened even more.

Hawkyns' Sorrowful Third Voyage

Hawkyns' third voyage left Plymouth on 2 October 1567 with two royal ships, the *Jesus of Lubeck* and the *Minion*, and four other vessels. The admiral, flying the Cross of St George and the queen's royal standard, led the fleet first for Guinea and then the West Indies, the same route as before.[21] Sailing again with Hawkyns was Francis Drake, this time in command of one of the smaller vessels, probably the 50-ton *Judith*.[22] Whereas on the first voyage John Hawkyns had sailed with a fleet of three and on the second, four, this voyage was made with six vessels in the hope of making an even bigger profit. Bad weather, bad fortune and stiff Spanish resistance were to dog them throughout.

In Guinea they watered and wooded, took on 400–500 slaves, and then set a westerly course on 3 February, 'continuing at the sea with a passage more hard than before'. After a long crossing of fifty-two days, the fleet reached Dominica on 27 March 1568. Despite the Spanish Crown's prohibition against traffic with foreigners, Hawkyns to this point had 'reasonable trade, and courteous entertainment, from the isle of Margarita unto Cartagena'. Hawkyns left Cartagena on 23 July, with the slaves and goods exchanged for gold, silver and jewels, according to his usual practice. It was not a moment too soon, for July was the start of the hurricane season, 'the time of their storms which then soon after began to reign, the which they call *furicanos*'.

The six ships rounded the west end of Cuba and were on course for Terra Florida, the name given to the area of North America south of the Chesapeake to México. On 12 August Hawkyns and his fleet met with

> an extreme storm which continued by the space of four days, which so beat the *Jesus*, that we cut down all her higher buildings, her rudder also was sore shaken, and with all was in so extreme a leak that we were rather upon the point to leave her then to keep her any longer, yet hoping to bring all to good pass, we sought the coast of Florida, where we found no place nor haven for our ships, because of the shallowness of the coast: thus being in greater despair, and taken with a new storm which continued another three days, we were enforced to take for our succor the port which serves the city of México called Saint John de Ulúa which stands in 19 degrees.[23]

It was hurricane season. August in the Caribbean generally has two to three hurricanes, September, four to five, or more than one a week.[24] The hull planking of the *Jesus*, working since the start of the voyage, was now leaking badly. Worse still, her rudder was disabled. Running for San Juan de Ulúa, Hawkyns captured three Spanish ships carrying 100 passengers, hoping that with these passengers he could better negotiate victuals for money and a quiet place to repair the fleet. On 16 September the English ships entered San Juan de Ulúa seeking refuge. Spanish officials, mistaking them for the fleet from Spain expected any day, came aboard. They were at first greatly dismayed but then relieved when Hawkyns let them know it was not pillage and plunder but only shelter and victuals he sought. He moored his ships at the port.

The next day, 17 September, Hawkyns and the English looked across the low island seaward in horror to see thirteen ships on the horizon. It was, by a most serious mischance, the *flota* from Spain. He sent word out in a boat to the Spanish admiral of the fleet that as an English fleet was already in the harbour the Spanish intended to enter, 'there should be some order of conditions pass between us for our own safe being there and maintenance of peace'.

Hawkyns describes this little refuge in much the same way Tomson had described it in the 1550s: as a poor port, but the only one along the coast, formed by an island of sand and shingle rising not 3ft above the water, two bow shots or more off the coast and just one bow shot, or half a mile, in length. The Spanish had built a wall on the island's lee side to which ships secured their mooring lines, setting their anchors ashore on the mainland. The moorage was so small that the English and Spanish fleets would both have to ride next to each other. Hawkyns, a seasoned commander, fully understood his vulnerable position:

> Here I began to bewail that which after followed, for now, said I, I am in two dangers, and forced to receive the one of them. That was, either I must have kept out the fleet from entering the port, the which with God's help I was very well able to do, or else suffer them to enter in with their accustomed treason, which they never fail to execute, where they may have opportunity, to compass it by any means: If I had kept them out, then had there been present shipwreck of all the fleet which amounted in value to six millions, which was in value of our money 180,000 pounds which I considered I was not able to answer, fearing [Her] Majesty's indignation in so weighty a matter. Thus with my self revolving the doubts, I thought rather better to abide the jut of the uncertainty, than the certainty.

Unknown to Hawkyns, the fleet of thirteen ships was bringing the viceroy of Nueva España, Don Martín Enríquez, to take up his new post. Leading the Spanish fleet was none other than Admiral Álvaro de Bazán (Baçan or Bacán), the officer who had destroyed the English fleet at Gibraltar and who was now under orders from Philip II to seek out and destroy Hawkyns and his ships. He was there to teach the English a lesson, as Ambassador Silva had advised the king the year before.

The English and the Spanish spent the weekend negotiating, and on Monday, with hostages exchanged, the Spanish ships were allowed to enter San Juan de Ulúa. The fleets saluted each other with cannon, 'as the manner of the sea doth require'. As Hawkyns writes: 'We laboured two days placing the English ships by themselves and the Spanish ships by themselves, the captains of each part and inferior men of their parts promising great amity of all sides: Which even as with all fidelity it was meant on our part, so the Spaniards meant nothing less on their parts.'

But on the mainland, the Spanish had secretly assembled 1,000 men and were planning to attack the English on the following Thursday at midday, while the English were at dinner. As the Spanish saw it, they had caught the English red-handed, poaching in Spanish waters.[25] To punish them for flouting the law, Viceroy Enríquez recorded in a deposition that once moored inside the harbour, the Spanish had met to 'determine ways and means to seize and punish [Hawkyns] and eject him from the island'. Enríquez laid out the plan. At about eleven on Thursday morning a large hulk should be brought up between the English and Spanish flagships. Hidden below would be 150 men armed with harquebuses, targets and other weapons. When the hulk was close enough to board, the general in charge should make a signal to the viceroy, who aboard the flagship would order a trumpet blown. At which signal Captain António Delgadillo with men from Vera Cruz, on one hand, and Captain Pedro de Yerba with men from the same town, on another, should assault the island and take the forts and artillery which the English had in them, trained on the fleet; and that forces from the fleet should come up in boats to reinforce the island and the hulk, 'and in this manner and in this order the enemy and his fleet and the island should be seized'.

Wednesday night, under the cover of darkness, the 150 men went aboard the hulk, and the next morning the general and admiral joined them to lay the hulk alongside the *Minion* in preparation for boarding. Hawkyns gives us his account of events:

> Yet we being not satisfied with this answer [Viceroy Enríquez's assurances of peace], because we suspected a great number of men to be hid in a great ship of 900 tons, which was moored next unto the *Minion*, sent again to the Viceroy the master of the *Jesus* which had the Spanish tongue, and required to be satisfied if any such thing were or not. The Viceroy now seeing that the treason must be discovered, forthwith stayed our master, blew the Trumpet, and of all sides set upon us: Our men which were ashore being stricken with sudden fear, gave place, fled, and sought to recover succour of the ships.

The Spaniards came ashore in great number, 'and slew all our men ashore without mercy, a few of them escaped aboard the *Jesus*'.[26]

According to the viceroy, Admiral Bazán had given the signal early, and under cover of their artillery the English were able to withdraw the *Minion* and a shallop, taking most of their goods and cargo, so the soldiers from the hulk were unable to board. Those vessels retired half a league from port, leaving behind the *Jesus of Lubeck* and four other vessels.[27]

Hawkyns writes that 300 men in the hulk fell onto the *Minion*, but 'by God's appointment' in half an hour's time the *Minion* released her headfasts, hauled away by her sternfasts, and got away, though at the cost of many men.[28] The Spanish then attempted to board the *Jesus*. Again the crew 'with very much ado and the loss of many of our men were defended and kept out'. Two other ships assaulted the *Jesus* at the same time, but the English again were able to cut the headfasts and haul on the sternfasts. 'Now when the *Jesus* and the *Minion* were gotten about two ships' lengths from the Spanish fleet, the fight began so hot on all sides that within one hour the Admiral of the Spaniards was supposed to be sunk, their Vice-admiral burned and one other of their principal ships supposed to be sunk, so that the ships were little able to annoy us.'

By then all the ordnance on the island was in Spanish hands, and Spanish gunners turned their cannon on the English, sank the smaller ships, and cut away the masts and yards of the *Jesus* so that there was no chance of carrying her away. Writes Hawkyns, 'we determined to place the *Jesus* on that side of the *Minion*, that she might abide all the battery from the land, and so be a defence for the *Minion* till night, and then to take such relief of victual and other necessaries from the *Jesus*, as the time would suffer us, and to leave her'. No sooner had Hawkyns moored the *Minion* out of the range of the cannon, than the Spanish sent two fire ships down onto the English. He writes:

Having no means to avoid the fire, it bred among our men a marvellous fear, so that some said, let us depart with the *Minion*, others said, let us see whither the wind will carry the fire from us. But to be short, the *Minion*'s men which had always their sails in a readiness, thought to make sure work, and so without either consent of the captain or master cut their sail, so that very hardly I was received into the *Minion*.

The crew left in the *Jesus* took to a small boat to follow the *Minion*, leaving many behind, Hawkyns writes, 'to abide the mercy of the Spaniards (which I doubt was very little) so with the *Minion* only and the *Judith* (a small bark of 50 tons) we escaped, which bark [commanded by Drake] the same night forsook us in our great misery: We were now removed with the *Minion* from the Spanish ships two bow-shoots, and there rode all that night'. The next morning they recovered an island a mile off from the Spaniards. The wind was northerly, and now with only two anchors and two cables (having lost two anchors and three cables in the battle), writes Hawkyns, 'we thought always upon death which ever was present, but God preserved us to a longer time'. Francis Drake, captain of the *Judith*, had sailed off in the night, leaving Hawkyns on his own in the *Minion* – a vessel of

less than 100 tons, greatly overcrowded, with little water and food and in great
distress. Francisco de Bustamente, royal lieutenant-treasurer from Vera Cruz, con-
firms the details.[29] He writes that the English ships had withdrawn under cover
of darkness outside the harbour, and during the night, very fortunately for the
English, 'the wind shifted to north and the north wind blew Friday and Saturday
following', so the Spanish ships could not follow.

The wind continued northerly, keeping the Spanish from leaving harbour
and pursuing the English. September winds near San Juan de Ulúa are typically
north-east to northerly and of reasonable strength, but during that September of
1568, the English and Spanish found themselves on the left (west) side of a major
tropical cyclone or hurricane, hence the powerful northerlies.[30] Hawkyns writes:

> The weather waxed reasonable, and the Saturday we set sail, and having a great
> number of men and little victuals our hope of life waxed less and less: Some
> desired to yield to the Spaniards, some rather desired to obtain a place where
> they might give themselves to the infidels, and some had rather abide with
> a little pittance to mercy of God at sea: So thus with many sorrowful hearts
> we wandered in an unknown sea by the space of fourteen days, till hunger
> enforced us to seek the land, for hides were thought very good meat, rats, cats,
> mice and dogs, none escaped that might be gotten, parrots and monkeys that
> were had in great price, were thought there very profitable if they served the
> turn one dinner.[31]

On 8 October they found themselves off the coast of Tamaulipas (about halfway
up the west coast of the Gulf of México, latitude 23° 30' N) where they hoped to
find help, victuals and a place to repair the *Minion*:

> [She was] so sore beaten with shot from our enemies and bruised with shoot-
> ing off our own ordinance, that our weary and weak arms were scarce able to
> defend and keep out water. But all things happened to the contrary, for we
> found neither people, victual, nor haven of relief, but a place where having fair
> weather with some peril we might land a boat: Our people being forced with
> hunger desired to be set on land, whereunto I consented.

Volunteers disembarked to take their chances on shore. 'And such as were willing
to land I put them apart, and such as were desirous to go homewards, I put apart,
so that they were indifferently parted a hundred of one side and a hundred of
the other side: these hundred men we set aland' to take in water. As for victuals,
only the most meagre of rations were aboard, and ashore, as Hawkyns recorded:
the sailors found 'neither people, victual, nor haven of relief'. The next day, when
Hawkyns was ashore with fifty of the remaining men filling water casks, another
storm hit the coast. For three days he and his shore party were stranded on the

beach, only able to watch the *Minion* pitching and rolling at anchor out in the roadstead. She was 'in such peril that every hour we looked for shipwreck'.

On 16 October, finally watered and provisioned as best as could be, Hawkyns set sail with those who had voted to return to England. The *Minion* sailed eastward through the Florida Straits and by 16 November had reached the Atlantic. Most of the men who had elected to go ashore ended up in local prisons. A few, such as Miles Phillips and Job Hortop, returned to England only after many years of misfortune. The newly appointed viceroy in Nueva España was at first hospitable to the castaways, but when the Inquisition came there in 1571, any English were hunted down, tortured, imprisoned, lashed naked, made to wear the penitent's garb, the San Benito, and burned at the stake. The few lucky ones were condemned for life, chained to the benches in the galleys.

For the *Minion* in the Atlantic foul weather followed fair, and food and water again became scarce. 'Growing near to the cold country', Hawkyns writes, 'our men being oppressed with famine, died continually, and they that were left, grew into such weakness that we were scantly able to manage our ship, and the wind being always ill for us to recover England, we determined to go with Galicia in Spain, with intent there to relieve our company and other extreme wants'. On 31 December 1568 the *Minion* reached Pontevedra, north of Vigo. There, writes Hawkyns, 'our men with excess of fresh meat grew into miserable diseases, and died a great part of them'.[32]

To keep the Spanish from learning just how weak his men were, Hawkyns did not give his crew shore leave. Still, he writes, 'our feebleness was known to them. Whereupon they ceased not to seek by all means to betray us.' He quickly left and sailed to nearby Vigo, where English ships provided him with twelve fresh crew and he was able to make repairs and reprovision victuals. On 20 January 1569 the *Minion* sailed north for England, arriving at Mount's Bay, Cornwall, five days later. 'Praised be God therefore', writes Hawkyns, 'if all the miseries and troublesome affairs of this sorrowful voyage should be perfectly and thoroughly written, there should need a painful man with his pen, and as great a time as he had that wrote the lives and deaths of the martyrs'. His third voyage had been a disaster, and for decades to come the year 1568 meant to the English sailor the Spanish perfidy at San Juan de Ulúa.

Francis Drake, in the faster and smaller *Judith*, had arrived back in Plymouth in December, nearly a month earlier. The year 1568 was to hound Drake for years to come. In the heat of battle and in his first command, young Drake had cut his cables and beat a fast retreat in the *Judith*, deserting his commander, mentor and kin. John Hawkyns had been left behind in the grossly overloaded and underprovisioned *Minion*.

This troublesome voyage, costing lives and cargo, also cost three vessels. The Spanish took Elizabeth's *Jesus of Lubeck* and two others, along with great quantities of silver and gold and brass cannon. To the English, San Juan de Ulúa was a piece of foul treachery to be revenged. Drake was to grow into the feared 'el Draque' who again and again would take his revenge upon the Spanish through-out the Caribbean. The storm swell of that tropical *furicano* through the Gulf of México in September 1568 was felt not only throughout the West Indies but ultimately on English beaches. Within twenty years, the long undeclared war that had smouldered for decades was to see open hostilities between England and Spain in 1585, when Elizabeth aided the Dutch Protestants and Drake's fleet rav-aged the Caribbean, and war was to break out into full flame in 1588 when Spain sent her Armada to invade England.

two

———— ✦✦✦ ————

STORM SWELL, 1569–76

We are as near to Heaven by sea as by land!
     Sir Humphrey Gilbert aboard the *Squirrel*, lost at sea, North Atlantic, 1583

Though pillage and plunder in Panamá and along the Spanish Main had been common, Nueva España to the north was a different story. Henry Hawks, like Robert Tomson in the 1550s, was an English merchant with strong Spanish ties. Hawks sailed in a Spanish hull to Nueva España, the land and coasts of México, in the 1560s and, according to Hakluyt, lived there for five years sometime before 1572. His account provides not only a merchant's perspective on profit but also on daily life in that land during those years. Hawks notes, for example, that after the battle in 1568, San Juan de Ulúa strengthened its defences, the shipyards on the Pacific coast at Culiacán were building seagoing vessels, and the Acapulco–Manila silk trade across the Mare Española was thriving.[1]

Despite their power, Spanish colonial authorities remained uneasy. At Nombre de Dios on 30 June 1569, they once again petitioned Spain for defence against foreign intruders.[2] Runaway black slaves were continuing to attack their former masters throughout Panamá, and from the coastal port of Ciudad de Panamá on 27 March 1570, Licentiate Carasa writes to the Spanish Crown that urgent action is needed to disperse these Cimarróns, renegades he calls 'black outlaws in rebellion' who are considered a 'great evil' to the country. One transgression is that they 'frequently carried off negresses at work washing clothes in the rivers from which the towns get their supply of water'.[3]

Ever more audacious, the English increased their pressure on the Spanish. Around February 1571 an English ship met a Spanish frigate off Nombre de Dios.[4] Just off the Caribbean coast, the English captain invited his Spanish counterpart to come and talk. 'We are surprised that you ran from us in that fashion', he said, noting that the Spanish would not talk under a flag of truce. 'And since you will not come courteously to talk with us, without evil or damage, you will find your frigate spoiled by your own fault.' On 1 March 1571 the widow Doña Juana de Estrada and Luis de Soto gave depositions in Nombre de Dios concerning pirates.[5] She and her husband Diego de Azevedo, a councillor in the *Audiencia* of Santo Domingo, had sailed from their home in Hispaniola bound for Nombre de Dios in company with Soto and others. At the Río Chagres on 21 February, they were attacked by French and English corsairs. Her husband and the others held off the attackers for three hours, using only rocks and two swords, but their vessel was taken. The corsairs shot Azevedo through the brows with an arrow, and he died within an hour. Another dozen aboard were either killed or wounded.

On 25 May 1571 the officials of the Ciudad de Panamá wrote to the Crown about their 'existing grave need' for defence, reminding them that their city was rich, as it handled 'all the gold, silver and pearls of Potosí, Chile and the rest of Perú, for shipment to Spain'. Their report says such wealth gives courage to English and French corsairs, 'many of them Lutherans, enemies of the holy Catholic faith', and that so bad are the depredations that 'traffic dares not sail from Santo Domingo thither, and trade and commerce are diminishing between the Windward Islands and this Main'.[6]

Drake's Caribbean Voyage

The English had most certainly not forgotten the massacre at San Juan de Ulúa in 1568. Four years later, in 1572, after two exploratory voyages in 1570 and 1571, Drake returned to the Caribbean with two ships and a crew of fifty-two.

Besides Hakluyt's account, this voyage was later colourfully documented in a pamphlet published in 1628 by his nephew, a latter Sir Francis Drake, who claims that the manuscript was reviewed by Drake before his death in early 1596.[7] It is a patriotic piece, puffed with bombast: *Sir Francis Drake Revived: Calling upon this Dull or Effeminate Age to follow his Noble steps for Gold and Silver.* The principal author was the preacher Philip Nichols, but others who were also on the voyage contributed too. This no doubt fanciful piece, together with the factual Spanish documents and the 1586 account by the Portuguese pilot Lopez Vaz, fill in the story.[8] *Drake Revived* reminds England of her earlier days of glory on the seas. In the affected Euphuistic style perpetuated from the 1580s, preacher Nichols begins this way: 'I have thought it necessary myself, as in a *Card*, to prick the principal points of the Counsels taken, attempts made, and success had, during the whole course of my employment in these services against the Spaniards, not as setting sail, for maintaining my reputation in men's judgement, but only as sitting at helm if occasion shall be, for conducting the like actions hereafter.'

On the evening of 24 May 1572, Drake, with five voyages to the Caribbean already under his keel, sailed from Plymouth with two ships, the admiral, *Pascoe*, 70 tons, a Hawkyns vessel commanded by Drake, and as vice-admiral the *Swan*, 25 tons, commanded by his brother, John Drake. The volunteer crew totalled seventy-three men and boys, forty-seven in the *Pascoe* and twenty-six in the *Swan*. Both vessels were 'richly furnished, with victuals and apparel for a whole year'. They were also both heavily armed and carried knocked down in the hold 'three dainty pinnaces', to be assembled once in the Caribbean.

Drake made a fast passage, reaching first Madeira and then the Canaries within two weeks. From there across the Atlantic, he says, 'we never struck sail, nor came to anchor, nor made any stay for any cause, neither there nor elsewhere, until twenty-five days after, when we had sight of the island of Guadeloupe [on 28 June], one of the islands of the West Indies, goodly high land'. On 29 June they landed, refreshed essential supplies, and on the afternoon of 1 July sailed for the Spanish Main. Drake reached Port Pheasant, on the Acla coast, on 12 July. Its narrow entrance was just half a cable or 360ft wide[9] and was flanked by two high hills, an ideal harbour. Inside was a bay perhaps 8 or 10 cables across, with depths of 10 or 12 fathoms. Fish were plentiful and the soil fruitful.

As the vessels made their way in, Drake saw smoke rising from a tree along the wooded shore. Armed and wary, the men landed. Nearby, Drake found a warning scratched onto a lead plate nailed to a tree by John Garret, a Plymouth man who had sailed there with him the year before: 'Captain Drake, if you fortune to come to this port make hast away, for the Spaniards which you had with you here the last year have betrayed this place, and taken away all that you left here. I departed from hence, this present 7 of July, 1572. Your very loving friend John Garret.' Garret had put up the warning and left just five days before Drake arrived, and the signal fire had been burning since then. Despite Garret's warning, Drake decided to stay at Port Pheasant at least long enough to reprovision, build a fort and assemble his pinnaces. While Drake's men were hard at work on the fort and pinnaces, a bark, a carvel and a shallop appeared on 13 July. The bark was English, from the Isle of Wight, with James Raunse, captain, and John Overy, master. The other two were Spanish prizes. Together, Drake and Raunse's men numbered 103 when the fleet sailed for Nombre de Dios.

Drake left Raunse at Isla de Piños and took three pinnaces and the shallop, heavily armed, their combined force of seventy-three men equipped with six firepikes, twelve pikes, six targets, twenty-four muskets and calivers, sixteen bows, six partizans, two drums and two trumpets. He reached Isla de Cativás, near Portobelo, landed his men, drilled them, re-embarked, and at sunset anchored within 2 leagues of the Río Francisco, still undetected by the Spanish. That night, with muffled oars, they rowed into the harbour. Just then, a Spanish vessel laden with Canary wines and other cargo sailed into the bay. She had not yet furled her sprit-sail when she spied four intruders – an alarming number – rowing into the harbour. Drake forced her *gundelo* to the far side of the harbour, landed his men and took over an artillery platform. The lone gunner fled for town to give the alarm. When the moon rose at three that morning, Drake told his men it was dawn and time to attack. John Drake and John Oxnam with sixteen men attacked from the east, and by the light of the moon and the firepikes, Drake's forces marched up the broad street into the marketplace of the town. The locals, he reported, 'stood amazed at so strange a sight, marvelling what the matter might be and imagining, by reason of our drums and trumpets sounding in so sundry places, that we had been a far greater number then we were'.

The townspeople (not soldiers, for at the time they had no garrison there) had hung lines with lighted matches to make it seem like there were very many of them ready to shoot, 'whereas indeed there was not past two or three that taught these lines to dance'. Once the English discovered the ruse, most of the citizens fled as Drake 'feathered them' with arrows. These were special arrows made in England, 'not great sheaf arrows, but fine roving shafts, very carefully reserved for the service'. They continued the attack with firepikes and short weapons and in short order thrashed the Spanish 'gallants' with their musket butts.

Drake came to the governor's house, according to Nichols, where he found the great door open, a candle lit at the top of the stairs, and a 'fair jennet ready saddled either for the governor himself, or some other of his household to carry it after him'. Through the doorway, by means of this light, up the stairs, Drake recalls that he 'saw a huge heap of silver in that nether room: Being a pile of bars of silver, of (as near as we could guess) seventy foot in length, of ten foot in breadth, and twelve foot in height, piled up against the wall. Each bar was between thirty-five and forty pound in weight.' At the treasurehouse by the waterside, the English found more jewels and gold than their four vessels could carry, writes Nichols. But was this really so? Drake was there in July. The galleons had left with the treasure weeks before, and the next armada was not due until the following January. There was no treasure.

At some point in the skirmish, Francis Drake was struck in the leg by a musket ball. According to Nichols:

> [Drake's] strength and sight and speech failed him, and he began to faint for want of blood, which as then we perceived, had in great quantity issued upon the sand out of a wound received in his leg in the first encounter … the blood having first filled the very prints which our foot-steps made, to the great dismay of all our company, who thought it not credible that one man should be able to spare so much blood and live.

Lopez Vaz, the Portuguese pilot taken earlier by Drake, has a somewhat different view. Vaz writes that Drake had attacked with four pinnaces and 150 men. Fourteen or fifteen of the Spanish, for the most part men of 'good discretion', had assembled in a corner of the marketplace, had killed the trumpeter and shot

Drake in the leg. The English, he writes, retreated to the pinnaces, carrying Drake. At the water's edge they put off their hose, 'swam and waded all to their pinnaces, and departed forth of the harbour, so that if the Spaniards had followed them, they might have slain them all'.

Drake, according to Vaz, barely harmed Nombre de Dios. Only one Spaniard was killed and one Englishman, the trumpeter, 'whom they left behind with his trumpet in his hand'. From there, the Portuguese pilot continues, Drake sailed to Darien, an area the Spanish had abandoned earlier 'because of the unholesomenesse of the place'. Vaz comments that some English think that by taking the South Sea, or Panamá, 'they could cut the gold and silver pipeline from Perú: Howbeit I do here most certainly assure you, that there be many ways to Perú'. Drake repaired to the isle of Bastimentos, a league (3 miles) from Nombre de Dios.

While Drake was there, the Spanish governor sent an emissary to enquire on several matters: was he really the feared Drake; did he use poisoned arrows and, if so, how might the Spanish cure their wounds; could the governor supply him with anything? Drake replied that he wanted only that 'harvest, which they get out of the earth, and send into Spain to trouble all the Earth'. Why, asked the envoy, since there was gold and silver to be taken from the town, did Drake not take it? Drake showed the governor's emissary his bandaged leg as answer.

Raunse and his ship left Drake, who made for Cartagena. On the evening of 13 August Drake took his three pinnaces into the harbour. A frigate was anchored in the roadstead, and standing anchor watch was just one old man, 'who, being demanded where the rest of his company was, answered that they were gone ashore in their *gundelo* that evening, to fight about a mistress'. He divulged that just two hours earlier, a pinnace, under sail and rowing as hard as possible, had called across to him asking if he had seen any English or French lately, and that when the old man replied no, they warned him to keep a sharp watch. Within the hour, the Cartagenians had hauled their vessels to safety under the artillery of the castle. The Spanish rang the church bell, shot off thirty cannon, mounted horse and fired calivers at the English, all to no effect except to deter Drake from attacking. Outside, he took a couple of frigates bound for Cartagena. All knew Drake was off the coast. The help of the Cimarróns was now essential.

Drake knew his men would fight better if there were no retreat. He also knew how loath they were to leave either of the two ships, as both were good sailers and well furnished. Drake sent for Thomas Moone, carpenter aboard the *Swan*, took him privately into his cabin and ordered that in the middle of the second watch, he was to go down secretly into the well of the ship (the bottom and centre of the hull, the bilge, where the pumps were), and with a large spike-gimlet bore three holes as close to the keel as he could. He was then to cover over the holes to conceal the water boiling up into the ship's hold. Moone was utterly dismayed. Why, Moone asked Drake, should he sink so good a bark, new and strong, a vessel in which he had made two rich and gainful voyages? If his brother, the master, and the rest of the ship's company should find out what he had done, Moone added, they would kill him. But the captain's order stood.

Early the next morning Drake took his pinnace to go fishing. He went aboard the *Swan*, where his brother was in command, and invited him to go along. As they were rowing off, Drake asked him why his *Swan* was floating so deep. John Drake sent a sailor to the steward to find out if there might be water in the bilges. The steward went below, found himself wet to the waist, and came up crying out that the ship was full of water. Some of the crew quickly manned the pumps while others searched for the leak. There was by then 6ft of water in the hold, even though in the six weeks before they had not had to pump twice. Drake left off with his fishing and offered to help, but the crew asked him to continue because they wanted fish for dinner. On returning, Drake found that the sailors had worked hard but the water level hadn't dropped, and by three in the afternoon, the water still had not dropped more than a foot and a half. There was no chance of finding the leak or of stopping it. Drake offered to take the pinnace out and capture a frigate so that his brother should be captain in the admiral and the *Swan*'s master should be there with him. And, Drake added for good measure, rather than have the Spanish take the *Swan*, he would fire her. First, though, her crew should take off anything they lacked or liked. The sailors were amazed, but followed orders. Thus, writes Nichols, 'Our Captain had his desire, and men enough for his pinnaces'. John Drake was given command of the *Pascoe*.

For the next several weeks, hidden away in the Gulf of Darien, Drake trimmed his vessels, trained his men for combat, built a fort and raided coastal traders for their food. Death was meanwhile gnawing away at Drake's numbers. His brother John Drake and Richard Allen were killed attacking a Spanish frigate, and another had died from disease. In January 1573 'half a score of our company fell down sick altogether, and the most of them died within two or three days', one being Joseph Drake, another brother. At one time, thirty were sick with this *calentura*, likely malaria. Francis Drake ordered an autopsy be performed on his brother Joseph. Ripped open by the surgeon, the cadaver's liver was 'found swollen, his heart as it were sodden, and his guts all fair'. Cause of death? Undetermined. As of Shrove Tuesday, 3 February, twenty-eight of the crew had died, but a few healthy men were left aboard, still free of fever.

The mule-trains bearing treasure from Venta de Cruces to Nombre de Dios were Drake's next target. While Captain Ellis Hixom looked after the ship, tended the sick and guarded the prisoners, Drake took a raiding party of eighteen English and thirty Cimarróns and marched overland for two weeks from sunrise until four each day. The skies were clear on 11 February 1573. The Cimarrón chief took Drake to the top of a high hill running east–west and 'prayed him to follow him, if he was desirous to see at once the two seas, which he had so long longed for'. The Cimarróns cut steps up into a tree and made a bower in which a dozen might sit. From there, the author of Drake's account writes, 'we might without any difficulty plainly see the Atlantic Ocean' and the Pacific 'so much desired'. Like Pizarro before him on first seeing the Pacific, so it was with Drake. Gazing out over that sea, 'of which he had heard such golden reports, he besought Almighty God of his goodness to give him life and leave to sail once in an English ship in that sea'. With him was John Oxnam, who vowed to help Drake to that end.[10] Within three years, Oxnam was to be the first to sail those waters.

A Cimarrón went into the town at dusk and returned with the information that tonight was the night the trains would be moving.[11] Drake set the ambush. Along one side of the road were Oxnam and his men, and on the opposite side, fifty paces further on, Drake and his men. They lay there in the dark for about an hour, and then heard the deep-sounding bells of the *recos*, the mule-trains, coming closer. Drake's orders to his men were that the English should stay concealed until all the *recos* that came from Venta de Cruces had passed by, as the first ones brought only merchandise. It was the following ones that carried treasure. Then one Robert Pike, who had drunk too much aqua vitae, forgot himself. He began to entice a Cimarrón to join him to show his forwardness as the first mules reached them. At that moment a cavalier from Venta de Cruces rode by with his page running at his side, and the sodden Pike rose up to see who was there. The Cimarrón quickly pulled Pike down and rolled on top of him – but not quickly enough. The Spaniard saw a white apparition in the woods, for the English had put on white shirts to know each other in the darkness, and he spurred his horse into a gallop to warn the others. The *recos* that had passed by carried only food, not gold. Those carrying treasure trotted back westward, and Drake came away with only two loads of silver. Pike's recklessness cost them 'a most rich booty'.

Drake entered Venta de Cruces, then a town of some forty or fifty houses as well as many warehouses to store goods. At the monastery, the English found a bundle of more than 1,000 papal bulls and pardons newly sent from Rome. Drake's raiders had been away nearly a fortnight with no booty and soon left the town to return to their vessels. On 22 February Drake sent a Cimarrón ahead to Hixom to announce his coming. The messenger 'shewed the tooth-pike of gold, which he said our captain had sent for a token to Hixom, with charge to meet him at such a river, though the master knew well the captain's toothpick yet by reason of his admonition and caveat given him at parting, he (though he betrayed no sign of distrusting the Cimarrón) yet stood as amazed, least something had befallen our captain otherwise than well'. The Cimarrón messenger told Hixom that as it was night when he was sent away, Drake could not send a letter but instead had taken his knife and inscribed a message on the toothpick. 'Thereupon the master looked upon it and saw written: *By me Francis Drake*, wherefore he believed.'

Drake learned that Oxnam and the *Beare* had taken a strong new 20-ton frigate of a good design in which was a great store of maize, 28 fat hogs and 200 hens. He careened and tallowed her, then fitted her with cannon from the pinnaces. With the newly tallowed frigate and the *Beare*, Drake set sail towards Isla de Cativás. Two days later, about noon, he made out a sail to the west, heading for the island. The captain was none other than the Protestant French captain Guillaume le Têtu (Testu) from Le Havre, the famous cartographer, pilot, corsair and explorer, then an old man aged over 60. He and his man-of-war, *Havre*, desperately needed Drake's aid. For five weeks the captain had been hunting for Drake along the coast. He had no water, having nothing but the wine and cider aboard from which his men had grown ill. Drake supplied him and had him follow to the next port for further provisioning. Once anchored, Têtu sent Drake a case of pistols and a gilt scimitar that had once belonged to the king of France. Drake, in turn, gave Têtu a gold chain and a tablet.

Têtu brought news of the recent massacre in Paris at the king of Navarre's marriage on Saint Bartholomew's Day and reported that France was 'now no longer France but frensy, even as if all Gaul were turned into wormwood and gall, Italian practices having overmastered the French simplicity'. Têtu had heard of Drake's successes and riches and wanted to join him in raiding the mule-trains. Twenty French, fifteen English and a number of Cimarróns manned the frigate and two pinnaces and sailed to the Río Francisco once again to attack the *recos* and their treasures. Lying in wait at night a mile from Nombre de Dios, the English could hear first the hammers and saws of shipwrights, then the sound of the bells on the pack mules coming overland from Panamá shores. This time, *this* time, they would capture more gold and silver than they could take away.

Three *recos* came on, guarded by forty-five soldiers, fifteen to each *reco*. One mule-train had fifty animals, and the other two had seventy each. Each mule carried three hundredweight, or 336lb, of silver – in all, nearly 30 tons. The English-French alliance attacked. As bullets and arrows flew back and forth, Têtu was wounded in the belly by hailshot. The Spanish retreated to call up help, abandoning the mules. The raiding party took a few bars and quoits of gold and for a couple of hours feverishly buried 15 tons of silver, partly in a burrow that giant land crabs had made under fallen trees and more in the sand of a shallow river-bed. They planned to return, but for now they had to leave. Spanish horses and footmen were pursuing them. The wounded Têtu could march no further and stopped to rest. Drake left him there. Two leagues further on, the French realised one of their men had gone missing. He had drunk too much wine and, weighted down with loot, was wandering in the woods. The raiding party later learned he had been captured by the Spanish that evening and had under torture revealed not only where the treasure had been buried but also where the English and French were to meet their pinnaces.

When the party arrived at the riverbank on 2 or 3 April, however, they saw not the two English pinnaces expected, but seven Spanish ones waiting for them. It had rained heavily the night before and, rowing hard against strong westerly winds the next morning, the English had got only halfway to the rendezvous. Not able to reach the English vessels by land, Drake figured the party might manage it by water. 'Let us therefore make a raft with the trees that are here in readiness, as offering themselves being brought down the river, happily this last storm, and put ourselves to sea. I will be one. Who will be the other?' John Smith stepped forward to join him, as well as two of the Frenchmen who could swim well. The Cimarróns agreed to trust to the raft, except for Pedro, who did not know how to row and wanted to be left behind. 'The raft was fitted and fast bound, a sail of a biscuit sack prepared; an oar was shaped out of a young tree to serve instead of a rudder, to direct their course before the wind.' As Drake and those with him set off on this *jangada*, he assured those left behind on the beach that if it pleased God to reach the frigate, he would see that they all got safely back as well, despite 'all the Spaniards in the Indies'.

They sailed some 3 leagues to an offshore island, 'sitting up to the waist continually in water and at every surge of the wave to the armpits, for the space of six hours, upon this raft. What with the parching of the sun and what with the beating of the salt water, they had all of their skins much fretted away.' As night was coming on they saw two of their pinnaces making for them, but wind and wave were increasing, and the pinnaces could not see the *jangada* riding low in the water. Soaked in brine, Drake watched the pinnaces making for cover behind the point. He quickly beached the raft and with three others ran along the shore around the point to the pinnaces. There he showed his men a gold quoit as a sign of the treasure, and thanked God for a profitable voyage. He informed the French that their captain, 'sore wounded', had stayed behind with two others, but that he would be rescued when they returned for the buried treasure.

The night of 4 April Drake and the crew rowed to Río Francisco to bring back the rest of the treasure. They worked feverishly through the night so that by the 'dawning of day' they were able to set sail back to the frigate, with treasure. Drake 'divided by weight the gold and silver into two even portions, one for the French and the other for the English'. The English-French alliance had proved profitable. But Têtu and other French were still out in the jungle. Two weeks after the attack, a French gentleman staggered into the camp. He had escaped the rage of the Spaniards only by throwing away all his gear and a box of jewels so he could run faster. But his servant with a 'covetous mind' had taken up the loot. Burdened, he could not run fast enough to escape the Spanish. The Frenchman reported that within half an hour after the ambush, Spanish soldiers had also captured Têtu and his servant. And the buried silver? The Spanish had recovered nearly all of it. Nearly 2,000 Spaniards and black men were out digging up what was left. Dismayed but not deterred, Oxnam and Sherwell's party set out anyway towards the buried treasure. At the site, for a full mile in every direction, the ground had been dug up. The English came away with only thirteen bars of silver and a few gold quoits missed by the Spanish.

It was now June, and with hurricane season approaching, it was time to return to England. Drake burned the pinnaces and gave their ironwork to the Cimarróns. Ill-provisioned again, he left, rounded Cabo San António, and off La Havana took a small bark 'in which were two or three hundred hides and one most necessary thing, which stood us in great stead, viz., a pump, which we set in our frigate'. Drake returned to Cabo San António, where he filled his water casks and took on great store of turtles' eggs, 200 by the day and another 50 by night, which they powdered and dried.

He sailed into Plymouth on 9 August 1573. It was a Sunday, and the parishioners were listening to the weekly sermon. The news of Drake's return 'did so speedily pass over all the church, and surpass their minds with desire and delight to see him, that very few or none remained with the preacher, all hastening to see the evidence of God's love and blessing towards our gracious Queen and country, by the fruit of our captain's labour and success. *Soli Deo gloria*. FINIS.' That day, to Drake as well as to God, went glory.

Drake's West Indian voyage of 1572–73 cost the investors the 25-ton pinnace *Swan* and three other pinnaces; more than thirty crew of the original seventy-three died in the fighting or of disease. Those lost in combat included the venerable French captain Guillaume le Têtu and Drake's brother John. His other brother Joseph succumbed to disease. Yet the voyage was a success, for Francis returned with £20,000 and two well-found Spanish frigates. The voyage made him rich.

English Pick Off Stray *Adviso*

By 12 September 1572 the *Audiencia* at Ciudad de Panamá was writing to the Crown about Drake's activities along the Spanish Main and the Isthmus of Panamá, an area equal in size to Spain and France together. For the previous six weeks Drake had been seizing Spanish vessels, and it was reported that the Portuguese Anton Couto had come from Spain on an *adviso* but had been captured by Drake. Blame was placed on the pilot for not following the prescribed route.[12] In a letter dated 27 November 1572 Couto wrote from La Havana to the Casa de Contratación (House of Trade) in Seville that the pilot had strayed off course and the caravel *Santa Catalina* had been attacked between La Tortuga and the mouth of the Río Acla by a pinnace carrying twenty-two English. Couto had destroyed his despatches to keep them from falling into English hands. He and others were held prisoners ashore for over forty days, from 14 July to 25 August, when they were given their ship back, but without sails and other essentials. With scraps of sail, they reached Nombre de Dios, where they made their way across land to Panamá.

On 20 February 1573 Diego Flores de Valdéz, commander of the Spanish Main fleet and armada, wrote to the Crown from Nombre de Dios about the unrest the French and English ships had caused. To patrol the coast and escort the brigantine, Valdéz had ordered another oared vessel be built. The English (Drake's men) had withdrawn to Acla inlet, he says, where they had rowing craft that had gone upriver to Venta de Cruces, within 3 or 4 leagues of the town of Panamá, where one morning they attacked a mule-train on its way towards Nombre de Dios, 'such has been their shamelessness'.[13] They had killed four Spaniards but missed taking a pack train that carried more than 100,000 pesos. That one had been warned and had returned to Ciudad de Panamá. Valdéz finds the English daring 'lamentable'. Worse, the English had recruited the help of the Cimarróns.

That same week, two days after the previous communication, the municipal officials of the Ciudad de Panamá wrote again to the Crown in a letter dated 24 February 1573 that the previous summer, on the night of 29 July 1572, Nombre de Dios was caught completely unprepared when 'four launches of Lutheran English, carrying about eighty men, fell upon that city'. In April 1573 Jorge Nuñez de Prado deposed at Panamá that in July 1572 'eighty English corsairs' had attacked Nombre de Dios.[14] Prado, adjutant to General Miguel Huertado, had stood sentry duty, as had Prado's servants. The Spanish had sent out a party to trap the English, but to no end. 'I crossed many rivers neck-deep in water', Prado writes, 'all of which I endured in person with my arms and servants, at my own expense, venturing my life and expending a large amount of money'. He complains that out of his own pocket he has spent 'a large sum in gold *pesos*' but has 'received no recognition nor any gratification' from the Crown.

Early in May 1573, Captain Cristóbal warns that if Drake and his ships take Nombre de Dios, 'Panamá is theirs as easily as the words are said'. The fears were not unfounded. In two years John Oxnam would build a vessel and raid along the Pacific coast.

The raids brought forth a flurry of letters from Panamá to the Crown.[15] The officials bemoaned the 'shamelessness of these persons' and feared that the English and French would return.

> It is a sad thing to contemplate the men who have been ruined by this attack. And what moves to greater compassion is the fact that many of them were retiring to Spain with their fortunes made by the labour of many years in other parts – some of them are from Chile, which are very remote and distant provinces – and only a league and a half from the city of Nombre de Dios to be robbed by corsairs and left destroyed, ruined!

Such pleas found the royal ear to be quite deaf.

Green Emerald Tied to Friar's Thigh

Andrew Barker was an English merchant mariner who had been doing business in the Canaries, on the island of Tenerife, where he trafficked in cloth, wines and sugar.[16] In 1575 his goods had been seized by the Spanish, and Barker had been imprisoned, interrogated by the Inquisition and fined. On his release, he sought in vain for redress and so took reprisal into his own hands. In 1576 Barker furnished two barks to sail to the Caribbean to attack the Spanish: the *Ragged Staffe*, with Barker himself as captain and Philip Roche as master, and the *Beare*, with William Coxe of Limehouse as captain and master.

The two ships left Plymouth on Whitsuntide of June 1576. Barker sailed first to the Cabo Verde islands, and then made for the West Indies, finding his landfall on Trinidad. In the bay of Tolú, west of Cartagena, Barker took a frigate and its treasure 'to the value of 500 pound, namely bars of gold, and ingots of silver, and some quantity of *corriento* or coin in rials of plate, and certain green stones called emeralds, whereof one very great, being set in gold, was found tied secretly about the thigh of a friar'. Illness struck his crew, and within two weeks eight or nine of his men died of a *calentura*, 'a hot and vehement fever'. Later, his crew mutinied and Barker was killed by the Spanish.

Undone by Chicken Feathers and a Lady

As Drake's trusted friend and captain, John Oxnam (sometimes given as Oxenham) had taken part in Drake's raid on the Spanish Main in 1572–73, and the Cimarróns had helped their small group climb the San Blas mountain range to gaze on the Pacific towards the south. Both men vowed that day to navigate the waters of the South Sea someday. It was Oxnam who did so first. Several accounts – English, Spanish and Portuguese – tell the story of this extraordinary Plymouth mariner, almost an exact contemporary of Drake.[17]

Oxnam set out from Plymouth for Panamá on 9 April 1576 as owner and captain of an eleven-gun frigate, 100–140 tons, name unknown, carrying two knocked-down pinnaces and a crew of some fifty-seven men. Oxnam, then about 40, was a gentleman of 'grave demeanour, much feared and respected and obeyed by his soldiers'. He came from an established Devon family and, like Drake, was known to be a 'bold sailor and fiery sea-captain', a man of 'courage and ability', of 'rude courage' – but unfortunately he was 'without fact or discretion' and 'excited the ill-will of his own men'.[18] He reached Panamá in the rainy season of late summer 1576, hid his frigate along the coast, and with his two pinnaces took a Spanish frigate, or possibly two prizes, and eighteen prisoners. He recovered his own frigate and sailed his vessels and the prizes to the Golfo de Acla, hiding them on Isla de Piños, north of Acla, and on the mainland, enlisting the help of the Cimarróns.

Meanwhile, the *Audiencia* in Panamá ordered out a frigate and a brigantine manned by twenty soldiers from Nombre de Dios to capture Oxnam. In August 1576 the Spanish found Oxnam's frigate (and the Spanish one), freed the Spanish prisoners and took Oxnam's cannon, supplies and the linen he intended for trade. With just the two pinnaces, Oxnam and his men then sailed to an inlet or creek mouth near Acla, the small coastal village deserted in 1532 by the Spanish. They buried what ordnance and stores they had left, opened the seacocks and sank the pinnaces to keep them safe until their return from the Pacific. The mission was a daring one: to cross the Cordillera de las San Blas, the mountainous backbone of the narrow Isthmus of Panamá, a distance of 6 or 7 leagues.[19] At the head of a navigable river that falls to the Pacific 13 or 14 leagues distant, they would build out of the forest timbers another pinnace for raiding the Southern Sea's coast. According to the Portuguese pilot Lopez Vaz, Cimarróns guided Oxnam across the mountains during the winter of 1576, taking 'two small pieces of ordnance, and his calivers, and good store of victuals'.[20] That winter, at the head of the Río Chucunaque (also called the Río Indios and Río Maize), the English crew of fifty, along with six or ten Cimarróns, felled and milled cedar to build a sailing pinnace, 45ft by the keel, of twenty-four (or twenty) oars. Balboa had set the example some sixty years earlier when he transported across the mountains of the isthmus two knocked-down brigantines (rowed vessels), with which he explored the coastline. Though the Spanish for some time had been building ships on the Mar del Sur coast, Oxnam was the first Englishman to build a vessel of local woods and sail her in Pacific waters.

Vaz and Oxnam call the vessel a pinnace. Spanish authorities variously call her a galliot, a barque, a galley, a launch or a shallop, names often interchanged by both Spanish and English writers. Swift pinnaces, often used as advice boats, were usually some 20 tons displacement, square-rigged on the fore- and mainmasts, and fore-and-aft rigged with three or four jibs, a fore-staysail, and on the mizzenmast, a lateen sail. According to Spanish accounts, Oxnam's pinnace had ten or twelve oars to a side and drew less than half a foot of water.

Sir Richard Hawkyns, later captured in 1593 by the Spanish off Cabo San Francisco, a short sail south of Panamá, picks up Oxnam's story in 1576.[21] Hawkyns notes that the Cimarróns were eager to help the English, to 'feed their insatiable revenges, [as they were] accustomed to roast and eat the hearts of all those Spaniards, whom at any time they could lay hand upon'. Oxnam, his English crew and the Cimarróns launched the pinnace in the upper reaches of the Río Chucunaque. Running down the Chucunaque and then the Río Tuira, the pinnace, armed with the two fast-loading cannon and manned by fifty English with calivers and some ten (or six) Cimarróns, entered the Golfo de San Miguel in late January 1577.[22] He sailed into the Golfo de Panamá and reached the Archipiélago de las Perlas on 20 February, Ash Wednesday, the day of penance – an irony not lost on Spanish officials at Nombre de Dios, who wrote on 17 April: 'Because of the sins which we who live in this land have committed, God permitted to befall what we have so long foreseen, and English corsairs allied with the *cimarrones* have crossed to the Pacific ... where they did great damage in carrying off the negroes and negresses they found there.'[23]

For ten days Oxnam lay hidden among the islands, just 25 leagues from Panamá, until a small bark from Guayaquil appeared from the south. Her cargo included 60,000 pesos of gold, writes Vaz, and 'much wine and bread'.[24] Six days later, another bark brought him a further 100,000 pesos in silver bars.

Hawkyns has a spicier account of seizing that Peruvian vessel from Guayaquil. He notes that Oxnam had taken two pieces of special value from her. One was a 'table of massive gold, with emeralds, sent for a present to the King; the other a Lady of singular beauty, married, and a mother of children. The latter grew to be his perdition,' he writes. The lady, unsurprisingly, is not mentioned by Vaz; nor do any of the Spanish accounts mention her.

> John Oxnam (I say) was taken with the love of this Lady, and to win her good will, what through her tears and persuasions, and what through fear and detestation of their barbarous inclinations, breaking promise with the Symarons, yielded to her request, which was to give the prisoners liberty with their ships, for that they were not useful for him. Notwithstanding Oxnam kept the Lady, who had in one of the restored ships, either a son or a nephew.

At this point Oxnam had outdone his former commander, Drake, the feared 'el Draque'. It was Oxnam who was the first Englishman to sail the Pacific. It was Oxnam who seized 160,000 pesos' worth of Spanish treasure, more than the worth of his and Drake's botched 1572–73 raids on the mule-trains four years earlier. In 1577 it was not Drake but Oxnam who was the real danger for the Spanish, terrorising the coast with his 45ft pinnace armed with two cannon. High in confidence, for the next week Oxnam raided the archipelago for its pearls and desecrated anything papist. His success had exceeded the wildest surmise. All that remained was to get his treasure back across to the Caribbean and return with it to England, there to enjoy all glory, laud and honour.

Meanwhile, Spanish documents show the response to the recent English pirates in the Caribbean.[25] From Veragua on 22 March 1577, Pedro Godinez Osorio wrote to the Crown in Madrid that the corsairs had 'been more numerous this year [1576] than in any since I came to the Indies'. Five vessels, the least of them with eighty crew, had plagued the coast. A frigate had taken on an English corsair with two vessels, got to windward and killed the best of the crew. But on the point of surrender, the Englishman had worked his ships to windward and escaped towards Río Chagres, where he put off a launch, attacked three barks and came away with 14,000 pesos.

Pork & Biscuits Along the Chucunaque

With his small pinnace heavily ballasted with gold, silver, pearls, prisoners and the persuasive Spanish *dueña*, Oxnam sailed from Las Perlas back to the Golfo de San Miguel and the Río Tuira, intending to return with lady and loot up the Río Chucunaque and across the cordillera to the Caribbean and then home. But rashly he set free the Spanish barks, their crews, the Pearl Islanders and the son (or nephew) of the lady of singular beauty. They quickly alerted the authorities in Panamá of the enemy pinnace in their Pacific waters.

Within hours Dr Gabriel de Loarte, president of the *Audiencia* of Panamá, ordered Captain Pedro de Ortega Valencia to take six vessels and 200 soldiers, nearly half of the 500 garrisoned there, to hunt down and capture Oxnam and the loot and, no doubt, to bring back the lady. At Las Perlas, Valencia learned that Oxnam had sailed for the Golfo de San Miguel and set off with his frigates in hot pursuit of the lone pinnace. The mouth of the Río Tuira branches where it empties into the gulf. 'The pursuers, approaching the river, were doubtful by which of the afore-remembered three mouths they should take their way,' writes Hawkyns. 'In this wavering one of the soldiers espied certain feathers, of hens and some boughs of trees (which they had cut off to make their way) swimming down one of the outlets.'[26]

Here were the clues they needed. The Spanish frigates entered a lesser branch, and for eight days made their way upstream until it became too shallow to navigate. Sixty men marched day and night for four days along the banks of the Río Chucunaque, until the morning of 2 April. At ten, as they reached the head of the river (near the confluence of the Río Tupisca or Río Chico), the Spanish came upon thirty English and eighty Cimarróns, Hawkyns says, 'making good cheer in their tents and divided in two partialities about the partition and sharing of their gold and silver. Thus were they surprised, and not one escaped.' On that particular morning, Oxnam was a few leagues away tending to the transfer of the loot across the San Blas Mountains towards the Caribbean, but the next day Valencia caught up with him. Oxnam was wounded but escaped, along with twenty others, into the bush. Three days later Oxnam and his men counterattacked but were forced to withdraw with heavy casualties, barely escaping Spanish capture. Vaz recounts that the Spanish put their prisoners aboard the English pinnace and returned to Ciudad de Panamá on the coast. 'So the voyage of that English man did not prosper with him, as he thought it would have done.' Torture elicited the information that the English planned to return with 2,000 men to settle there and, with the Cimarróns, further 'infest the Pacific'.[27]

In its report to the Crown, the council of the Ciudad de Panamá corroborates Hawkyns' account.[28] Captain Valencia had by 'Divine touch' noticed chicken feathers floating down one branch of the river. For eight days he had tracked the feathers upstream until he at last 'found the trail of the English, who had left pork and biscuits, which they carried', on the riverbank where they stopped to eat. After four days, at ten on Tuesday morning of Holy Week, the captain saw some thirty English and more than eighty Cimarróns cooking 'a quantity of pork in kettles and amusing themselves together. They had a canvas awning stretched, where they were unloading the biscuit and everything else they had in the launch. Being of light draft (drawing little over a palm of water) it had been able to navigate so far up.'

The report says Valencia attacked at once, killing more than twenty-five English and many Cimarróns. As the Spanish officials proudly declared to the Crown:

> We certify to your majesty that Pedro Menéndez did not merit more recognition, nor do as much in killing Jean Ribaut and all his company in Florida, as Pedro de Ortega Valencia has done in defeating and capturing John Oxnam ... For had Oxnam succeeded in his undertaking, it would have entailed the total ruin of this realm and the utmost damage and disturbance through all Perú.

To the Spanish authorities in Panamá, an English attack on the peninsula was far more dangerous than any threat from the French or English in Terra Florida.

No Roasted Spanish Hearts

In coastal anchorages of the Main and in the islands, the Spanish were on alert. On 7 June the Ciudad de Panamá reported to Viceroy Don Francisco de Toledo in Perú that Captain Melo and forty men had recently found Oxnam's two pinnaces 'half submerged in an inlet, hidden under certain trees'.[29] Next day, 8 June, Dr Loarte, for the *Audiencia*, wrote from Panamá to the viceroy that there were just twenty English still uncaptured but that these 'were left unarmed – having not a knife, not a weapon, not a harquebus, bow nor arrows – and without subsistence, tar, cordage, nails or tools'.[30] No threat, he was suggesting, but the viceroy thought otherwise and in short order sent his own commander to stamp out every last Englishman. This was General Diego de Frias Trejo, equerry to the viceroy of Perú and a seasoned soldier who had fought the Incas and the Chiriguanaes.[31] From Panamá, Trejo wrote to the Crown that Dr Loarte would not receive him and claimed he outranked the viceroy. Loarte, Trejo complained, would not even supply subsistence for the soldiers. 'I can not carry a sufficient supply with me, for lack of slaves. The President will not support me, I fear, judging by the little assistance he has given me thus far.'

In the end, says Vaz, the Cimarróns betrayed the English. Himself a prisoner of the Spanish fifteen years later, Hawkyns notes that the Cimarróns had turned Oxnam and the other survivors over to the Spanish because Oxnam had broken his promise to let them roast and eat Spanish prisoners' hearts.[32] Hawkyns observes:

This may be a good example to others in like occasions: First, to shun such notorious sins, which cannot escape punishment in this life, nor in the life to come: for the breach of faith is reputed amongst the greatest faults which a man can commit. Secondly, not to abuse another man's wife; much less to force her, both being odious to God and man. Thirdly, to beware of mutinies, which seldom or never are seen to come to better ends; for where such trees flourish, the fruit of force must either be bitter, sweet, or very sour. And therefore, seeing we vaunt ourselves to be Christians and make profession of his law, who forbideth all such vanities, let us faithfully shun them, that we may partake the end of that hope which our profession teacheth and promiseth.

As for Oxnam's 'lady of singular beauty', her dark attractions, her fortunes and her fate all remain a mystery, lost deep in the steamy shadows of the Panamanian jungle.

'Surrender Dog!'

Nearly nine months after his February raids in Las Perlas, Oxnam was finally tracked down and captured in a banana grove with seven (or nine) other Englishmen. He was caught in the Vallano region near the Río Banique, and details of his capture in the September emerged ten months later on 12 July 1578, when the *Audiencia* in Panamá took Oxnam's deposition.[33] The royal notary wrote: 'The Englishman said that his name was John Oxnam, English by birth, forty-two years old, and that he was the captain of the English who crossed this ocean, and that he is a Christian and has been baptized.' (This deposition was being recorded just five days after Francis Drake, prior to transiting the Strait of Magellan, had beheaded a mutinous Thomas Doughtie at Port Julian, 7 July 1578.)

On the day of his capture, Oxnam and four other Englishmen were in a banana grove in Vallano when they learned of a party advancing through the bush. Oxnam had been aware that the Spanish (campmaster Pedro Arana and his men) were pursuing them. Oxnam had seen them earlier and realised they had seen him too.

He fled, seeking to hide behind a cabuya or bejuco tree, but could not reach it. While so endeavouring, he looked and saw a soldier, whom they call Gonzalo, and a negro. Gonzalo was armed with a sword and shield, and the negro with a bow and arrows. Deponent gripped a lance and advanced on the soldier and on the negro, and they gave back.

Oxnam sought cover. When he saw Don Gomez de Rojas' match lighted on the serpentine, his harquebus aimed and ready to fire, Oxnam threw up his hands and cried out to Rojas: 'For the love of God, don't kill me!' Rojas ordered Oxnam to drop his lance, then he and the others seized Oxnam, cuffed him, and 'wounded his head many times with a knife'.

Temporarily, at least, the Spanish had stopped the English. But Oxnam's daring raid showed the Spanish that the English were a real threat to their hegemony in the American tropics.

three

━━━❮❮❮❯❯❯━━━

NEAR GALE, 1577–81

In largest seas are sorest tempests.

George Pettie, Petite Palace, 1576

*W*hile the Spanish were holding Oxnam and his men prisoner, Drake was in Plymouth finishing preparations for his next voyage to the tropics.[1] This voyage to the South Sea was to be Drake's greatest success and a wildly profitable venture for his investors, including the queen, not to mention a serious blow to Spain's source of wealth in Perú. By rounding Cape Horn to get to the Pacific side of the tropical Americas, Drake was to have and to hold a huge fortune, much larger than the one that had slipped through Oxnam's fingers thanks to the *dueña's* soft touch. Returning via the Cape of Good Hope may not have been part of Drake's original plan, but terrorising the Pacific coast of Spanish America certainly was.

Hakluyt's account, including that of Vaz, was published in 1589 and was augmented in 1598–1600, when England was still at war with Spain. It is notably circumspect. Editor Purchas, long after the Anglo-Spanish treaty in 1604, gives more details than Hakluyt; author Nichols has patriotic fervour; and author/mariner Carder expresses the horror of it all. Peter Carder and John Wynter (whose author is Edward Cliffe, another mariner) both left Drake near Tierra del Fuego.

Wynter's (Cliffe's) account begins on 17 September 1577, when 'one good and new ship', the *Elizabeth*, 80 tons burden, commanded by John Wynter, and a small pinnace, the *Benedict*, 12 tons, sailed out of the Thames for Plymouth. They joined the admiral, *Pelican*, 120 tons, commanded by Drake (his ship was later rechristened the *Golden Hinde*), the bark *Marigold*, 30 tons, and a flyboat, 50 tons. Drake's was not a large fleet either in number or tonnage – two ships, one barque, a flyboat and a pinnace – in all, five vessels, great and small, with a crew totalling 164 that included both 'gentlemen and sailors'. Its tonnage of 292 tons total was less

than half that of one single large ship such as the queen's 700-ton *Jesus of Lubeck*,
lost to the Spanish nine years earlier at San Juan de Ulúa.

Drake's fleet left Plymouth on 15 November 1577, 'giving out his pretended
voyage for Alexandria'. An autumn storm forced them into Falmouth, then back
to Plymouth for repairs. They set out again on 13 December. Along the African
coast, Drake kidnapped the Portuguese captain Nuño da Silva and kept him as
pilot for nearly sixteen months.[2] On 2 February they set a course westward from
Africa across the Atlantic. For three weeks they were becalmed in the doldrums,
where victuals and water ran low and tempers ran high. Rank was the bone of
contention. John Wynter, Thomas Doughtie (Doughty) and Drake were equals,
but Drake claimed that his authority was above theirs since his came directly
from the queen, though never during the voyage did he produce any royal commission to support his claim. Without that, or any letter of marque, Drake was
arguably a pirate.

In Panamá, some of Oxnam's men were still loose in the jungle. On 18 February
1578, five months after Oxnam's capture, General Trejo wrote from San Miguel
de Vallano to the Crown that, on 7 December 1577, he had come across six
English in a canoe, paddling upstream, their intention being to cross the peninsula
to the Caribbean and escape.[3] Trejo had fallen upon them at night, capturing five:
'One of them is the most important man among all who came over, because he is
the most astute and sagacious of them all, and acted as their pilot and interpreter.
He is a very clever pilot, and speaks Spanish and other languages well; they call
him Chalona [John Butler] and by this name he is well known and famous.'

Fifty-four days after leaving Africa, Drake's vessels reached the Brazilian coast
on 5 April.[4] By 14 April they were anchored in the Rio de la Plata, and by 27 April
were on a course SSW towards the Strait of Magellan.[5]

The issue of authority that had arisen during the long crossing was not to be
resolved until the fleet reached Port St Julian, Magellan's southern hemisphere
rendezvous, before undertaking the narrow passages of the strait. Drake wintered
there from 20 June to 17 August, refitting his fleet and sorting out matters of
authority and discipline.

On 21 May Pedro de Araña, a veteran soldier of thirty-eight years' service in
both Europe and South America, wrote from Panamá to the Crown summarising the Vallano War, the name being given to the mopping-up operation against
Oxnam and his men.[6] Viceroy Toledo believed it was essential to stop the English.
Besides Trejo, Toledo had commissioned others to seek out the English. As funds
were scarce, the viceroy had also commissioned Don Diego de Mora, 'a rich
young man, son of a deceased resident of the city of Trujillo', to be admiral of the
fleet. Viceroy Toledo had raised a force of a further 145 soldiers by 'forcibly req-
uisitioning sixty half-breeds, mulattoes and negroes to serve them' and shipped
them off in two large vessels – hardly seasoned officers and soldiers, these. He had
also ordered that two of the pearl-fishing barques at Manta on the Puerto Viejo

coast be converted to brigantines that could be rowed into coastal inlets and up rivers or, if at sea, could assist ships in battle.

Araña feared that Dr Loarte had some 'private interest of his own' for ordering the return of the forces to Panamá and suspected that Loarte was trying to take over the forces himself in order to get all the credit for expelling and killing the English. The royal high court in Panamá nevertheless gave Araña forty more soldiers and some black carriers, and Araña sailed for the Vallano region. He did indeed catch the English captain, plus seven other English sailors and five black men. The hunt was at last over; the victory was Spain's. Spanish colonials had stopped the English infidels, all 'Lutheran heretics'.

Beheading, Brazilian Sugar, Bedding

While Drake was wintering in Port St Julian in Brazil, English merchant John Whithall was quietly starting a trading enterprise between England and Brazil.[7] In 1578 England and Portugal were still trading together; Spain's hostile takeover of the country was to come two years later. In a letter dated 26 June 1578 written from Santos, the port for São Paulo, he writes to his friend in England, Richard Staper, that he had at first intended to return to England from Portugal but had come across a chance to live in Brazil and take his 'choice of three or four' eligible young women in marriage. Writes Whithall: 'So that I am about three days ago consorted with an Italian gentleman to marry with his daughter within these four days. This my friend and father-in-law Signor Ioffo Dore is born in the city of Genoa in Italy.' Dore had a daughter and thought Whithall would make a better husband than

> any Portugal in all the country, and does give with her in marriage to me part of an *ingenio* [sugar plantation] which he hath, that makes every year a thousand roves of sugar. Thus my marriage will be worth to me two thousand ducats, little more or less. Also Signor Ioffo Dore my father-in-law doth intend to put into my hands the whole *ingenio* with sixty or seventy slaves, and thereof to make me factor for us both.

Silver and gold mines, Whithall writes, have recently been discovered at São Vicente, and Brazil, he finds, is a country 'very healthful without sickness'. As he is now a free denizen in Brazil, he wants to engage in trade and instructs that a bark of 60 or 70 tons be laden with wares and sent to Brazil, for such a passage would be 'as good as any Perú voyage'. Cargo? Hampshire and Devonshire kersies, or lengths of ribbed woolen cloth, to be sold in the Canaries. With the proceeds, the request is to 'lade fifteen tons of wine and six dozen Cordovan hides (orange, tawny, yellow, red, and very fine black, take saffron to dye the skins), [and] sixteen quintals of Canary pitch'. Whithall also instructs Staper to 'bring four dozen scissors and twenty dozen knives, eight or ten dozen hats (half trimmed with taffeta, the other plain), with bands of cypress, and other finery', along with tools, 'and four masses of gittern strings'. For the return voyage, he will ship sugar from his own fields and mills.

About the same time the *Audiencia* at Panamá took Oxnam's deposition on 7 July 1578, Oxnam's friend Francis Drake on 2 July, in ironic coincidence, was presiding over his own court, sitting in judgement on his sometime friend Thomas Doughtie, a gentleman close to Sir Christopher Hatton and other powerful men in England.[8] Doughtie was quickly tried for treason and condemned. A day and a half later he was beheaded, in the shadow of the gallows erected by the Portuguese admiral Magellan fifty-eight years earlier during his ship's voyage around the world. Magellan had had to sort out his own mutinies before negotiating the treacherous strait and had executed Captain Quesada, one of three mutinous Spanish captains in his own fleet of five ships. Once Doughtie had been despatched, Drake ordered the sailors and gentlemen to confess and take Communion. Further, all gentlemen would hereafter work shoulder to shoulder with the sailors, as he himself did. He relieved all the officers of their commands and, for the most part, reinstated them to serve under his authority. Uneasy, especially at sea, is the head that wears command.

Drake's fleet was now three: the *Pelican*, with himself in command; the *Marigold*, with Captain John Thomas; and the *Elizabeth*, with John Wynter as captain. It may be about this time that the *Pelican*, named for that ancient symbol of Christian sacrifice so beloved to Elizabeth, was rechristened as the *Golden Hinde* in honour of Drake's patron, the same Sir Christopher Hatton who was supportive of Doughtie.

By early July Drake's fleet was nearing the Strait of Magellan. Coasting along within a harquebus shot of land, Hakluyt writes that the sailors could see giant Indians, one of whom cried out: '*Magallanes, Esta he minha Terra,* that is, Magallanes, this is my country.'[9] Such was the Indian hatred of their Spanish conquerors. On 21 or 24 August the winds turned favourable. Drake entered the strait, and by the ancient English custom of 'turf and twig', claimed it for England.[10] Purchas, on Wynter's recollection years later in 1618, writes that 'formal possession was then and there taken of the said Straits and territories, with Turf and Twig, after the English manner; Captain Drake delivering him the said possession, in the name and to the use of Queen Elizabeth, and her successors'.[11] The fleet reached Cape Deseado at the western end of the strait on 6 September. There, with the Pacific before them, they were hit by a severe storm that battered the fleet for more than a week. On 8 October Drake writes that he lost sight of Wynter and the *Elizabeth*.

On the night of 8 October Captain Wynter's *Elizabeth* lost company with Drake.[12] The next day, Wynter entered the strait again and anchored in an open bay, where for two days he made large signal fires on shore to catch Drake's attention. He next made for a more protected sound, where he stayed for three weeks, awaiting Drake. On 1 November, still without seeing him, Wynter turned back eastward through the strait. One of the pinnaces with its crew of eight, including Peter Carder, was separated from Drake possibly in that same storm (or more likely, from the *Elizabeth* in another storm off the coast of Brazil). After some years, Carder managed to return to England and tell his extraordinary tale to the queen.

Drake Takes *Cacafuego*

On 1 November Drake started northward up the Pacific coast of South America in the *Pelican* – alone. At Valparaíso on 5 December, he seized the aged vessel, *La Capitana*, once the flagship for Pedro Sarmiento de Gamboa, and kidnapped her pilot, Juan Griego (most likely the Greek mariner Juan de Fuca, Ioánnis Fokás) and his *derrotero* (chart). From *La Capitana* Drake took many casks of wine and nearly 200,000 pesos of gold stored in four large chests. Off Arica, now at the northern border of Chile, he seized another Spanish ship with 13,000 pesos of silver. On the beach at Tarapacá (Tarapaza, then in Perú, now in Chile), Drake found a Spaniard asleep, and next to him, thirteen bars of silver worth 4,000 ducats: 'We took the silver, and left the man.' Pillaging his way northwards, Drake crossed into the Viceroyalty of Perú, source of the better half of Spain's New World wealth.

On 13 February 1579 the *Pelican* anchored at Callao, port for Lima. The Spanish inspectors boarded and were stunned to see her bristling with cannon. Never expecting to see the English in their port, they quickly jumped down into their launch and rowed madly for shore, shouting 'Frenchmen!' Drake sent his pinnace to search the harbour for two ships supposedly carrying silver, but they could not be found. The crew cut the cables on the eight or nine ships already anchored there, hoping to exchange them as Drake's bargaining chips in a ransom deal. From Spanish prisoners, Drake had learned that his old friend Captain John Oxnam, as well as ship's master Thomas Sherwell and John and Henry Butler, were imprisoned nearby in Lima, less than two hours' march away. Drake indeed commanded the most powerful warship in the Pacific, fitted with eighteen cannon, but he had only thirty or so men fit to march and fight. The feared 'el Draque' was powerless against the Peruvians.

Drake along the way had earnestly been enquiring after a treasure ship, and at this point heard that the ship of Captain Juan de Antón, heavily laden to her lines with treasure, had only recently left Lima bound for Panamá. He immediately ordered the *Pelican* and the pinnace to weigh anchor and make sail in hot pursuit. Just as Drake had deserted his commander, John Hawkyns, in the heat of battle off the shores of Nueva España in 1568, Drake now left his captain, Oxnam, a prisoner in Lima in order to chase down the Spanish ship.[13]

On reaching Paita, he learned his prey had recently cleared for Panamá. Drake pressed on after her, seizing and plundering as he went. He announced to the company that whoever first sighted Antón's ship should have his gold chain and, as it turned out, it was John Drake who saw her from aloft at three in the afternoon. For three hours they gained on her and, after about six hours, came up to her off Cabo San Francisco, about 150 leagues from Panamá, at latitude 1° N. This was the same headland that Oxnam, as prisoner, had doubled only months before on his way to prison in Lima. On the evening of 1 March 1578 Drake cleared for action. He was about to engage Antón's *Nuestra Señora de la Concepción*, known to sailors by her nickname *Cacafuego* (*Shitfire*). She was the treasure ship he had been hunting since Lima.

The *Pelican* had been lumbering along, trailing warps to slow her speed, and Antón, thinking she was a friendly vessel, struck his sails and stood by for her to catch up. But when Drake drew closer, Antón was horrified to see that the *Pelican* 'was none of that coast, and then he began to hoist his sails, but could by no means get from Captain Drake because he was within the reach of his great ordnance'. Drake shot away the mizzenmast and wounded the captain. The Spaniards, 'not having so much as a rapier to defend themselves, were soon constrained to yield'. On boarding, the English found the *Cacafuego* laden with great riches. The ship's pilot, Francisco, had two fair bowls of silver. 'Our general said: "Señor Pilot, you have here two silver cups, but I must needs have one of them".' As the pilot could not choose between them, he gave Drake one and the other to the steward. 'When this pilot departed from us, his boy said thus unto our general, "Captain, our ship shall be called no more the *Cacafuego*, but the *Cacaplata*, and your ship shall be called the *Cacafuego*": which pretty speech of the pilot's boy ministered a matter of laughter to us, both then and long after.'

The treasure they seized was extraordinary. Antón valued it at more than 400,000 pesos' worth of gold, silver bars and coin. Some belonged to the Crown, some to private individuals. They counted 80lb of gold, 1,300 bars of silver and 14 chests of silver *reales*. Additionally, says Vaz, what other treasure there was, 'uncustomed', he does not know, 'for many times they carry almost as much more as they pay custom for; otherwise the king would take it from them, if they should be known to have any great sum; wherefore every ship carries his bill of custom, that the king may see it'. Besides gold and silver, the haul included pearls, precious stones and other things of great worth and weight – indeed, so much that the crew threw the *Pelican*'s stone ballast into the sea and replaced it with silver. It took five days to transfer the treasure to the *Pelican*. In a now familiar litany, Vaz comments: 'Surely this was a great plague of God justly inflicted upon us for our sins.' Presciently, he predicts that such acts are 'an especial cause of all the dangerous wars that are likely to ensue between Spain and England', as happened nine years later.

When Drake finally got under way, he bypassed Panamá and went straight for Nueva España. The Peruvian viceroy had sent three ships under the command of Pedro Sarmiento, Perú's finest navigator, to pursue and capture Drake and the *Pelican*. Sarmiento arrived at Cabo San Francisco twenty days after Drake had seized the Spanish treasure ship. When the Spanish admiral learned that Drake was not bound for Panamá, he concluded (wrongly) that he must be returning to the Strait of Magellan. Sarmiento sailed south in quick pursuit, while Drake sailed north.

What had happened to the remainder of Drake's fleet, separated in October off the Strait of Magellan? What of Captain Wynter in the *Elizabeth* and Peter Carder in the pinnace *Marigold*? Edward Cliffe records that on 20 January 1579, while making his way back to England, Wynter was near São Vicente at latitude 24° S, 'almost under the Tropic of Capricorn'.[14] He encountered foul weather and lost a pinnace and eight men (probably Carder's pinnace). On 30 May they were off Saint Ives, Cornwall, and on 2 June 1579 Wynter and crew arrived at Ilfracombe, on the north coast of Devon, 'safe into our own native country to enjoy the presence of our dear friends and kinsfolks'.

Carder Among the Tupinambás

Peter Carder, the sailor from St Verian, Cornwall, had his own version of parting from Drake. The *Marigold*, a 5-ton, eight-oared pinnace, had separated from Francis Drake's fleet after negotiating the Strait of Magellan from the Atlantic to the South Sea.[15] When the *Elizabeth* parted from the *Pelican* in the storm that drove them southwards, according to Purchas, Drake ordered Carder's *Marigold* to find the *Elizabeth*. For fifteen days Carder tried in vain, and with no compass and not even a day's victuals, he and his mates found they had lost both the *Elizabeth* and the *Pelican*. On their own with just eight oars and a sail, he and his men made for the coast, surviving on mussels, oysters, crabs, some edible roots and fresh water.

Carder writes that the eight men sailed back through the strait and northward from the eastern opening of the Strait of Magellan to Port St Julian, then to the north side of the Rio de la Plata. When the Tupí Indians attacked them, only William Pitcher and Carder himself survived. Beset by foul weather off an island, their pinnace was driven ashore and dashed against the rocks. Carder and Pitcher, now castaways, were trapped on the desert island for two months, surviving on fruit, white crabs and small eels. There was no water:

> We were driven to drink our own urine, which we saved in some shards of certain jars, which we had out of our pinnace, and set our urine all night to cool therein, to drink it the next morning, which thus being drunk often, and often avoided, became in a while exceeding red, in all this time we had no rain.

Tying other wood to a 10ft driftwood plank with withes, the two struck out for
the mainland. Two poles served as oars. They hoped the flood tide would carry
them to the coast about 3 leagues away. After three days and two nights they
reached the beach. Ashore, Carder and Pitcher found fresh water at a small river,
but a frantic Pitcher 'over drank himself, being pinched before with extreme
thirst, and to my unspeakable grief and discomfort, within half an hour after died
in my presence, whom I buried as well as I could in the sand'. Carder, alone with
a sword and shield, began walking north along the coastline towards whatever
succour Brazil might offer.

He writes that he was taken in by the Tupinambás and lived with them for six
months, and was part of an attack against the Tapwees (Tapuias), their enemies.
The tribes of Tupinambás had attacked with 300 or 400 bowmen. They tied their
prisoners to a stake, quaffed down a liquor 'like to an ale', a brew that at feasts they
would drink 'till they be as drunk as apes', then bashed their prisoners' brains out.
After battle, the Tupinambás king had taken the prisoners and would cause 'many
of thir carcasses to be broiled upon the coals and eaten'. Others brought home
were 'killed, roasted and eaten' later. It was much the same with the Portuguese
and 'certain Negroes', who 'were brained with clubs, broiled and eaten'. Such was
to become the tale of Othello's anthropophagi, first told by Carder.

The Tupinambás king eventually let Carder go to seek passage on an English
or French ship. Peter Carder surrendered himself to the Portuguese, who imprisoned and then released him to work as an overseer of fields of sugar cane, of
ginger, of cotton, of red and white peppers, and groves of brazilwood. His master
had a small coasting bark and, as a sailor, Carder was soon signed aboard to work
there. At the end of their second cruise, when arriving back in Spirito Santo, the
kindly Portuguese warned Carder that a ship would soon be arriving to transport
him as a prisoner to Portugal and they gave Carder his boat and four black slaves
to escape. Carder writes of 'pretending to go on fishing to the sea; and so of purpose going much to leeward of the place, I put in to Fernambuc' (Pernambuco),
where he hid for some months until a hulk with a crew of eight English and
fourteen Portuguese arrived. Carder shipped aboard. At the Azores two English
ships of war attacked. Carder was taken first to Baltimore, in Ireland, then up the
Channel to Chichester. He arrived in late November 1586, as he says, 'nine years
and fourteen days after my departure out of England with Sir Francis Drake in his
voyage about the world', a hero.

He told his tales to Charles Howard, Lord High Admiral of England, who took
him before Elizabeth I at Whitehall, 'where it pleased her to talk with me a long
hour's space of my travails and wonderful escape, and among other things of the
manner of M. Doughtie's execution; and afterward bestowed twenty-two angels
on me, willing my Lord to have consideration of me: With many gracious words
I was dismissed; humbly thanking the Almighty for my miraculous preservation,
and safe return into my native country'.

Carder's return six years after Drake's own triumphant one is a story not unlike those of Job Hortop and Miles Phillips, survivors of Hawkyns' ill-fated third voyage and the slaughter at San Juan de Ulúa in 1568. Hortop suffered Spanish torture, imprisonment and twelve years in the galleys. He was not to return to Portsmouth until 2 December 1590, twenty-two years after sailing with Hawkyns from England. Phillips was rescued by Cumberland in the Rio de la Plata on 3 April 1587, nineteen years after he went ashore in Nueva España. (Another source has him returning to Europe in the Spanish *flota* of 1582.)

But Carder's account to the point when he reaches Bahia must be considered together with the writings of 'Edward Cliffe' on John Wynter's *Elizabeth*. The Cliffe account tells a somewhat different story.[16] It says that after being parted from Drake, Wynter passed back through the strait, reprovisioned with seal meat, assembled a pinnace, and set sail for England on 1 January 1579. On 20 January during a storm, writes Cliffe, the *Elizabeth* lost sight of the pinnace off São Vicente, just south of the Tropic of Capricorn. The Cliffe account has it that the pinnace and her eight men were never seen again. This version counters Carder's claim to have sailed solo for some 1,900 miles.

A Spanish account corroborates the Cliffe story. Galician navigator Captain Pedro Sarmiento de Gamboa, in his *Relación y derrotero* written to the Crown in 1580, says that on 19 July 1580 his ship, the *Nuestra Señora de la Esperanza*, was moored in the port of Angra on the Azorean island of Terceira, where two Portuguese ships arrived from Brazil. Their captains reported that off Bahia, on the eastern tip of Brazil, five Portuguese and fifteen Indians had found ten Englishmen drying their boat's sails at the mouth of the Rio das Contas. In the skirmish, two of the seven English on land were taken. Five others were wounded but escaped to the boat being guarded by three other sailors. The Portuguese next saw them on Quiepe Island, Camamu Bay, where the five wounded men had been left to die. These men were later captured and confessed that they had been part of an English fleet that had passed through the Strait of Magellan into the Pacific, then turned back to the Atlantic. They said they were lucky to be on shore, for in a storm, their ship had run aground. Afterwards, they sailed to Porto Seguro, then to the Rio das Contas. An English sailor, a '30-year-old, very skillful lad and great mathematician' and others had been captured along the coast of Bahia.

This man may have been Carder. It seems likely that Carder sailed the strait in the *Elizabeth*, and after being cast away was eventually taken prisoner in Bahia. Author Amilcar d'Avila de Mello finds that Carder's account, as published by Purchas, has numerous inconsistencies. Carder, says Mello, was not attacked by the Tupinambás in the Rio de la Plata, but his accurate description of a Tupí village and the Indians' language instead fits the time he was a prisoner of the Portuguese in Bahia.

Pelican Bound for England

Since taking the *Cacafuego* in March, Francis Drake's course had been north-north-westerly. At the Nueva España port of Huatulco (then Guatulco), along with a number of Spaniards, Drake set ashore Nuño da Silva, the Portuguese pilot kidnapped in the Cabo Verde islands more than fifteen months earlier.[17] The details of the rest of Drake's voyage are sketchy, particularly those published by Hakluyt in 1598–1600, for England and Spain were then still at war.

Drake thought it good not to return via the Strait of Magellan for two reasons: the Spanish would be there in numbers and strength to capture him and the *Pelican*; and the western mouth of the strait was a place of 'continual storms reigning and blustering, as he found by experience, besides the shoals and sands upon the coast, he thought it not a good course to adventure that way'. He resolved to avoid these hazards and to go to the Moluccas and carry on past the Cape of Good Hope to return home. From 16 April to 3 June he sailed northward to catch a favourable wind for crossing.

The author of Drake's account writes that on 5 June the *Pelican* found herself at latitude 43° N, progressing towards the Arctic on the back side of America, where:

> we found the air so cold, that our men being grievously pinched with the same, complained of the extremity thereof, and the further we went, the more the cold increased upon us. Whereupon we thought it best for that time to seek the land, and did so, finding it not mountainous, but low plain land, till we came within 38 degrees towards the line. In which height it pleased God to send us into a fair and good bay, with a good wind to enter the same.[18]

He had reached what would later be called Alta California, but in those early years he was safely beyond the pale of the Spanish. On 17 June, at about latitude 38° N, near San Francisco, Drake found a harbour, careened and graved the *Pelican*, probably in Drake's Estero, within Drake's Bay.

On 26 June a delegation of Indians came down to the ship. The Indian chief swore fealty to Drake and Queen Elizabeth, and Drake claimed the land for England, naming it Nova Albion – England's first possession in North America. Its white banks and cliffs facing the sea reminded Drake and author Francis Fletcher of Dover. The account claims 'there is no part of earth here to be taken up, wherein there is not some probable show of gold or silver'. Hakluyt, editing in the 1590s, underscores the point in his sidenote: 'Gold and silver in the earth of Nova Albion.' Before leaving, Drake set up a monument, 'namely a plate, nailed upon a fair great post, whereupon was engraved her Majesty's name, the day and year of our arrival there, with the free giving up of the province and people into her Majesty's hands, together with her Highness' picture and arms, in a piece is sixpence of current English money under the plate, whereunder was also written the name of our general'.

Drake may have set out from Nova Albion across the Pacific as early as 25 July 1579, or it may have been later, in August.[19] The sources differ. The *Pelican* was among the islands of the Far East by October 1579.

In Panamá, on 2 October, Dr Diego de Villanueva Zapata wrote to the Spanish Crown that some of the Cimarróns had negotiated for peace in exchange for a site on the Río Francisco to be administered by the Spanish.[20] Resettlement was the answer for these renegade black people. For the Cimarróns of Vallano, it was a different story: 'Having given great evidence of a desire for peace, and of humility and Christianity, the blacks of Vallano have failed of their promise and withdrawn and revolted … These are unreliable people, changeable and unreasonable … Finally troops were sent against them.'

On the same day that Drake doubled the Cape of Good Hope, leaving the Indian Ocean for the Atlantic, Licentiate Cepeda, president of the *Audiencia* in Panamá, was writing to the Crown that his jurisdiction, 'washed by both the Pacific and the Atlantic', could expect the English to return.[21] Cepeda adds that he plans to build a garrison at Acla. As for those Cimarróns of Portobelo, the highwaymen who repeatedly commit robberies, he writes, now 'have been brought to obedience and your majesty's service'.

Drake, his crew and the *Pelican*, heavy with ballast of silver bars and a cargo of silver, gold, silks, pearls and spices, arrived back in Plymouth (or Portsmouth) on 26 September 1580 (or October or November), in 'the third year of our departure'. Drake's voyage had made him the first captain to circumnavigate the globe in his own ship. His riches bought him a knighthood, Buckland Abbey and the queen's lasting gratitude.

A Crown, Gallows, Walnut Bed

Significant political changes were taking place in Europe as Drake was making his way homeward up the west coast of Africa. With the death in 1579 of the Portuguese king, Dom Henrique, and with no direct heir to the throne in sight, many of the nobles and others favoured the accession of the Spanish monarch, Philip II, to rule both countries. Spain was to rule Portugal from 1580 to 1640, when the Duke of Bragança was accepted by the Portuguese as the king of Portugal. As late as 1668, the Spanish were contesting Portugal's independence.

Drake's Devon friend and lieutenant, Captain John Oxnam, and the three with him who had been left in a Lima prison were viewed by the Spanish not only as Protestants and heretics but as pirates. The Inquisition was at pains to convert these 'Lutheran heretics' to Catholicism. Once converted, their penance for heresy was to be a lifetime of repentance in the galleys. Viceroy Toledo, however, had other ideas. He condemned to death as pirates John Oxnam, John Butler, and ship's master Thomas Sherwell. John Butler's younger brother

Henry Butler was sentenced to the galleys. In October 1580, as winter was giving way to summer in Perú and just days after Drake had sailed triumphantly into Plymouth harbour, that other fiery Plymouth captain and two of his men were hanged. The remains of Oxnam, John Butler and Sherwell lie unmarked somewhere in Peruvian soil. What happened to young Henry Butler we do not know.

Captain Oxnam remains the first Englishman to build a vessel from New World timber, the first to sail that pinnace as the first English warship on the Pacific, and the first to seize a treasure of Spanish gold and silver in those waters. Ashore, Oxnam led legions of Spanish soldiers on a chase through the Panamanian jungle for fully half a year, offering the first sustained English challenge to Spanish rule in the Americas.

About a month after Drake reached Plymouth Sound, Captain Stephen Hare slipped the lines of the *Minion* at a dock in Harwich. Her cargo included copper cauldrons, iron tools, cloths, and finery for John Whithall in Brazil, and she arrived in Santos on 3 February 1581. *Minion*'s mariners brought Whithall the news: 'The Islands, Indies, and Portugal itself was molested and troubled by the Spaniards, and … the Portugals had both English and Frenchmen to Lisbon to defend them against Spain.' Portugal was now under Spanish rule, though the Azores were still holding out, and Dom António, the Pretender, might take the throne back if the English would support him.[22]

English adventurers had sent Whithall his goods as ordered and, in exchange, were to receive the 'best, finest, and whitest dry sugars 32 pound of our weight for a ducat at the most'. Out of the hold the crew brought ashore a token of goodwill from the investors to the newly-weds: 'a field bed of walnut tree, with the canopy, valence, curtains, and gilt knobs.' Just as Robert Tomson had wedded wealthily with the Spanish woman of Nueva España, so Whithall had wedded to great advantage in Brazil.[23]

In one of Richard Hakluyt's earliest tracts, 'A Discourse of the commodity of the Taking of the Strait of Magellanus', the author, then a young English curate of 28, argues that Europe is compromised if Spain and Portugal are allowed to control the East and West Indies.[24] To prevent this, among other things, he urges the English to control the strait at both ends, and to take and garrison Cabo São Vicente, Brazil. Control of the strait, he says, should be by some English pirate and not acknowledged officially by the government. Hakluyt's plan was not accepted by the Crown.

In 1582 Hakluyt published *Divers Voyages Touching the Discoverie of America*. In its dedication to Sir Philip Sidney, he criticises the English for allowing the Spanish and Portuguese to claim the Americas exclusively for themselves.[25] In this, his first publication, he writes that colonisation is one's Christian obligation, as it is an opportunity to save the souls of the Indians. Further, by transporting undesirables to the Americas, England could not only clear out its prisons but could also give convicts a chance for redemption. Put God first and gold will follow. All for England, for a Protestant God and Profit.

By the early 1580s England was openly challenging Spain in the Americas. Though Oxnam and his men had been hunted down, Drake had terrorised the Pacific and had taken the largest haul of treasure to date.

four

SEVERE GALE, 1582–88

To prognosticate as the dolphin that some storm or tempest approaches.

Sixteenth-century proverb

On 9 April 1582 Edward Fenton received instructions for his voyage to the East Indies by way of the Strait of Magellan.[1] He was to command a fleet of four vessels: the galleon *Beare*, the *Edward Bonaventure*, the bark *Francis* and a small frigate or pinnace. He was to provision for 200 able men. Besides gentlemen and their servants, ministers, surgeons, merchants and others, 'which said number is no way to be exceeded, whereof as many as may be [of that 200], to be seamen'. He was not to sign on any 'disordered or mutinous person, but that upon knowledge had, you shall remove him before your departure hence, or by the way as soon as you can conveniently avoid him, and receive better in his place'. In all important matters, Fenton was to consult a council of eight ships' captains. Only with just cause was Fenton to relieve any of the captains of command. Fenton was secretly to rank the gentlemen, 'written in parchment, included in balls of wax, sealed with her Majesty's signet, put into two coffers locked with three several locks'. Each ship would keep an inventory of 'tackle, munition, and furniture'.

Fenton was to make for the Moluccas 'for the better discovery of the Northwest passage'. He was to establish rendezvous points but must not 'spoil or take anything from any of the Queen's Majesty's friends or allies, or any Christians, without paying justly for the same'. On the voyage, Fenton and the factors are to deal 'like good and honest merchants, trafficking and exchanging ware for ware, with all courtesy to the nations you shall deal with, as well ethnics as others'. Further, Fenton was encouraged to arrange for future trading and, to that end, to learn the 'tongue and secrets of the countries' and to take and leave hostages, 'being careful that equal rank is observed'. Charts are to be kept close, and they are to be turned over upon return. Minister Richard Madox is to keep a 'particular and true note' of the voyage. Finally, to assure God's blessing on the enterprise, ministers aboard should be allowed to practise their calling.

The author of the account printed by Hakluyt was Vice-Admiral Luke Ward, captain of the vice-admiral *Edward Bonaventure*, 300 tons, Thomas Perrie, master.[2] She cast off from Blackwall on 1 April. On 19 April Ward was at Nettle Road in Hampton, where he joined the admiral, the galleon *Leicester*, 400 tons, commanded by Edward Fenton as captain-general, and in her, William Hawkyns the Younger as lieutenant-general, and Christopher Hall as master. Aboard the *Francis*, 40 tons, were John Drake, captain, and William Markam (Markham), master. On the *Elizabeth*, 50 tons, was Thomas Skevington, captain, and Ralph Crane, master. The fleet set out on the morning of 1 May, bound for China and the East Indies.

At the beginning of August the fleet was off the coast of Guinea, and at about six on the morning of 1 December Fenton saw Brazil, 8 leagues off, at the height of about latitude 28° S. He was south of Florianópolis, anchoring in 8 fathoms, half a mile off the land. When Fenton learned there that the Spanish had fortified the Strait of Magellan, he called Ward, Hawkyns, Drake and the two pilots together. After dining in his cabin, he proposed two courses: either to transit the strait, knowing the Spanish were there in force, or to turn back. All agreed the first course was foolhardy. According to Lopez Vaz, the fleet turned back either from foul weather or 'fear of the king's ships'.[3]

In turning back for São Vicente to reprovision, Fenton lost Drake in the *Francis*. On the night of 22 December the *Francis* had 'gone room' (fallen off) from the fleet and was cast away on shoals in the Rio de la Plata. Drake and his men swam ashore and lived for fifteen months with the Indians before being captured by the Spanish. Drake, as an important prisoner, was sent to Perú for interrogation, trial and sentencing by the viceroy.

On 20 January Fenton was off São Vicente, and with the ships' boats, the fleet sounded its way in over the bar, anchoring in 7 fathoms. Fenton and the other captains sent the governor 'three yards of fine scarlet, and three yards of fine murry-cloth', and to Whithall, Dory and others 'three yards of fine black cloth' each. Fenton also met Joseph Dory, John Whithall's Genoese father-in-law. Then before dawn on the 24th, Whithall came to warn Fenton that Spanish warships were on their way and at four that afternoon, three Spanish galleons manned by some 600 men came around the point. They anchored on the bar and despite a fierce battle, the English beat off the Spanish.

Early in February the fleet was hit by a 'stout gale'. One man died of the bloody flux, and water and victuals were low. The journal records that on 11 April carpenter George Coxe had broken into the hold, stolen wine, and 'drunken himself drunk, being taken in the room, leaped overboard out of the beakhead and so drowned himself'. On 12 April they 'spied our foremast to be perished in the hounds, and durst not bear our foretop sail upon it, but went hence with our sails, next hand, North all day and night'. North homeward it was, and on 27 May they were off the Scilly Isles. At 1900 hours Ward notes they 'saw the land's end of England, which bare East by North off us'. On the 29th they were off Plymouth within a league of Ram Head, becalmed in thick fog. On the last day of May, at nine in the morning, Ward dropped the *Edward Bonaventure*'s anchor near Millbrook. 'Thus I ended a troublesome voyage.'

Cannon, Women, Cattle

Colonisation and further depredations by the English continued to trouble the Spanish. On 30 July 1583 the governor of the island of San Juan de Puerto Rico, Diego Menéndez de Valdéz, wrote to the Crown that on Monday 22 July, seven vessels (William Hawkyns' fleet), 'five of them being large ships, one a shallop and one pinnace', had anchored near the settlement of San German at Guadianilla. Governor Valdéz writes that the English asked 'if they wanted to barter for women', for there were many women aboard, and adds that the fleet is strong and intends to find a site for settlement.[4]

In England, meanwhile, Hakluyt was once again trumpeting the cause of colonisation, this time at the suggestion of Sir Walter Ralegh.[5] Hakluyt puts pen to paper in his *Discourse of Western Planting* and urges as before, in religious terms, that the queen should support colonies in America, particularly Ralegh's, as it undermines the Papists.

Spanish intelligence about the English was usually accurate. The Spanish were well aware of Sir Francis Drake's plan to raid the West Indies again. While Drake's fleet was off the islands of Bayona in Galicia, the High Admiral of Spain, Don Álvaro de Bazán, Marqués of Santa Cruz, was writing to the Crown on 26 October 1585 from Lisbon that he expected Drake to attack the Madeiras, the Canaries and Cabo Verdes, then head for Rio de Janeiro, a 'haven capable of many ships and very safe, where there is water, wood and flesh'. A fort should be built on the island in the Bay of Guanabara, he says, and in the Caribbean the colonies must be warned.[6]

Don Diego de Alcega, commander of the Nueva España fleet, had left San Juan de Ulúa on 19 May and on arriving in La Havana wrote to the president and officials of the Casa de Contratación there.[7] On the high seas south of Bermuda, Richard Grenville had captured the *Santa Maria de San Vicente* on course from Santo Domingo for Spain. He had seized her cargo of gold, silver and pearls totalling more than 40,000 ducats, as well as '200 boxes of sugar of forty *arrobas* each, and 7,000 hides, and a thousand hundredweight of ginger and other merchandise, to a total value of 120,000 ducats'.

Grenville, Alcega writes, seemed a man of quality, one who ate on silver and gold plate, had servants, and dined to music provided by a consort of instruments.

He learned from passengers that Grenville had gone in five ships to Florida, where he had disembarked about 300 men and set them to building a fort, and planned to settle northwards towards the Newfoundland fishing banks.

Licentiate Francisco de Aliaga, fiscal or Crown counsel of the *Audiencia* of Santo Domingo, adds in a letter dated 30 November to the Crown that the English had with them thirty pieces of artillery, 500 men and some women, as well as plants, horses and cattle of all kinds.[8] It was evident that by the mid-1580s the English were bent on colonisation, while at the same time attacking the Spanish at sea or in port.

Drake's West Indian Voyage

Drake's retaliatory voyage to the West Indies in 1585 and 1586 was rightly feared by the Spanish.[9] The fleet was truly an armada of nearly three dozen vessels sent into the heart of the sources for Spain's gold and silver in the West Indies and the Americas – the largest undertaking to date by the English to the Caribbean. It was organised largely by the Hawkyns family, with the queen's open support. The official records show that Francis Drake supplied £1,200, Walter Ralegh's brother Carew Ralegh (probably as agent for younger brother Walter) £400, John Hawkyns £1,600, and his nephew, William Hawkyns, £300. The queen provided £10,000 in cash, in addition to her two (greatly overvalued) royal ships. The endeavour was underwritten by £13,500. A tallying puts the total support, including cash, ships and supplies, at £23,900: Drake, £7,000; John Hawkyns, £2,500; William Hawkyns, £1,000; Walter Ralegh, £400; Robert Dudley, Earl of Leicester, £3,000; and the queen, £10,000 cash plus two ships. This royal English armada was to raid the West Indies three years before the much larger Spanish counterpart sailed up the English Channel to invade England. It is this voyage in 1585, as much as Elizabeth's support of the Protestants in Europe, which brought the war with Spain to flame.

The journals written on board three of the ships, giving details of the voyage, were by ships' officers, not Drake. The best first-hand account is the journal of Captain Walter Bigges, first published in Latin in 1588, and then translated into English in 1589. Bigges' journal is unfinished, as he died of fever at sea en route from Cartagena to Cuba.

The two royal vessels were the *Elizabeth Bonaventure*, 600 tons, rebuilt as a galleon and serving as Drake's admiral, and the *Aide*, 200–250 tons. Other vessels were the galleon *Leicester*, 400 tons; the *Primrose*, 300–400 tons; and the *Tiger*, 150–200 tons. Ten other ships had tonnages between 100 and 200 tons. The rest were smaller vessels and included the *Francis*, a smaller *Elizabeth*, 60–70 tons, and the *Duck*, a galliot of 20 tons. In all, the fleet comprised fifteen ships plus smaller vessels, totalling some 2,000 tons of shipping. Here was truly an English armada.

The vice-admiral *Primrose*, one of Hawkyns' ships, was commanded by Martin Frobisher. Christopher Carleill, Walsingham's stepson, was captain of the *Tiger* and was later named lieutenant-general for all land operations. Thomas Fenner was captain of the admiral, the *Bonaventure*, under Drake. Francis Knollys, younger son of the treasurer of the Royal Household and brother-in-law of the Earl of Leicester, was captain of the *Leicester* and listed as rear-admiral for parts of the voyage. Others in on the enterprise were Edward Wynter, son of Sir William Wynter; the courtier Fulke Greville; the elder William Hawkyns; Thomas, the young brother of Francis Drake; the young William Hawkyns; and John Hawkyns' son, Richard. Three of the crew had been with Drake on his circumnavigation: George Fortescue, John Martin and Thomas Moone, carpenter with Drake on his 1573 voyage. Drake had aboard as chaplain Philip Nichols. The fleet's company, totalling 1,925 men, were mostly West Country men.

On the morning of 14 September, the NNE winds were favourable for departure. As Elizabeth had not at that point stayed the fleet from sailing, Drake seized his chance and slipped his lines at 0800 hours without full supplies of water and food and without detailed sailing orders for his ships' captains. This was Drake's largest command to date, and he improvised as he sailed. Under way, he called his officers together to decide course and plan of attack, and to establish disciplinary rules, initiating a practice later adopted by England's Royal Navy. On long voyages, as Drake well knew from past experience, discipline and loyalty were especially important. With Plymouth still in sight, Drake was happy to see ashore (on the queen's orders) Sir Philip Sidney, Fulke Greville, Richard Drake, the Portuguese Pretender Dom António and others.

They reached the Ilhas Cabo Verdes on 17 November and at last fully provisioned the fleet. Two days later Drake made his officers swear oaths of allegiance. First was the usual oath of supremacy. The second was that of the lieutenant-general of the land forces to the general, Drake. The third was the captains' oath to the general, Drake, and the fourth was that of the private passengers to the captain of their ships and their officers. Knollys objected that the oaths could 'hazard many men's souls', at which Drake 'grew in exceeding fury'. Knollys defended the loyalty of his men and asked that he be given a ship for himself so that he and his men could go their own way. Drake agreed, no doubt recalling his trouble with Thomas Doughtie's loyalty seven years earlier. While in the Cabo Verdes, a court martial was called to deal with discipline. One man, having killed an officer, was hanged for mutiny. The second was the steward in the bark *Talbot*, Thomas Ogle, who had sodomised two boys in his cabin. He was convicted and hanged from a gibbet: 'The man confessed the fact and died very penitently.' Knollys was discharged from these courts martial proceedings.

The fleet sailed mid-afternoon on Monday 28 November, not a moment too soon. The Cabo Verdes were notorious for pestilence, the 'island fever', and just a few days afterwards Drake's fleet was hit by disease, a *calentura* with delirium that makes sailors mistake the sea for green fields. It was accompanied by chills and presented spots similar to those of bubonic or pneumonic plague.[10] On the *Bonaventure* 100 were ill, and throughout the fleet of overcrowded ships for nearly two weeks, a couple of men died every day. In all, between 300 and 500 men were soon lost, a heavy toll that was later to compromise the fleet's ability to fight.

Their course was westward for some 550 leagues, in 'very fair weather'. Drake made his landfall at Dominica on 18 December after a fast passage of nineteen or twenty days. On 21 December the fleet reached Saint Christopher's, where Drake aired the ships, refreshed the sick and celebrated Christmas. Though twenty more men died there on the island most of the remaining crew recovered.

On 30 December he reached Hispaniola. Its capital, Santo Domingo, was one of the three most important cities in Spanish America. Though in 1585 it was a poor city, the *cortes* and the Casa de Contratación were still there, and no doubt the city still had enough old wealth to make it attractive to Drake. On Friday 31 December, at about three in the afternoon, his men embarked in the pinnaces, sailing and rowing all night, their guide a Greek pilot kidnapped from a Spanish ship. They made for a deserted cove, Boca de Hayna, 3 leagues from Santo Domingo.

The Spanish did not expect Drake's plan of attack. At eight in the morning of Saturday 1 January 1586, Christopher Carleill, land-general, landed about 1,000 soldiers and marched them towards the city. Drake returned to the ships and sailed them to a position off Santo Domingo within range of his cannon. About mid-morning, as Carleill's men attacked the city, Drake fired on it, catching the Spanish completely by surprise.

As the English entered by the city's upper gate, the Spanish fired back, killing two. But by late afternoon the English had taken the town, except for a few pockets of resistance. The town's ordnance consisted of sixty-six cannon, 'all brass very fair', and in a Spanish report, others totalling 'over 70 pieces of artillery' – a fine haul for Drake. In Santo Domingo, he writes, there were as well 'so many dry hides in this town that it was wonderful, great store also of sugar which we esteemed not, it was so plentiful'. Besides hides, sugar and ordnance, the English took church bells, three ships (leaving behind two of the older English ones) and eighty slaves.

Finding no gold and silver, Drake demanded ransom. When the Spanish procrastinated, Drake replied by burning a different part of the town each day. Finally, the factor for the Crown and spokesman for the citizens, García Fernández de Torrequemada, arranged for a ransom of 25,000 ducats to be paid for the portion of the town still standing (less than half, possibly just a third, of the old city). He asked for the return of a silk escutcheon taken from the *Audiencia*'s building. Drake declined to return it, saying its value as a token of the damage he had done to Spain's pride was greater than any ransom he might be offered for it. Emblazoned on it was King Philip's motto, *Orbis Non Sufficit* ('the world is not enough'). To the English, the motto's presumption fired the sort of strong anti-Spanish propaganda that figures in the *Summarie*, published in 1588 and 1589. Drake's raid was worth a candle – cannon, church bells, hides, ransom *and* the silk escutcheon. As he wrote, 'the Spaniards gave us the town for a New Year's gift', and so he was to name one of the Spanish vessels seized.

While the English occupied Santo Domingo, not far away at an *ingenio de azúcar* (sugar mill) at Xagua, Licentiate Aliaga wrote to the Crown on 3 January 1586 that two days earlier Drake had landed nine companies, 1,400 men in all, and the day after at about two o'clock, he had taken the city and about 50,000 ducats from the royal treasury. No more than a hundred foot soldiers and fifty horse had stood up to the enemy: 'It was indeed pitiful to see the women and children, nuns and friars, and the invalids, wandering lost through the bush and along the roads.'[11]

On 4 January licentiates Fernández de Mercado and Baltazar de Villafañe, both of them judges of the *Audiencia*, wrote to the Crown from Hispaniola that the enemy was so terrifying, 'not a man stood his ground to fire his harquebus'.[12] That same day, Mercado and Villafañe also wrote to Don Diego de Zuñiga, president of the Casa de Contratación in Seville.[13] With a Biblical twist, the licentiates write, 'we are wandering through the bush in such misfortune and nakedness that God alone suffices to give us patience'.

On 12 January 1586 Alonso Rodriguez de Azebedo, serving under the commander of the galleys, Don Diego Osorio, wrote to Diego Fernandez de Quiñones from Bayaha.[14] Azebedo had been sent by Osorio to fetch slaves who had deserted from the galleys.

> For the love of God, let your honour fortify yourself strongly! This traitor is strong. He has 32 large galleons and now from here he will take as booty over seventy pieces of artillery, including five culverins and eleven cannon larger than Little Saint Lorenzo, and three extra large perriers, and all the munitions the fort and city had, for these damned fools did not throw them into the sea, but ran and left everything.

As for Drake's own officers, the trouble long brewing with Captain Knollys came to a head. At dinner on 14 January, Drake raised a toast to Knollys, wanting to know his decision. Knollys, who since the Cabo Verdes had refused to take the loyalty oath, answered that he had not changed his mind about the oath and would accept Drake's offer to take a ship and leave. On 27 January Knollys and his men were given the *Hawkyns*, where 'the only provision was wine and meal, as well for gentlemen as for mariners. The general sent aboard a mutton and quarter of beef for my master and a 1,000 poor John [salted dried hake].' Knollys was relieved of his command within the fleet and was to return to England.

Santo Domingo, Cartagena Sacked

The Spaniards in Santo Domingo began to bring in the ransom, first in 'beeves and muttons', then in 'gold, silver, and pearl'. A Spanish official recorded 50,000 ducats having been taken from their royal treasury, and the handover as a whole was estimated at 200,000 ducats. The Spanish finished paying the ransom on 30 January.

Francis Drake had occupied Santo Domingo for thirty-one days and had traded his *Scout*, *Hope* and *Benjamin*, all older ships, for better Spanish ones lying in the harbour. One was a 400-ton vessel he renamed the *New Year's Gift*, loading her with the seventy cannon and other ordnance taken. Another Spanish ship they renamed *New Hope* and loaded with the rest of the booty. Drake freed the 400 slaves chained to the royal galley, sent them ashore, then towed the galley to sea and set her afire. Before leaving, Drake also burned the rest of the Spanish ships, including an old ship of 600–700 tons, as well as many small barks, spoiling more than twenty vessels in all.

The news spread fast of Drake's sacking of Spain's premier city in the Caribbean, 'that strong thing, Santo Domingo, which is the key to all of the Indies', and Cartagena, La Havana and other ports quickly strengthened their defences. The fall of Santo Domingo underscored for Philip II the seriousness of the English threat.

On 14 February 1586 the seven members of the *Audiencia* of Santo Domingo, echoing other reports, wrote to the Crown summarising the recent English attack.[15] The licentiates reiterated that Santo Domingo was ill-prepared to defend itself against 5,000 or 6,000 troops. These were 'very well armed and equipped, and so well-disciplined that within a few hours they had so fortified themselves that a great force would have been required to retake the city'. Drake as a leader? He is 'a cautious commander, equal to any undertaking. He brings with him veteran captains and soldiers from among the richest and most honoured in England'. His thirty or thirty-one vessels 'have the best possible armament and equipment, munitions and choicest powder' in abundance. 'There are ships of over 700 tons, armament some seventy heavy guns, most of them bronze, not counting those they took from us.'

On 31 January Drake's fleet, now twenty-four vessels, set sail for Cartagena. Cartagena had been warned.[16] One correspondent there wrote:

> Your honour can imagine the condition of this city. So far what has been done is to make trenches, ditches and greatly to strengthen its defence; and now we are busy making wills and arranging all our affairs for a stand to the death …
> And so this city awaits the enemy every hour, arms in hand. The governor has 600 harquebusiers, fifty horse, 800 Indians, 200 hundredweight of powder, exclusive of the strength of the galleys which is 150 soldiers, not counting the galley slaves.

Nine years earlier on another Ash Wednesday, 1577, Oxnam had attacked Las Perlas. On this later Ash Wednesday, about noon on 9 February 1586 (not 11 February, as the English record it),[17] Drake was off Cartagena, a town about half the size of Santo Domingo and equally weak.[18] At three in the afternoon (some say four or five o'clock), he hoisted the counsel flag aboard the admiral to set up a meeting of officers, who agreed on landing at two the next morning. To defend the inner harbour, Don Pedro Vique, the commander of the Spanish galleys, 'ordered the galleys to swing a chain, which had been made of iron, across the channel from the fort at its entrance to the other side. Because a few links were lacking they went to the jail and brought the chain which was there, with which they supplied what was missing, and fastened it to floats in such a manner that no launch nor any ship could enter.' The Cartagenians dug a trench, erected a barricade and planted poisoned stakes (possibly boxthorn) to hinder a land attack along the beach. Two leagues from the town, at the west end of the point, 'were set an infinite number of pricks, poisoned and set in the sand of length a foot and a half and so thick that a man could not get clear if he came among them'.

Though the Spanish knew the English were coming, Drake still surprised them. They did not expect him to attack in the dead of night. Under cover of darkness, he landed some 550 to 1,200 men, according to Spanish sources (Carleill gives 1,700 men, probably exaggerated). Shoal water off the town's coast prevented the larger vessels from sailing in close enough to bombard it, and the smaller pinnaces were prevented from entering the narrow Boquerón Channel, just two ships' lengths wide, barricaded with a chain, and covered from the castle by sixteen cannon and on the other side by another six at the fort. An eyewitness with Frobisher's pinnaces records that the enemy fire was effective: 'We had the rudder of our pinnace stroke away and men's hats from their heads and the top of our main mast beaten in pieces, the oars stricken out of our men's hands as they rowed and our captain like to have been slain.' Should the English get past all that, 499 armed Spanish horsemen and footmen defended the corridor leading into town.

More important to the English was that it was low tide when they landed, so soldiers could march in the surf, water up to their navels, and avoid the poisoned stakes planted in the beach. Low tide further meant that both the Spanish royal galleys ran aground, and their commander ordered them burned to keep them and their cannon from English hands. One caught fire when a keg of gunpowder exploded, and the Spanish unchained the slaves, many of whom went over to the English side. Indians loyal to the Spanish shot poisoned arrows 'coming very thick'. By dawn, the English had entered Cartagena. Their casualties were high, but by mid-morning the city had fallen.

On 12 March 1586 the governor of Cartagena, Pedro Fernández de Busto, wrote to the *Audiencia* at Ciudad de Panamá: 'I do not know how to begin to tell your lordship of my misfortune and of the loss of Cartagena. I can only say that it must be God's chastisement of my sins and of those of others. Our Lord be praised for all!' Busto had faced the much greater English numbers with only 220 men. 'It was', he wrote, 'the blackest night I have ever seen in my life'. Drake set up his new defences in a priory near the city and occupied the fort by the water-side. On 15 February the Spanish came with a flag of truce to ransom the town, and Drake and the Spanish officials dined together to discuss the details. Drake demanded 400,000 ducats. The Spanish countered with 5,000 (the numbers vary, but the disparity is consistent). After five weeks and three days, negotiations for ransom had stalled. Drake did as he had done before in Santo Domingo, setting fire to sections of the town and taking the brass cannon (a French account mentions six or seven score) and the church bells.

Fever then struck the English, killing 100. Seven hundred men were now left, and of those 150 were sick or wounded. Drake told his prisoner, Captain Alonso Bravo, that since the start of the voyage, 500 in all had been lost.[19] His plan to attack Nombre de Dios or Panamá would have to be scrapped. Drake had moved into the house of Captain Bravo, whose wife presented Drake with 'a very rich suit of buttons of gold and pearl, and a very fair jewel set with emeralds and a ring with an emerald and another emerald set in a pendant'.[20] Through her husband, she also sent the lieutenant-general 'a fair jewel set with emerald and a fair ring with an emerald', and to the vice-admiral 'a fair ring with an emerald'. She died during the time Drake was staying in their home, and he allowed her to be buried in the priory of St Francis in Cartagena, honouring her memory by firing off a volley in her name. In February, with his characteristic mix of cruelty and kindness, Drake put out a general order that strangers in the city, namely Frenchmen, Turks and black men, be used well.

According to Kelsey, slavery, and especially women slaves, had been a problem throughout the voyage.[21] Black female slaves had been taken aboard at the Cabo Verdes, more at Santo Domingo, and now at Cartagena still others. Most of the slaves brought aboard there were female. In the West Indies, slavery and prostitution flourished, and venereal disease was rampant. Indian and black slave women, and later Spanish women, worked as prostitutes. To quell dissent among the ranks, Drake ordered that no one under the rank of ensign could have a slave, male or female.

On 11 March the ransom arrived. 'There came in twenty mules laden with silver wedges; eight of them were a load, four one each side. There was likewise some gold and jewels brought. The most of the wedges wayed fifty pounds.' Ransom came to 107,000 ducats. About 15 March Drake resolved to sail for England and loaded aboard victuals, wood and water. He had been in Cartagena for seven weeks.

In the early morning of Maundy Thursday, 31 March, Drake set sail for Cuba.[22] The winds were south-easterly, the weather foul. But 'there fell such a leak in one of our ships that we were driven to go back again to Cartagena and there to take out all our ordnance, goods and other furniture and so set her on fire'. This

was the *New Year's Gift*, Corço's new ship captured by Thomas Drake at Santo
Domingo, the ship that carried all the captured ordnance. Drake returned to
Cartagena on 4 April. This time, the Spanish co-operated with Drake, the sooner
to see him gone. For a week the cooks baked sea biscuit, and crews transferred
cargo and cannon to the other ships. On Wednesday 13 April, when the transfer
of booty was completed, the Spanish prize ship was set on fire. At about four
in the morning of 14 April, Drake and the fleet left Cartagena a second time.[23]
The wind was south-east, a small gale. On 20 April the fleet reached Río Grande
Cayman, where the men refreshed themselves with alligator and tortoise meat.
Drake doubled Cabo San António, but bypassed La Havana. His numbers were
too few to attack the port.

After two weeks of beating eastward, the fleet ran back to Cabo San António
for water and firewood. 'The scarcity of fresh water being grown somewhat
greater with us, we were fain to take such water as we found in the moorish
[marshy] ground, by making of pits, and out of them to take up the water that
would gather together in them.'[24] That and rainwater filled the casks. Drake's fleet
started east again on 13 May. Their destination was San Agustín, the Spanish settlement on the eastern Florida coast.

Spanish Reactions to Drake's Raid

The Spanish beat their breasts over the disaster. On 8 April 1586 Diego Daça, lieu-
tenant-governor under Pedro Fernández de Busto, wrote from Punta de la Canoa
to the municipal authorities in La Havana that Drake's attack on Cartagena was
'heaven's punishment for our sins'.[25] On 6 February 1586 Don Juan Fernandez
wrote from Cartagena to Alonso de la Torre, a judge of the *Audiencia* of Panamá,
informing him as well of Drake's attack.[26] The English commander, he says,
'would rather ransom the city for a lady's ring', and as a condition of the ransom
laid down that he would not return the escutcheon he took from the *Audiencia*.

From 20 April to 5 May 1586, further depositions flesh out the raid and continue the finger-pointing.[27] Special judge Diego Hildago Montemayor wrote to
the Crown from Cartagena on 23 May 1586.[28] The letter, badly burned around the
edges of the pages, describes Drake as 46 and 'red complexioned, under medium
in stature' and says residents were blaming one another for the disaster. 'Each one
lays the onus on the others', insisting it was others who fled. The governor, to
'exculpate himself, reports that the enemy was strong'.

The ransom, paid in part from the royal treasury, was a touchy subject. On
4 June 1586 the officials of the city of Cartagena, including Pedro Fernández de
Busto and Alonso Bravo Montemayor, wrote to the Crown to justify the ransom
they paid Drake, seeking six years to repay the money taken from the royal treasury as well as asking for two new galleys, two frigates and 300 soldiers to man the

garrison against any future attack.[29] The city's authorities argue that as the Spanish fleet had carried back to Spain all the money the city had, they had no recourse except to borrow 'from Your Majesty's royal treasury 80,000 ducats left here by a ship which was driven in from General Don António Osorio's fleet, its master Gerónimo de Ojeda. That this ship should have been forced in seems to have been an act of Divine Providence', for otherwise, the entire city would have been burned. 'What was taken from the royal strongbox', they write, 'shall return this money by next Christmas Day'. As for Cartagena's defences, they say, 'Cartagena is left so stripped and so unable to defend itself that it has not a single piece of artillery. The enemy took it all.'

Heaven's Punishment for our Sins

On 27 May[30] (some sources say 28 May), Drake sighted a watchtower on the Florida coast, in latitude 30° N at San Agustín.[31] He planned his attack. As the moon rose that night, Drake used his pinnaces to land the men away from the fort while bombarding the town itself from the ships. During the bombardment, a Frenchman escaped from the Spanish and came to the English in a small boat, playing on a fife the tune of the Protestant Prince of Orange (probably 'Wilhelmus van Nassouwe'),[32] bringing news that the Spanish had fled the fort.

Drake destroyed the fort, burned the settlement, and took away twelve large brass cannon, a treasure chest filled with 6,000 ducats, various tools, forty pipes of meal and some barley. The fleet made for Croatoan, where the year before Richard Grenville had left the colonists for Ralegh's new settlement.

As he sailed north, Drake looked for a signal fire from the English settlers, hoping 'to have a sight if it might be of our English men planted in Virginia'. On 9 June Drake at last saw a fire and sent his skiff ashore. He had found Ralegh's colonists and the 'place where those men did live that Sir Walter Ralegh had sent thither to inhabit the year before'.[33] Some of Drake's larger vessels drew too much to enter the sound, so all anchored outside, in a 'wild road at sea, about two miles from shore'. Meeting the colonists, he offered to leave them the *Francis* and a month's supplies from the materials taken from San Agustín. Three days later, as he was preparing to send provisions ashore, a storm 'extraordinary and very strange' battered the coast for four days, and some of Drake's ships, including the *Francis*, were forced to put to sea. Richard Hawkyns' vessel, possibly the *Duck*, was separated from the fleet and sailed to England on her own, spreading the first news of Drake's great successes at Santo Domingo and Cartagena when he arrived on 21 or 22 July. Drake offered Governor Lane and the colonists the *Bonner* and provisions or passage back to England. They chose to return.

Drake's fleet entered Portsmouth harbour on 27 (or 28) July 1586, then continued up the Channel and the North Sea into the Thames. The Caribbean raid brought £62,100 in bullion, plate, pearls, ordnance, ships, hides, lead and iron, but the auditors soon found that Drake's 'great wealth' could not cover the expedition's costs. The sailors and soldiers would have to wait for their pay. The seamen's pay was calculated at £17,500, leaving a net valuation of £47,900 from which other expenses had to be taken.[34] Investors, including the queen, got only 15s return on the pound. Worse still, of the 1,925 men at the start of the voyage, Drake had lost some 750 men to disease or combat, nearly 40 per cent of his crew.[35] In financial, military and human terms, the voyage was disastrous.

Measured in terms of politics, though, it was decidedly successful. One of Walsingham's agents was heard to say that it was 'certain that one year of war in the Indies will cost the Spaniards more than two or three in the Low countries'. Because of Drake's raid, Philip II had to divert increasingly scarce money from Europe to the New World to strengthen defences against another attack by 'el Draque' or others. After Drake's 1585–86 voyage, as far as Philip was concerned war in Europe was inevitable.

The day before Drake's fleet sailed into Portsmouth, another fleet quite independently left Gravesend for the American tropics. It was the first of twelve voyages for George Clifford, 3rd Earl of Cumberland, voyages that he hoped would repair his family's fortunes. Being a courtier Queen Elizabeth was proving to be a most expensive and fickle proposition, as others of her favourites had found or were to find.

The earl set out on 26 June 1586 with three ships and a pinnace, his intended destination the South Sea. The *Red Dragon*, 260 tons, was admiral, carried 130 men and was commanded by Captain Robert Withrington. The bark *Clifford*, 130 tons, was vice-admiral, with seventy men, commanded by Captain Christopher Lister. The *Roe*, rear-admiral, was commanded by Captain Hawes. The *Dorothee*, a small pinnace, captain unknown, belonged to Sir Walter Ralegh.

John Sarracoll, merchant on board, narrates Cumberland's voyage.[36] The fleet sailed first to the Canaries, then to Sierra Leone, where they took no goods or slaves. Before Cumberland set sail from West Africa for the Strait of Magellan on 17 November, writes Sarracoll, 'divers of our men fell sick of a disease in the belly, which for the time was extreme, but (God be thanked) it was of small continuance'. On 24 November, he reports that 'one or two of our men died, and others also were sick of a *calentura*'. They reached South America and, by 3 February 1587, had sailed to latitude 41° S, some 6° south of the Rio de la Plata.

There they met contrary winds, cold and long nights. Cumberland writes: 'Our bread [is] so consumed that we have not left above two months' biscuit, our drink in a manner all spent, so that we have nothing but water, which in so cold a country as the Straits, if we should get in, and be forced there to winter, would no doubt be a great weakening to our men, and a hazard of the overthrow of the voyage.' Cumberland turned back towards Brazil to resupply, 'both with wine which is our greatest want, and other necessaries'. On 3 April 1587 at the Rio de la Plata, Sarracoll writes that Cumberland picked up Miles Phillips, survivor from Hawkyns' disastrous defeat at San Juan de Ulúa in 1568 (though another account has him returning to Europe with a Spanish *flota*). They called at Bahia, where on the day before Easter they took four Portuguese ships. For Cumberland, as for Drake and Oxnam, the Lenten season seemed an ideal time for such attacks.

Cumberland stayed in the area until June, at which point he and others abandoned the idea of reaching the South Sea. On 29 September they 'reached the coast of England after an unprofitable and unfortunate voyage'. Water, victuals, wills and weather had proved the undoing on this first of Cumberland's many voyages. He was to make two others to the American tropics, one in 1593 and another in 1597–98.

Cavendish Circumnavigates the Earth

The lure of the South Sea drew yet another mariner to sail in 1586. Just a day after Cumberland had left for the tropics, Thomas Cavendish, then 28, set out from Harwich on 27 June 1586 with a fleet of three vessels.[37] Cavendish was well connected. He left Cambridge to spend eight years running through the family fortune. Like Cumberland, he hoped to repair the damages by going to sea. Emulating Drake, his aim was to circumnavigate the earth's oceans. The modest fleet included Cavendish's new vessel, the *Desire* (120 tons), the bark *Hugh Gallant* (40 tons), and the *Content* (20 tons) with, in all, 123 men aboard, including surgeons. The voyage is chronicled by Master Francis Pretty, gentleman.

Cavendish provisioned for two years at sea. In 1586 the cost of victualling four vessels for two years was £20,984 – a vast amount. For some years the price of food had been increasing. Beef that had cost a penny for 3lb in 1532, for example, was a penny a pound in 1565 and, two or three years later, more than twopence halfpenny a pound.[38] In West Africa Cavendish loaded his ships with lemons and, when he reached the Strait of Magellan, reported no cases of scurvy. He thus became, as far as is known, the first Englishman to use lemons to prevent scurvy. Though it had been Spanish practice since the 1540s, the efficacy of ascorbic acid was not accepted in England until James Lind published his findings in 1762. Only later, in 1794, did the Royal Navy make it policy.

Cavendish reached the Pacific on 27 February 1587 and sailed northwards, plundering three towns and thirteen ships en route. Off Cabo San Lucas, in the Sea of Cortés, he took the 600-ton Manila galleon *Santa Ana* and her treasure of 122,000 silver dollars, the richest plunder seized by an English vessel to date. He kidnapped a Spanish pilot to get across the Pacific. After two years, on 9 September 1588, four weeks after the Spanish Armada had sailed up through the Channel, Cavendish arrived back home in just one vessel, the *Desire*, very rich.

Drake: 'Heaven's Punishment'

Drake's voyage to the West Indies in 1585–86 drew another score of letters from the Spanish. After Drake had destroyed the fort and settlement at San Agustín, the Spanish captain-general there, Pedro Menéndez Marqués, pleaded on 17 June 1586 to the president of the Casa de Contratación: 'We are all left with the clothes we stood in, and in the open country with a little munition which was hidden. We are without food of any sort except six hogsheads of flour which will last twenty days at half a pound per head.'[39] Alonso Suarez de Toledo wrote from La Havana to the Crown on 27 June 1586 about a fledgling colony of English settlers many leagues to the north.[40] Drake's raid on Santo Domingo had hit the Spanish in their coffers, which drew further immediate response. On 30 June 1586, Rodrigo Fernández de Ribera, royal accountant for Hispaniola, wrote from Santo Domingo to the Crown regarding the sacking the previous January.[41] Accountant Ribera, only two months into his new job, swears on his word as a treasurer, 'a Christian conscientious man', that on the third night after the city fell, and at 'great danger' to himself, he had retrieved the official record books. 'Not a note was lost concerning amounts to be collected and debited.' All this was at personal cost. 'All my personal belongings I lost, as is well known; nothing was saved. In addition, they burned my house because they learned that I had rescued the royal books and papers.'

Preoccupied with empty coffers, His Spanish Majesty's accountant in Florida, Alonso Sancho Saez, wrote to the Crown from San Agustín on 12 July 1586, bemoaning the loss of paperwork, especially that of the deceased, as it meant loss of money for the government and especially for himself.[42] 'Having in Fort San Juan lost the papers of the accountant's office and the funds from the deceased persons' estates which were in my charge, this represented nothing more or less than the culmination of my poverty and other persons fared as badly, having trusted solely in that fort.'

The sack of Cartagena brought on the dismissal of Governor Pedro Fernández de Busto. A letter to the Crown dated 30 July 1586 from Don Pedro de Lodeña, the new governor, claims that Busto had botched the job of defending Cartagena from Drake.[43] He reports that Drake did more than 400,000 ducats' worth of damage and the town's officials are still blaming one another for the debacle. Worse still, Drake plans another attack.

On 8 August 1586, Francisco de Ávila wrote to the Crown from Cartagena, noting that a third of the men were not from Cartagena and yet were compelled to defend the port.[44] The rest were merchants and traders,

> whose felicity is rather in their merchandise than in the profit to be had from opportunities. Persons little accustomed to noble acts are disconcerted by occasions for such. Those who are not merchants (as are even Your Majesty's

royal officials) are retail dealers in the food supplies produced by the country. Therefore I admit recalling Romulus' way of thinking – that the government of the *res publica* should be left to the old and military affairs to the young – and, considering that the Chinese put their fortresses in charge of natives of the place, I don't know who could have been entrusted with either, here.

And the defences? The governor and commander of the galleys were both unarmed and asleep when Drake attacked. The rich had sent away all their possessions and had their horses saddled that night, ready to retreat, as did many of the infantry captains. An 'evil outcome was prognosticated'; Drake was Heaven's punishment.

Ávila continues to write that those in the galleys were 'creatures of little fortune and less conscience'. They made up for their number with their sins, 'both public and secret, with killings, robberies, insolences and unrighteous intercourse between the Moors of these galleys and slave women and Christian Indians, and even other women of other sort, moved by desire which overmasters every other consideration'. Nor were they punished, given the friendship between the governor and commander of galleys. Rather than resist the corsair, the colonials secretly began to negotiate a ransom, and when Drake finally left, these people provided him with meat and vegetables. 'Thus the rich profited and we poor remained without a roof or shelter over us, because they burned and demolished the half of the town which lay outside the line of their entrenchment. They occupied the best part, where were the houses of those who negotiated the ransom, for these were the principal citizens.' The rich in Cartagena, says Ávila, are reporting falsely. Ávila apologises for 'the imperfections of this indiscreet communication and those of its author' as the king's 'least vassal' in Cartagena de Indias.

Mouldy Spanish Pikes & Rusty Swords

As 1587 began, all England knew that Spain would attack. Elizabeth drew back her naval forces to protect England's coasts, and very few English hulls sailed for the tropics that year or the next. The tactics used in fighting the Spanish in the Caribbean would soon be put to the test in the waters of the English Channel against a far more powerful fleet – the Invincible Spanish Armada. The English would be greatly outnumbered in tonnage, in close-in artillery and in men, but they had manoeuvrability, longer-range firepower and hit-and-run tactics, all sharpened and tempered in battles against the Spanish in American tropical waters.

In England, Elizabeth was afraid of a Spanish attack; in the Caribbean, Philip feared an English one. The Spanish factor and inspector to the royal treasury for Hispaniola, García Fernández de Torrequemada, wrote on 1 February to the Crown from Santo Domingo that even the venerable port was vulnerable to attack 'if reliance is placed in force, arms, defensive measures, and the military prowess of this people, for among them there is not a soldier, nor a captain, who knows what war is, or strategy, or has seen or perhaps even heard of such'.[45] When musters are called, he writes, 'some are litigants and others are merchants, some are haggling shopkeepers and others those who find their profit and support in rural parts'. The cavalry are 'unarmed except for a sort of lance of little worth and a poorly cinched wooden saddle'. As for horses not being shod, they are good only for work in the fields. To assemble a couple of dozen horses for a tourney is impossible, for 'a mount in a proper stable represents a cost of 200 ducats a year. Few persons can afford it.'

Foot soldiers have only harquebuses, and mounted soldiers have only lances and shields, mostly without munitions. Their pikes are mouldy, their swords rusty. The climate 'is such that every harquebus, sword and halberd needs a man with no other occupation, to keep it clean. I speak of this from such experience that I assure Your Majesty that the sword I carry in my belt is cleaned every time I return home and nevertheless it rusts.' Torrequemada informs the Crown that merchants and shopkeepers or litigants who come to Santo Domingo remain only until they earn enough to return to Castile, or if they are resident in the colony, the subject 'seeks only to feed his wife and family, inasmuch as the misery and poverty of this land yields no further profit, and even this only at the price of much sweat and exertion and sickness'.

It was Torrequemada who had negotiated Cartagena's ransom. He and Drake met in a room for some hours (while dining, according to one source) along with nine or ten English officers. The conversation had occasionally turned sour, with 'an heretical animosity inclined rather to destruction' of the city. As for 'el Draque':

> Francis Drake knows no language but English and I talked with him through interpreters in Latin or French or Italian. He had with him an Englishman who understood Spanish a little and sometimes acted as interpreter. Drake is a man of medium stature, blonde, rather heavy than slender, merry, careful. He commands and governs imperiously [and] is feared and obeyed by his men. He punishes resolutely. Sharp, restless, well-spoken, inclined to liberality and to ambition, vainglorious, boastful, not very cruel. These are qualities I noted in him during my negotiations with him.

Though England was on a war footing in the spring of 1588, sometime after 8 March, but before the Crown stayed shipping at month's end, four ships set out from England for the West Indies.[46] These were the *Drake*, belonging to John Watts, the London merchant-ship owner; the *Examiner* belonging to Watts, his son John, Thomas Sewell and Robert FitzWilliams; and the *Hope* and the *Chance*, owners unknown. Watts was the major underwriter of the expedition. His ships had been active in both privateering and trading, and he had contributed to West Indian ventures since 1585. The pilot, Roger Kingsnode (Kingson), was unusual in that he was one of the few Englishmen who knew the West Indies, even the Old Channel along the north coast of Cuba.

Spanish documents note that two ships and two pinnaces, English privateers, were in the Old Channel from about the end of June that year to the second or third week of July. These were probably Watts' ships. The voyage was not successful, taking only a cargo of Canary wines. They continued to sail the Caribbean.

The Spanish Armada

The Spanish and English had been at their undeclared war, at least as far as the American tropics were concerned, since the first English vessel entered a Caribbean port in 1516. The issues were trading rights, piracy and territory. Drake's 1585–86 West Indian raid stirred a reluctant Philip II to marshal his army and his fleet for a direct invasion of England. With the Treaty of Nonsuch in 1585, in which the English aided Continental Protestants, and with the execution of Catholic Mary, Queen of Scots in February 1587, it was clear to Philip that returning England to the true faith could only be accomplished if he were to take both the Scottish and English thrones. That required force.

On the evening of 30 May 1588, in light winds, 130 Spanish vessels left the Río Tejo bound for England with 27,000 seamen and soldiers, arguably to date the largest naval force in history. England would be facing this gigantic fleet with 190 vessels but only 16,000 men, just over half the Spanish number. From fighting in the American tropics, the English had come to use their ships less as barges for soldiers and more as manoeuvrable artillery platforms. The Spanish had just over 1,000 cannon, but for the English, double that number, nearly 2,000. The Spanish had about 45 per cent in heavy short-range artillery and 55 per cent for light long-range fire, appropriate for the tactics of close-in engagement and boarding, whereas the English artillery had only 5 per cent for heavy short-range fire and 95 per cent for light long-range fire. Boarding, as the English knew from the West Indies, was effective only when there were overwhelmingly favourable odds, and only rarely in the Caribbean had they had that advantage. Better to batter the enemy into submission first with ordnance than to board with marines.

On 22 July the Spanish Armada in tight crescent formation appeared off the Lizard. The winds were light. A week later that crescent of ships was off the Eddystone. The English fleet warped its way out of Plymouth, crossing the Spanish fleet, and gaining the weather gauge. At long range the English opened fire off Plymouth on 31 July, off the Portland Bill on 2 August and the Isle of Wight on 4 August. But though English cannon had the range, they did not have the power to damage the Spanish hulls. On 6 August the Spanish anchored off

Calais, as did the English, still to windward. A day later the English sent six fire ships into the Spanish fleet, missing the ships but forcing them to cut their cables and drift eastward. On 8 August off Gravelines, the English closed, and now the cannon were effective, destroying three vessels and impairing others. The wind shifted from north-west to south-west, and the Spanish were able to sail off the lee shore into the North Sea. The English pursued the Armada fleet into the North Sea until 12 August and then returned home.

The Spanish fleet was mortally wounded. Stricken by typhus, low on food and water, with their anchors and cables lost off Calais, they were hardly in fit shape to face a stormy North Atlantic on their homeward passage. Of the Spanish fleet of 130 ships, a quarter were lost to English firepower and to storms encountered on the return to Spain around the north of Great Britain. The defeat of the Invincible Armada of Spain saved the Reformation, and it saved England. This was the first great European naval battle exclusively between sailing vessels employing the tactic of both short- and long-range naval gunnery. For sixty years the Caribbean had been England's naval proving ground. The lessons learned there proved their worth in the English Channel.

Fears of a Spanish invasion were lifted, but for only a time. Philip II was still intent on crushing England, Protestantism and any threat to his American empire from privateers who could cut his supply of gold and silver from Nueva España and Perú. The two aged monarchs, Philip and Elizabeth, were wary of each other from opposite sides of the church aisle. Philip was to make further attempts to invade England in the next several years, and in response, Elizabeth shored up her land defences and issued letters patent to private vessels. An unprecedented number of vessels flying the Cross of St George sailed for the West Indies to attack the Spanish at the source of her wealth. Peace was not to come until 1604, under James I, and even then it was, in the Americas, at best a most imperfect peace.

five

―――∞∞∞―――

PROFIT IN PIRACY, 1589–91

Ships be but boards, sailors but men:
there be land-rats and water-rats, land-thieves and water thieves.
                    Shakespeare, *The Merchant of Venice*, 1596–98

There were at least 235 voyages to the Cabo Verdes and to the Americas in the years 1588–91, but little is known of them. As far as is known, all the English voyages to the Caribbean in those years were made by privateers, except for one promoted by John Watts in 1590, one by Sir Robert Dudley in 1594 and one commanded by Hawkyns and Drake for the Crown in 1595. Andrews provides details of a few of these voyages.[1]

The period 1588–95 saw the greatest number of privateering voyages of any seven-year period of English tropical voyaging in the century marked from 1516 to 1618. Drake's West Indies raid in 1585–86, though a financial loss, nevertheless proved its political worth. After the Armada, royal vessels were few, and to meet the very real threat of another Spanish attack, the Crown thus issued 'letters of reprisal' to private ships. At little cost, reasoned Whitehall, privateers in the Caribbean could continue putting pressure on Spain.

Letters of reprisal were issued to subjects who had been wronged by the Spanish. The terms 'privateer' and 'privateering', appearing first in the seventeenth century, are here used for sixteenth-century voyages as well. In a point of fine distinction of rank, which was lost once at sea, 'letters patent' were issued to the Earl of Cumberland or Sir John Chidley. Privateering became more attractive after 1585, for it became easier to prove loss before the Admiralty Court. Writes Andrews, there is 'no indication that anyone who applied for letters of reprisal was ever refused'.[2] Once licence had been granted, the captains or masters had to enter recognisances or bonds, usually £3,000 for each ship, to be forfeited to the

Lord Admiral if the terms of the bond were broken. Privateers often considered the bond (and its forfeiture) simply a normal expense of the voyage. The bond had little effect on controlling depredations committed at sea.

Privateers, notes Andrews, usually sailed alone or in pairs, though in the longer voyages to the Caribbean three or four vessels, with a pinnace, would sail together. Privateers sailing European waters would use a smaller merchantman (to about 100 tons) and add more cannon to her. They did not rebuild the ship. There was no heavy artillery. Since prizes taken would need crew to sail them home, the crew of forty was large.

Vessels sailing Mediterranean, Guinean and Caribbean waters were between 100 and 300 tons, and sometimes engaged in both trade and plunder during a voyage. Like a royal warship of similar tonnage, these would have heavy battery cannon such as 18-pound culverins and 10-pound demi-culverins, 5½-pound sakers and smaller ordnance. There were also a few men-of-war, such as those of Cumberland, Ralegh and Howard. Voyages in the 1590s continued to include pinnaces using both oar and sail, critical for unknown waters and for coastal raiding. These vessels were seaworthy despite their small size, and could also serve as swift yet powerful small vessels of war.

Caribbean voyages were expensive (a 300-ton privateer typically cost some £3,000 to provision for six months), and once back in home port, repairs and refitting were expensive. The owners took two-thirds of the profit and the remaining third went to the crew. Reward for the crew came from prizes taken, and dividing the spoils caused the most trouble. Jewels, money, gold and silver were the preferred loot, as these were easily hidden from the owners or customs officials.

As with other vessels, privateers usually sailed with both a captain and master, and sometimes a pilot. Captain and crew were often equals. The chance for striking it rich, and the certainty of fewer floggings but more flagons of wine and spirits, was reason enough to sign on. 'A lot of drunkards' and a 'low lot' is what the governor of La Havana thought of them – a view shared by Captain Richard Hawkyns.

To catch the Spanish fleet, privateers would usually leave England in March or April, first south to the Canaries or Cabo Verdes, then west on the trade winds to the Caribbean, where they would usually make for Hispaniola or Puerto Rico. Other privateers would sail for the Spanish Main, calling at La Margarita and other islands before raiding Río de la Hacha, Cartagena and Nombre de Dios. From there the usual route home was by way of Cabo San António.

Privateers usually worked independently, and Caribbean privateering was profitable. London merchants regularly put money towards those voyages, and some were highly successful.[3] The aim for most was profit; not politics or heroics, but business. The choicest prey was the most defenceless vessel. Smaller barks and caravels to 100 tons were easily taken at sea by larger ships and, along the coast, by fast manoeuvrable pinnaces. Privateers found raiding *fazendas* (ranches) and cattle farms easy pickings. The usual haul brought in sugar and hides. Silver, gold, pearls and jewels were rare. Only once, notes Andrews, is tobacco mentioned.[4]

Diego de Ybarra, the treasurer of Santo Domingo, wrote to the Crown on 14 October 1595 that for the past four years, corsairs were 'as numerous and as assiduous as though these were ports of their own countries'.[5] They lie in wait along the sailing routes, especially those that converge on Santo Domingo:

> Coming or going, we always have a corsair in sight. Not a ship coming up from the outside escapes them; nor does any which leaves the harbour get past them. If this continues, either this island will be depopulated or they will compel us to do business with them rather than with Spain … They make their incursions safely and find persons with whom to barter, for the land is sparsely settled and full of horned cattle, so that anywhere that they put in, they find opportunity awaiting in the presence of negroes and other wretched delinquents who live outside the law in the bush, certain that neither the special judge nor any other representatives of justice can lay hands on them.

The treasurer finds the only way to get rid of these corsairs is by protecting the coasts with galleys. During this period, when a new ship's keel was laid she was built as a heavily armed merchantman, following the earlier practice of the Portuguese in their East Indian trade.

In autumn 1588, after the threat of the Armada was gone, privateering resumed. On 4 October Cumberland set forth in a royal ship, the *Golden Lion*, provisioned at his own cost.[6] He took one ship from Dunkirk laden with cargo for Spain and sent her back to England. Bad weather ended Cumberland's second voyage.

The case of the *Black Dogge* stirred up fierce anti-Spanish sentiment in England. The *Black Dogge*, 70 tons, was armed and carried forty crew. William Michelson was captain, William Mace of Ratcliffe, master. Roger Kingsnode, who had been on Watts' voyage the year before, was pilot.[7] The *Dogge* went directly for the West Indies. In May 1589 she was off the coast of Cuba between Cabo San António and La Havana, where she took a Spanish merchantman. The Spanish captain called for a truce and came aboard the Englishman, where he and his officers 'received reasonable entertainment'. The English were then invited to the Spaniard as if to 'requite the English courtesy'. It was, however, writes Hakluyt, a piece of 'Spanish treason'. Hakluyt gives this example to show that the English must be circumspect in dealing with that 'subtle enemy, and never to trust the Spanish further, than that their own strength shall be able to master them: For otherwise whosoever shall through simplicity trust their courtesy, shall by trial taste of their assured cruelty'.

Robert Abraham, later a master of his own vessel, writes that when Kingsnode, Mace, the master, the surgeon and three or four others ferried the Spanish captain

back to his ship, by 'sugar speeches [the English] were enticed to go on board the
Spanish ship to be feasted by the Spaniards in like sort'. In the captain's cabin the
Spaniard made them good cheer. He came to the pilot, and

> embracing him with many thanks, drew his dagger and stabbed the said pilot
> to the heart and presently a number more were ready at the cabin door with
> rapiers and stabbed him likewise, together with John Hughes the surgeon and
> Edmund Bense the corporal: And William Mace the master and two others did
> leap overboard and were taken up by the boat and saved, although all wounded
> by the said Spaniards.

In producing the first edition of Hakluyt's great work, printer George Bishop
stopped his press to add leaves on Drake's 1577–80 circumnavigation. From the
publication of *Principall Navigations, Voiages and Discoveries of the English Nation*,
Hakluyt was granted the rectory of Witheringsett-cum-Brockford, Suffolk. This
was the first launch, appearing in two volumes in 1589, of his famous book.[8]

Cumberland's Third Voyage, for Azores

Purchas narrates the third voyage of Sir George Clifford, 3rd Earl of Cumberland,
with great enthusiasm:[9] 'His spirit remaining nevertheless higher than the winds,
and more resolutely by storms compact and united in itself', Cumberland set out
from Plymouth on 18 June with the queen's vessel *Victory*, as well as the *Meg*, the
Margaret and a caravel. He was for Spain, via the Azores.[10] En route to the Azores
Cumberland seized French and Dutch vessels, taking Newfoundland fish and
goods 'to the value of £4,500 of a Jew of Lisbon'. He reached the islands about
1 August, and flying a Spanish flag took four carracks on 27 August. At Terceira,
under fire from the fort's cannon, Cumberland took cargoes of elephants' teeth,
grain, coconuts and Guinean goat skins. At Faial, finding the town deserted, he set
a guard to preserve the churches, took the fort's fifty-eight cannon, and demanded
and got a ransom of 2,000 ducats, mostly in church plate.

    The governor of Graciosa, partial to the English and knowing that water was
scarce, welcomed Cumberland with sixty butts of wine. The Mainland fleet (the
Tierra Firme fleet) was due in shortly. Cumberland put to sea, beating back and
forth for three or four days in rough conditions. Then to weather of him he saw
fifteen sail going into the port of Angra, on Terceira. He could not attack. At São
Miguel he was denied water and had to sail on to Saint Maria, where he found
two ships laden with Brazil sugar. But worse, 'His Lordship received three shot
upon his target, and a fourth on the side, not deep, his head also broken with
stones that the blood covered his face, both it and his legs likewise burned with
fire-balls'. English losses were heavy, over eighty.

Cumberland left the Azores for Spain. Along the way he took a Portuguese and a Spaniard from Nueva España that yielded a rich haul of cochineal, sugar and some silver. 'Thus full of joy they resolved homewards, but sea-fortunes are variable, having two inconstant parents, air and water.' Cumberland's Spanish prize was wrecked on the rocks of Cornwall, and captain and crew, except five or six, were drowned. Out of water and beer, Cumberland steered for Ireland:

> Three spoonfuls of vinegar were allowed to each man at a meal with some small relief squeezed out of the lees of their wine vessels: Which continued fourteen days without other supply than the drops of hail and rain, carefully saved with sheets and napkins. Some drank up the soiled running water at the scupper-holes; others saved by device the runnings down the masts and tarred ropes; and many licked the moist boards, rails, and masts with their tongues like dogs. Yet was that rain so intermingled with the spray of the foaming seas in that extreme storm, that it could not be healthful: Yea, some in their extremity of thirst drank themselves to death with their cans of saltwater in their hands.

Each night ten or twelve died. The storm raged on and tore away at Cumberland's cabin and the dining room, so that the earl himself 'was forced to seek a new lodging in the hold'. Eventually, he put into Ventre Haven on the west coast of Ireland to refresh himself and his crew, and on 20 December sailed for England. He had taken thirteen prizes, to great profit. On reaching London there was news of his family. His eldest son had died, and a daughter had been born.

Chidley and the Desire for Strait

John Chidley, a gentleman adventurer from Devon, received a special 'letter patent' from the queen, help from the Privy Council, from Lord Hunsdon and most likely from his kinsman Sir Walter Ralegh.[11] Chidley hoped to repeat Cavendish's successful circumnavigation of the year before, but his fate was to be otherwise. He sailed with five or six ships, some 800 tons of shipping, and a crew of between 400 and 500 men. Near the equator disease hit his fleet, killing Chidley on 6 November. One ship deserted and returned to England. Two others carried on for Trinidad, arriving shortly before 20 January 1590, and the fleet's navigator took the pinnace and returned home.

Without Chidley the *Delight*, the smallest ship in the fleet, continued on alone. Her first landfall was Port Desire, at latitude 48° S. Thus far, writes the voyage's author Magoths, disease had killed sixteen. The ship resupplied and she entered the Strait of Magellan on 1 January 1590. At Penguin Island the crew took and salted hogsheads of that bird, 'which must be eaten with speed: For we found them to be of no long continuance'. In six weeks a further thirty-eight died from sickness and due to hostile Indians. The *Delight* lost three anchors and had just one left. The crew, down to just a small store of victuals, was mutinous and insisted on returning home. The officers, it became evident, had been hoarding the best food and had locked up all the weapons. Besides the new captain and his mate (whom the crew did not trust), only six were able to sail the ship. They turned back out of the strait on about 14 February 1590, reached the Rio de la Plata, steered for Cabo Verde, the Azores and the Channel island of Alderney.

Of the ninety-one who set out on the *Delight*, only six were still alive. Magoths survived to tell the tale:

> The master and his two mates and chief mariners being dead, we ran in with Monville de Hage eight miles to the west of Cherbourg in Normandy. Where the next day after our coming to an anchor, having but one in all left, being the last of August 1590 by the foul weather that rose the anchor came home, and our ship drove on the rocks.

Cast away and stranded, Magoths and three other English crew (leaving in France a Portuguese and a Breton) made their way to Cherbourg and found passage on an English bark from Weymouth. The mortality rate for this voyage was a sobering 93 per cent. There was no profit for queen, lords or knights.

Spanish Letters Seized

Meanwhile, in the Americas and West Indies, the Spanish colonists were having problems of their own, as shown in a parcel of Spanish letters seized by privateer John Watts. Bartholomew Cano wrote to Peter de Tapia in Seville from México on 30 May 1590, that the Armada sent to England in 1588 'was all spoiled and cast away', so that for 1590 there would be no fleet from Spain.[12] 'And this is the cause that all linen cloth is very dear in these parts. Wines also are very dear; for they are sold for ninety and one hundred deminas a pipe.' Despite the disaster, frigates left Nueva España in August carrying cochineal, hides and 'much treasure, more than has been sent to Spain in many years'.

Another letter intercepted by Watts, dated 20 June 1590, comes from Nueva España. Sebastian Biscaino wrote to his father, António Biscaino of Corchio in Spain, that there was great profit to be made from the China-México trade.[13] In the fine port of Acapulco lie ships of 600 and 800 tons that make the passage of 2,000 leagues, a return voyage that takes thirteen or fourteen months. Biscaino has sold Spanish and Flemish commodities worth 200 ducats for 1,400 ducats in Nueva España. Those, along with silks from China, have brought him 2,500 ducats for the voyage and, he reports:

[he] had gotten more, if one pack of fine silks had not been spoiled with salt water. So as I said, there is great gain to be gotten if that a man return in safety. But the year 1588 I had great mischance, coming in a ship from China to Nueva España: Which being laden with rich commodities, was taken by an Englishman [Cavendish, on his circumnavigation, 1586–88] which robbed us and afterward burned our ship, wherein I lost a great deal of treasure and commodities.

Lope de Vega Portocarrero, the governor and captain-general of Hispaniola and president of the *Audiencia* of Santo Domingo, writes from Santo Domingo to the Crown on 4 July 1590 that the galleys on the northern coast of the island are out of commission.[14] They are worthless, 'have cost 90,000 ducats', and have left the port only two times. Steven (Stefano) de Tresio writes from Panamá to Alonso Martínes Vaca in Seville, on 21 August 1590, that the word is that His Majesty is preparing another armada against England.[15] In Panamá, Tresio and the other dwellers are in 'such a perplexity and confusion' since they have sent money (some 600,000 pesos, some less) and commodities to Spain, and that under the king's seal, if the Crown needs the money, it may well take the merchandise itself. But the colonists cannot lend the king their money, for in Panamá things are dear, food is scarce, and the people poor.

On 23 August 1590 Juan de Oribe Apallua, commander of the West Indies armada of twenty-three sail, writes from La Havana to the Crown that English ships have blockaded the port, cut off food and taken cargoes of hides and indigo.[16] On 7 July English corsairs off Cabo Tiburón had attacked a fleet of thirteen vessels out of Santo Domingo. They took one vessel's sugar, hides, ginger and other merchandise bound for Spain. The English corsairs 'place their reliance on their artillery and musketry' rather than boarding. Apallua learned that on the day of the attack, one of the English ships had been 'just thirty days out of London and brought news that seventeen Queen's ships were being made ready to sail, as were many other vessels privately owned'. This fleet was intended for Cabo San António and the Spanish treasure fleet, but with information that a Spanish armada was making ready, the queen had postponed the fleet's departure. Apallua adds that it is believed Elizabeth of England will attack La Havana in 1591 with a fleet of 150 sail.

From Panamá, Hieronymo de Nabares wrote to licentiate John Alonso from Valladolid to his address in Seville, concerning the gainfulness of the lucrative trade with the Philippines and their fear of the English: 'For every hundred ducats a man shall get 600 ducats clearly.'[17] At Panamá there are great ships of up to 500 tons and small coastal barks. 'I can certify your worship of no news, but only, that all this country is in such extreme fear of the Englishmen our enemies, that the like was never seen or heard of: For in seeing a sail, presently here are alarms in all the country.' On 24 August 1590 Diego de la Ribera, admiral in command of the Tierra Firme (Mainland) fleet, wrote from La Havana to the Crown that off the Organos, the English took a ship that had left Nueva España as part of Rodrigo de Rada's fleet, laden with hides and cochineal, and near Cabo San António took another laden with flour and biscuit. 'They carried off the biscuit but left the flour.'[18]

From La Havana on 17 October 1590 a servant wrote to John Lopez Canavate, alderman, residing in Canavate, Spain.[19] The servant hoped to find a friend to convey him away from Cuba. 'This country is so close and narrow, that if a man steal not away hidden in some ship, it is not possible for him to escape, nor to go a league out of the town, no way but by sea. And because the harbour is so close, it is the best harbour and the surest in the world.' Despite La Havana's three forts, manned by a thousand soldiers and protected by two galleys, 'the audacious Englishmen being without all shame are not afraid to come and dare us at our own doors'. The plan outlined is this:

> Our journey to go for England [with a second armada] is most certain in the year 1592. Here are making with great expedition eighteen ships, which are called frigates for that effect. They are very strong ships, and will draw but very little water, whereby they may enter amongst the shoals on the banks of Flanders: They are built the higher because here is great store of timber and excellent good and incorruptible. It is reported that the fleet will depart from hence in February, by reason that at that time the Englishmen are not departed out of their own country.

For perhaps the first time, Spanish America is building and supplying warships for use in European waters.

Admiral of the Fleet Juan de Orimo reports from La Havana to the Crown that one of the frigates built for the 1592 attack on England was launched on 18 October 1590:

> They are very big and excellent of sail, which will carry 150 men apiece with soldiers and mariners. And having good ordnance, there are few or none of our enemies that can offend us … But it behooves your Majesty to send both soldiers and mariners to man the frigates. For we have great want of soldiers and mariners, with tackling, anchors, powder, shot, calivers, and all kinds of furniture for them. For these things are not here to be had for money: And likewise to send some great ordnance for the *zabras* [small Spanish sailing vessels]. For the merchants ships are so weak and so unprovided, that they have almost none to defend themselves. Also we shall be constrained to give the *carena* [to careen, scrape, caulk] again unto all the ships; for they are very weak by reason of the long voyage.[20]

On 20 October 1590 the governor of La Havana, Juan de Texeda, wrote to the king about the port's needs.[21] He asks for 200 'Negro' labourers and dares not take men from the galleys. Send tools of iron, he asks, send 'powder and match to furnish these forts', and send money to pay the soldiers sent from Spain and Nueva España. To aid in the forthcoming attack on England, he writes that Cuba is building five frigates as fast as possible, but as of yet their rigging and sails have not arrived. The king 'shall not have upon the sea such good ships as these are'. On 20 November 1590 Don Diego Menéndez de Valdéz, governor of San Juan de Puerto Rico (the island), wrote to Don Pedro de Xibar, one of the king's counsellors of the West Indies, and states that a new fort (Il Morro) is under construction on a high elevation overlooking the entrance to San Juan's harbour.[22] It is big enough to contain 300 persons. The island has 400 pioneers continually at work, but to maintain their schedule the governor has written to Nueva España for more supplies. 'The most principal thing of all is, to send more Negroes' to build the fort.

The fort is to be a triangle and reach into the bay. Inside there shall be forty pieces of good ordnance, which the master of the field has promised to send from La Havana. At present the governor has nearly 1,500 fighting men and 80 horsemen. Once built, the fort will be 'the strongest that his Majesty has in all the Indies. And now the people of the country sleep in security. For commonly before, the Englishmen would come and beard us to the haven's mouth.'

Cumberland's Fourth Voyage

For his fourth voyage[23] the Earl of Cumberland took command of the queen's new ship, the *Garland*, 600 tons, serving as admiral. The vice-admiral, one of Cumberland's own ships, was the *Samson*, 260 tons, John Morton, captain; and the rear-admiral was the *Golden Noble*, Edward Partridge, captain. To these was added the *Allagarta*, 80 tons, Balie, captain, and the *Discoverie*, a small 12-ton pinnace owned by Cumberland, with Nicholas Lynche as captain. Friends supplied 'other good ships' to make up the fleet.

Cumberland set out in May 1591. At Saint Thomas he took a ship laden with sugars, but she was so leaky he had to cast her off. Another prize making her way back to England encountered contrary winds and, for want of victuals, had to put in to a Spanish port. Two other ships had more unfortunate fates. One night in calm seas Spanish galleys attacked, killed one captain and took prisoner the other, along with crew. Cumberland learned of a 'great Armada prepared in the Groyne' (in A Coruña, Galicia) to be sent against the English. Cumberland, 'weakened by disadventure', returned to England.

Watts' Privateers in the Indies

At least eleven English privateers were cruising the West Indies in 1591. Five of these were sent out by John Watts and his partners, three by Sir George Carey, two others by a group of London merchants, and one by another. The privateers did not act as a fleet, though their paths often crossed. Watts' vessels included the *Centaur*, commanded by the leader of the expedition William Lane, with John Gall, master; the *Pegasus*, Stephen Michell, captain, and Abicocke Perry, master; the *Hopewell*, under William Craston and George Kennell; the *John*, under Michael Geare and William Bendes; and the *Fifth Part*, a pinnace. In all it was a substantial force of some 500 tons burden with its leaders all well-seasoned mariners. Watts was the major shareholder, and Sir Walter Ralegh the most eminent supporter.

Carey's fleet included the *Bark Burr*, 130 tons burden, commanded by Captain William Irish; the *Swallow*, 35 tons burden, Ralph Lee, captain, and Anthony Daniel, master; and the *Content*, 30 tons burden, under Nicholas Lisle and William King. The third fleet had two ships, the *Margaret*, 60 tons, commanded by Christopher Newport, with Cuthbert Grippe as master; and the *Prudence*, 50 tons, under John Brough and Thomas Harding. Christopher Newport, aged 31, was in command of the vessels in the third fleet.

Carey sailed in late March or early April 1591. By the end of May he was between Dominica and Puerto Rico. Lane and his ships left Plymouth on 5 April with Lord Thomas Howard in command. Before long, Watts' fleet lost Howard – Andrews believes intentionally – and soon after, off Cádiz, the fleet took a large prize of hides, money, bullion, precious stones and other valuables. The prize was sold at Tenerife before the ships set sail for the West Indies. At the end of May Newport's *Margaret* and the *Prudence* took the *Nuestra Señora del Rosario* off La Yaguana, Hispaniola.

About that time, the ships of Craston and Kennell joined with those of Irish, Lee and Lisle, and were in position on 13 June between Cabo Corrientes and Cabo San António, at the west end of Cuba. There they were attacked by a vastly superior Spanish fleet commanded by Diego de la Ribera. The *Bark Burr* was lost. The other ships escaped. On 19 June at Cabo Corrientes, the *Hopewell*, *Swallow*, *Centaur*, *Pegasus*, *John*, *Prudence* and *Lion* joined forces. Three days later, some of the privateers took three prizes bound for La Havana from Santo Domingo with hides, sugar and ginger. The captains of the seven ships and the pinnace agreed to sail as a fleet for a week. On 6 July the English fleet took the richest prize of the cruise. She was the *Trinity*, of Seville, part of the Nueva España *flota*, with a cargo worth £20,000 in silver, cochineal and hides.

With such rich plunder, the privateers quickly left the Caribbean. The *Prudence* arrived in Plymouth by 26 August, and Watts' ships were home by mid-September. Watts' ships had taken eight prizes in the course of their voyage, five of them brought to England. The *Lion* and the *Swallow* each brought home a prize. Despite embezzlement of some of the prizes, Watts' voyage was profitable for the investors, with the net value of the goods at nearly £32,000. The *Trinity* alone yielded some £20,000. Altogether the eight prizes, after pilferage by the crews, were worth some £40,000. It was a heady profit of over 200 per cent for owners and investors.

Shipwrecked on Bermuda Islands

On 10 April 1591 'three tall ships' set out from Plymouth for the East Indies, via the Cape of Good Hope.[24] These were the *Penelope*, admiral, commanded by Captain Raimond; the *Merchant Royal*, vice-admiral, with Captain Samuel Foxcroft; and the *Edward Bonaventure*, rear-admiral, with Captain James Lancaster. Additionally, there was a small pinnace. Henry May wrote the account of the undertaking.

Sickness sent one ship and the pinnace back to England from Africa, but two ships doubled the Cape of Good Hope on 8 September. Four days later a great sea broke over the admiral, *Penelope*, and 'their light struck out: And after that we never saw them any more'. Lancaster in the *Edward Bonaventure* now sailed on alone for the East Indies, plagued by short rations and sickness. Lancaster became gravely ill, and the crew of thirty-three men and boys were 'much wasted and diminished', but the hold was rich with cinnamon and diamonds when, on 8 December 1592, the *Edward Bonaventure* set sail westward, homeward bound. The ship reached Trinidad in June 1593, but as the Spanish were there, there was to be no refreshment. The ship was low on victuals and her crew were ready to abandon ship when at Mona a French ship refreshed them with bread, provisions and sails. Here author May stayed with the French, and Lancaster carried on in the *Edward Bonaventure*.

On 30 November Henry May left Laguna, Hispaniola, with the French. Off Bermuda on 17 December, the noon sight proved to be wrong, for that night about midnight the Frenchman was cast away on the north-western coast of the Bermuda Islands. May tells the tale: The pilots' noon sights determined that the ships were south of the islands by 12 leagues, and so 'demanded of him their wine of height: The which they had. And being, as it should seem, after they had their wine, careless of their charge which they took in hand, being as it were drunken, through their negligence a number of good men were cast away'. May was the sole Englishman among fifty or so Frenchmen. They all thought they had been cast away close to shore and the high cliffs but soon found they were fully 7 leagues off the coastline:

> But with our boat and a raft which we had made and towed at our boat's stern, we were saved some twenty-six of us; among whom were no more English

but myself. Now being among so many strangers, and seeing not room for the one half, I durst neither press into the boat, nor upon the raft, for fear lest they should have cast me overboard, or else have killed me: So I stayed in the ship which was almost full of water, until the captain being entered the boat, called me unto him being at hand, for that it stood upon life or death: And so I presently entered, leaving the better half of our company to the mercy of the sea. After this we rowed all the day until an hour or two before night where we could come on land, towing the raft with the boat.

The castaways landed and found fresh water.

Now it pleased God before our ship did split, that we saved our carpenter's tools, or else I think we had been there to this day: And having recovered the aforesaid tools, we went roundly about the cutting down of trees, and in the end built a small bark of some eighteen ton, for the most part with trunnels [wooden tree nails] and very few nails. As for tackling we made a voyage aboard the ship before she split, and cut down her shrouds, and so we tackled our bark, and rigged her. In stead of pitch we made lime, and mixed it with the oil of tortoises; and as soon as the carpenters had caulked, I and another, with each of us a small stick in our hands, did plaster the mortar into the seams, and being in April [1594], when it was warm and fair weather, we could no sooner lay it on, but it was dry, and as hard as stone.

It was very hot, and May feared they would not have enough water. Before leaving, the castaways made two great chests, caulked them, and stowed them either side of the mainmast, for rainwater, and thirteen live tortoises for food. They intended for Newfoundland. The east side of Bermuda, writes May, has good harbours, so that 'a ship of 200 ton may ride there landlocked, without any danger, and with water enough'. The pearls and fishing are as good as anywhere in the Indies. Castaways for some five months, May and the French cleared the island on 11 May. On 20 May they reached land near Cape Breton, and sailed up a river where for four hours they took on water, wood and ballast. Indians came to them, 'being clothed all in furs, with the furred side unto their skins, and brought with them furs of sundry sorts to sell, besides great store of wild ducks'. Henry May eventually joined an English bark, and in August 1591 reached Falmouth.

Content Beats Off Spanish Attack

The 'memorable fight' of the *Content* off Cabo de Corrientes, near Cuba's western end, on 13 June 1591[25] ranks as one of the finest accounts of an Elizabethan sea battle, equal to Hawkyns' disaster and escape in the *Minion* at San Juan de Ulúa in 1568, to Ralegh's account of the last fight of Grenville's *Revenge* off Flores in August 1591, and to Richard Hawkyns' loss of the *Daintie* off Perú in 1594. Andrews suggests that the author may be William King, master of the *Content*, who was later to write the account of his own voyage as captain the following year, 1592.

At five in the morning of Sunday 13 June 1591, Sir George Carey's *Hopewell*, *Swallow* and *Content* were off Cabo de Corrientes, at the south-west point of Cuba, when the watch sighted six Spanish sail and two galleys. The Spanish admiral and vice-admiral were each 700 tons, two were 600 and two small ships were about 100 tons each. King says the sight 'made us joyful, hoping that they should make our voyage', thinking that this was the Cartagena treasure *flota*. But as soon as the Spanish saw the English, they gathered their fleet together, close on the wind (it was easterly), and prepared for attack. At six in the morning the English first prayed, then cleared for action. Battle formation was taken up, with the admiral at the head, and the others to leeward. William King, master of the *Content* (Nicholas Lisle was captain) writes that his vessel was at that point 'broadside aweather' of the Spanish vice-admiral. The *Content* gave the Spaniard a volley of muskets and the ship's great ordnance. 'Then coming up with another small ship ahead of the former we hailed her in such sort, that she paid room' (pay round, changed course, or 'going room or large', falling off the wind). While firing away at the little ship, King saw smoke billowing up from the English admiral, but before the *Content* could reach her two of the small Spanish ships had worked to weather of King, with the intention of boarding. The fight raged on for three hours. The *Hopewell* and *Swallow* not coming to her aid, the *Content* was forced to stand for the north. Meanwhile, the English admiral was fighting off the Spanish vice-admiral and another great ship:

> All this time we were forced to the northwards with two of their great ships and one of their small. They having a loom gale [an easy wind] (we being altogether becalmed) with both their great ships came up fair by us, shot at us, and on the sudden furled their spritsails and mainsails, thinking that we could not escape them. Then falling to prayer, we shipped our oars that we might row to shore, and anchor in shallow water where their great ships could not come nie us, for other refuge we had none. Then one of their small ships being manned from one of their great, and having a boat to row themselves in, shipped her oars likewise and rowed after us, thinking with their small shot to have put us from our oars, until the great ships might come up with us: But by the time she was within musket shot, the Lord of his mercy did send us a fair gale of wind at the northwest off the shore. What time (they being all to leeward of us) we stood to the east. The small ship was under our lee within falcon shot, and another great ship lay to the westward, so that we could no way possibly escape them

upon that board [tack]: then (we thinking to avoid them by casting about to the westwards) the other great ship got under our lee, and the small ship on our weather quarter, purposing to make us pay room [fall off] with the great ship, by force of her small and great shot. Then (we being larboard tacked, and they starboard) we made her spring her luff [luff her up, to windward, in irons], and by a fortunate shot which our gunner made, pierced her betwixt wind and water. Hereupon she was forced to lay herself upon the carena [heel over], and to stand with one of the other ships for aid.

Afterward (commending ourselves to almighty God in prayer, and giving him thanks for the wind which he had sent us for our deliverance) we looked forth and descried two sail more to the offing: These we thought to have been the *Hopewell*, and the *Swallow* that had stood in to aid us: But it proved far otherwise, for they were two of the King's galleys. Now having a loom [gentle] gale of wind, we shipped our oars, and rowed off the shore: And our watch was no sooner set, but we espied one galley under our lee hard by us, boging up [falling off the wind] with us. Then (because it was evening) one of the great ships discharged six great shot at us, to the end the galleys should know that we were the ship they looked for. Then the galley came up, and (hailing us of whence our ship was) a Portugal which we had with us, made them answer, that we were of the fleet of Tierra Firma, and of Seville: With that they bid us 'amain English dogs', and came upon our quarter starboard: And giving us five cast pieces out of her prow, they sought to lay us aboard: But we so galled them with our muskets, that we put them from our quarter.

Then they winding their galley [turning around], came up into our stern, and with the way that the galley had, did so violently thrust in the boards of our captain's cabin, that her nose came into it, minding to give us all their prow, and so to sink us. But we being resolute, so plied them with our small shot, that they could have no time to discharge their great ordnance: And when they began to approach, we heaved into them a ball of fire, and by that means put them off: Whereupon they once again fell astern of us, and gave us a prow. Then having a second time put them off, we went to prayer, and sang the first part of the twenty-fifth Psalm, praising God for our safe deliverance.

This being done, we might see two galleys and a frigate all three of them bending themselves together to encounter us: Hereupon we (eftsoons commending our estate into the hands of God) armed ourselves, and resolved (for the honour of God, her Majesty, and our country) to fight it out till the last man. Then shaking a pike of fire in defiance of the enemy, and waving them amain [brandishing a sword or fire pike to signal the enemy to strike his topsail and surrender], we bade them come aboard: And an Englishman in the galley made answer, that they would come aboard presently. So managing ourselves to our furniture [clearing for action], and every moment expecting the assault, we heard them parl to this effect, that they determined to keep us company till the morning, and then to make an end with us: Then giving us another shot from one of the galleys, they fell astern.

Thus our fight continued with the ships and with the galleys, from seven of the clock in the morning till eleven at night. Howbeit God (which never fails them that put their trust in him) sent us a gale of wind about two of the clock in the morning at east-northeast, which was for the preventing of their cruelty, and the saving of our lives. Also (the Lord be praised for it) in all this dangerous fight, we had not one man slain, and but two hurt: But our sails and ropes were so rent with their shot, that it was wonderful to behold: Our mainmast also was shot clean through, whereby we were in exceeding great danger. Thus our consorts forsook us, and left us in these extremities.

The next day being the 14 of June in the morning, we saw all our adversaries to leeward of us, and they espying us, chased us till ten of the clock, and then seeing they could not prevail, gave us over. So that day about five of the clock in the afternoon, we bore up to the southwest, in hope to find our consorts, but we had no sight of them at that time, nor afterward. Then stood we in all that night for the Cape of Saint Anthony, hoping there to see our admiral according to his direction. The fifteenth day of June early in the morning, we descried the Spanish fleet again, being within five leagues of Cape Saint Anthony. Then (having no sight of our consorts) we stood for the place according to the direction of our owner Sir George Carey, where we did ply for the space of twenty-three days, and never could see any sail but two frigates, which we gave chase unto the twenty-fourth of June, and could not fetch them up. Thus we give God most humble thanks for our safe deliverance from the cruel enemy, which hath been more mighty by the providence of God, then any tongue can express: To whom be all praise, honour, and glory, both now and ever, Amen.

King adds that the *Content* had one minion, one falcon, one saker and two port-bases, and that with this meagre ordnance held off from seven in the morning until sunset three warships of 600 and 700 tons each, and one small ship of 100 tons, never being out of musket range from them or the two galleys that joined the attack in the late afternoon. The large warships had shot their great cannon continually,

not so few as 500 times. And the sides, hull, and masts of the *Content* were sowed thick with musket bullets. Moreover, all her sheets, tops and shrouds were almost cut asunder with their great and small shot. There passed from the galleys (each whereof came thrice up to her, and discharged five great pieces at a time, out of every their prows forthright, within three yards of her poop) through her mainsail nineteen great shot, through her main topsail four: Through her foresail seven: Through her foretopsail five: And through her mainmast one. The upper part of the *Content* was hurt in five places. Only thirteen men continued this fight, the rest being in hold. A frigate of the Spaniards (being afterward taken) confessed, that there were in the galleys above forty Spaniards slain, and many were hurt in that combat.

The English gunner who fired on the galleys, allowing the *Content* to escape, was William Clement from Weymouth. He later became captain of two vessels.

Last Fight of the *Revenge*

As one of the greatest naval battles of the period, and as another attempt by the English to take the annual Spanish *flota*, the last fight of Sir Richard Grenville's *Revenge* off Flores, in the Azores, fits squarely within the history of the tropical Americas.[26] The Azores are key to a transatlantic passage from the Caribbean to Europe. In May 1591 Lord Thomas Howard, as admiral, sailed from Plymouth with an English fleet of some twenty-five vessels to lie in wait for the treasure fleet, doubly rich that year. Sir Richard Grenville was vice-admiral, in the *Revenge*. The *Revenge*, launched in 1577, was three-masted, race-built, with a burden of about 440 tons, heavily armed with forty-two bronze cannon and manned by a crew of 260. In her fourteen years this fine vessel had faced the Spanish in both American and European waters.

The Spanish fleet of fifty-nine vessels included the 'Twelve Apostles', each about 1,000 tons burden, new ships launched by the previous April. The fleet was commanded by Don Álonzo de Bazán, brother of the much more famous Admiral Álvaro de Bazán, 1st Marqués of Santa Cruz, he of the battles off Gibraltar and San Juan de Ulúa. Though the fleet of Don Álonzo was short on firepower, its crew numbered 3,000, with 4,000 marines.

The English fleet at the end of August was reballasting at Flores and had disembarked her sick crew ashore to refresh. Having been on station in the Azores for three months, Grenville had some ninety crew sick, leaving about 160 fit to fight. The Spanish fleet was sighted by the English, who at first thought it was the annual *flota* arriving. The Spanish split into two squadrons to round the island from both sides and catch the English fleet in harbour. Howard's fleet managed to sail out and escape, but the *Revenge*, 2 miles astern, was cut off. Grenville had two choices: to fall off and run, or to continue on ahead in the hope of battering his way through the Spanish fleet. He chose the latter course, and his defeat was within months immortalised by Ralegh (who originally was to have been vice-admiral of the fleet) in *A Report of the Truth of the Fight about the Isles of Azores*, 1591, and much later by Alfred Lord Tennyson's ballad, *The Revenge*.

The Spanish found Grenville to be the 'most arrogant man in the world', with 'intolerable pride and insatiable ambition', in short, full of '*arrogancia*'. He was then about 50, as fiery as Drake and as unlucky as his relative, Ralegh.

On 30 August 1591 the Spanish fleet appeared at about five in the afternoon. Grenville nearly broke through the Spanish fleet but was engaged and blanketed and rammed by the *San Felipe*, then grappled and fired on by the *San Barnabe*, rammed and boarded by the *San Cristobel*, and grappled by the *Asunción*. The battle raged on throughout the night. By dawn the *Revenge's* three masts had been shot away, her decks were shattered and many crew lay dead. No English ship to date had been boarded by a Spaniard, and Grenville, wounded by a musket ball, cried 'Fight on! Fight on! No surrender!' He ordered his master gunner to blow up the ship. The captain and master countered the order. Semi-conscious, having been shot in the head, Grenville was taken aboard the *San Pablo* and died two days later. The *Revenge* was repaired and sailed on 15 September for Terceira. When the fleet was hit by a storm, the *Revenge* was lost on the rocks at Terceira.

Spanish Crown Orders Frigates Built

Return now to the Caribbean, and to the summer of 1591. On 15 June 1591, two days after King's sea battle off Cuba's Cabo Corrientes, Lope de Vega Portocarrero wrote from Santo Domingo to the Crown, reporting that the Spanish fleet had been detained in port because of news of enemy vessels in the area.[27] Nevertheless, he took the flagship and another vessel out to sea before dawn, and when day broke was attacked by five English ships, saved only by a galley that had come to his rescue. 'Corsairs have been more numerous than usual this year. In the last fifteen days more than twenty sail have passed here or along the north coast.'

Pedro Alvarez de Ruesga, captain of the *Brava*, one of the two galleys that defended Cuba, testified in a certificate dated 23 June 1591 that he knew Fernando Menendez Carrasco, from Baeza in Spain, a soldier aboard the flag galley *San Agustín*, and that in 1591 the galleys off Cabo Corrientes had engaged an English vessel (the *Content*).[28] Carrasco, he writes, is a soldier of good record and honest character, 'medium sized, good face, blond beard'. While 'fighting bravely, arms in hand, in the right wales of the flag galley, [he] was shot through the left leg below the knee. The wound left him markedly lame although still of service.' Ruesga provided the soldier with this certificate.

Various depositions were made in La Havana from 23 September to 11 October 1591 regarding the naval action the previous June off Cabo Corrientes in fighting the *Content*.[29] Francisco Moncayo, royal accountant for the galleys, testified that Miguel Romero had taken part in all the galleys' encounters against English and French corsairs, 'always fighting like a good soldier, until lately when he was shot twice in the right leg engaging the English off Cabo Corrientes'. Romero, in the flag-galley when he was wounded, was 'in the post of most danger, that is, in the bow in the wales with his harquebus and arms, fighting with great spirit'.

On 27 July 1591 the governor of the city, Juan de Texeda, wrote to the Casa de Contratación from La Havana.[30] He had received one cannon, just the thing, though he wishes there were more like it. 'As it is, these English are losing all respect for me, for every hour they sail under my nose and because the galleys are in Cabo San António waiting for Pedro Menéndez, I cannot scare them off.' He asks the king to take back the two galleys in exchange for the four frigates he is building. These will clear the coast and will 'punish any enemy loitering here in such manner that they will not send me love-messages and compliments as these drunkards did'. Two of the frigates ordered by the Crown were ready. As for the other six frigates ordered to be built, some carpenters have been hired, he writes, but there is no money to pay them, nor do they have tools: 'In the warehouse there are only forty-five cases of assorted nails and eight barrels of tar and a little iron.'

Those three years between 1589 and 1591 saw privateers especially put strong pressure on the Spanish in the Caribbean, helping to stall another armada from attacking England.

six

⸺⸺

Indigo, Sugar, Penguins, 1591–93

Praise the sea; on shore remain.

John Florio, *Second Frutes*, 1591

*J*ohn Jane, 'a man of good observation' as described by Hakluyt, reports on the last voyage of Thomas Cavendish (Candish), intended for the South Seas, the Philippines and China, undertaken with three ships and two barks.[1] In the *Galleon Leicester*, 400 tons, the admiral, Cavendish sailed as commander of the expedition; in the *Roebuck*, 240 tons, vice-admiral, John Cooke (Cocke) was captain; in the *Desire*, 120 tons, rear-admiral, John Davis, captain (with whom author Jane sailed); the bark *Daintie*, 60 tons, Randolfe Cotton as captain; and the *Blacke Pinnace*, 20–40 tons, captain unknown (named 'black' as she had transported the body of Sir Philip Sidney back to England). In all, Cavendish put out nearly £13,000 for his five vessels, their provisions and 350 men.

Cavendish set off on 26 August 1591 from Plymouth. It was a slow crossing, since near the equator his fleet was caught in the doldrums for twenty-seven days. On 29 November Cavendish's fleet fell in with the bay of Salvador on the coast of Brazil, 12 leagues north of Cabo Frio. Off Salvador, the fleet again lay becalmed until 2 December, 'at which time we took a small bark bound for the River of Plate with sugar, haberdash wares, and Negroes'. On 24 January he set sail for the Strait of Magellan and arrived at Port Desire on 6 March, provisions running low. While at sea, Cavendish aboard the *Galleon* had a ship's boat built, for his longboat and lighthorseman had been lost in bad weather. Ashore at Santos, he also had a pinnace built. Pinnaces, with their shallow draft, sail and oars, could go where the larger vessel could not and were necessary for sounding unknown waters.

On 20 March the fleet left Port Desire, and after many storms fell in with the Strait of Magellan on 8 April 1592. There, writes Jane, highly critical of Cavendish:

> we indured extreme storms, with perpetual snow, where many of our men died with cursed famine, and miserable cold, not having wherewith to cover their bodies, nor to fill their bellies, but living by muscles [mussels], water, and weeds of the sea, with a small relief of the ship's store in meal sometimes. And all the sick men in the *Galleon* were most uncharitably put ashore into the woods in the snow, rain, and cold, when men of good health could scarcely endure it, where they ended their lives in the highest degree of misery, Master Cavendish all this while being aboard the *Desire*.

The officers persuaded Cavendish to turn back from the strait. On the 18th of the month they were at Cape Froward. One night Jane's vessel, the *Desire*, lost her ship's boat at the stern. Split, 'sore spoiled', her oars lost, she sank. Two nights later, in altering course off Port Desire, Cavendish lost the rest of the fleet when it did not follow him. 'For in the evening he stood close by a wind to seaward, having the wind at north-northeast, and we standing the same way, the wind not altering, could not the next day see him: So that we then persuaded ourselves, that he was gone for Port Desire to relieve himself, or that he had sustained some mischance at sea, and was gone thither to remedy it.' When John Jane and the *Desire* arrived at Port Desire on 26 May, Cavendish was not there.

As for Captain Davis and the *Desire*, Jane writes: 'Being most slenderly victualled, without sails, boat, oars, nails, cordage, and all the other necessaries for our relief, we were stricken into a deadly sorrow.' The captain was now faced with famine, a mutinous crew and the foul weather. On 26 August 1591 Davis and thirty-eight of the ship's company gathered and signed a testimonial bearing on the loss of Cavendish and the fleet. It reads:

> And now being here moored in Port Desire, our shrouds are all rotten, not having a running rope whereto we may trust, and being provided only of one shift of sails all worn, our topsails not able to abide any stress of weather, neither have we any pitch, tar, or nails, nor any store for the supplying of these wants; and we live only upon seals and mussels, having but five hogsheads of pork within board, and meal three ounces for a man a day, with water for to drink.

In attempting the strait, a storm drove the *Desire* to the north-east some 50 leagues. On 14 August they reached unknown islands. These were the Falklands, which Davis claimed for England. Again they made for the Strait of Magellan and were driven back. Finally, on 22 August, they entered it, and three weeks later, on 13 September, the crew saw the South Sea before them. Their ship was a wreck. 'Now had we but one anchor which had but one whole fluke, a cable spliced in two places, and a piece of an old cable' that soon was held by only one strand. Davis consulted his crew, saying that they should proceed, for if they returned 'there is nothing but death to be hoped for'. The crew reluctantly agreed to keep on going.

On the night of 2 October another storm hit them. The 4th found the *Blacke Pinnace* lying ahull, unable to follow the *Desire*. 'We durst not hull in that unmerciful storm, but sometimes tried under our maincourse, sometime with a haddock of our sail, for our ship was very leeward, and most laboursome in the sea. This night we lost the pinnace, and never saw her again.' The next day the *Desire's* foresail split and was torn to shreds. To balance the ship, the master hoisted the mizzensail onto the foremast stay, and mended the foresail with canvas from the spritsail. The storm raged on 'without all reason in fury, with hail, snow, rain, and wind such and so mighty, as that in nature it could not possibly be more, the seas such and so lofty, with continual breach, that many times we were doubtful whether our ship did sink or swim'.

By 10 October all were prepared for death. Davis sat pensive in the gallery. As his captain was cold to the bone, Jane brought him some *rosa solis*, a cordial brewed from the bog plant sundew, thought to stir up lust and to lift one's spirits. He drank it and prayed for deliverance, thinking of giving over the voyage and returning home. 'And so suddenly, before I went from him the sun shined clear; so that he and the master both observed the true elevation of the Pole [the Cruzeiro do Sul, the Southern Cross], whereby they knew by what course to recover the Straits.' All rejoiced, officers and crew.

The master being a man of good spirit resolutely made quick dispatch and set sails. Our sails had not been half an hour aboard, but the footrope of our foresail broke, so that nothing held but the eyelet holes. The seas continually broke over the ship's poop, and flew into the sails with such violence, that we still expected the tearing of our sails, or oversetting of the ship, and withall to our utter discomfort, we perceived that we fell still more and more to leeward, so that we could not double the cape: We were now come within half a mile of the cape, and so near the shore, that the counter-suffe [surf] of the sea would rebound against the ship's side, so that we were much dismayed with the horror of our present end.

Being thus at the very pinch of death, the wind and seas raging beyond measure, our master veered [let out] some of the mainsheet; and whether it was by that occasion, or by some current, or by the wonderful power of God, as we verily think it was, the ship quickened her way, and shot past that rock, where we thought she would have shored. Then between the cape and the point there was a little bay; so that we were somewhat farther from the shore: And when we were come so far as the cape, we yielded to death: Yet our good God the Father

of all mercies delivered us, and we doubled the cape about the length of our
ship, or very little more.

Being shot past the cape, we presently took in our sails, which only God had
preserved unto us: And when we were shot in between the high lands, the wind
blowing trade, without any inch of sail, we spooned before the sea, three men
being not able to guide the helm, and in six hours we were put five and twenty
leagues within the Straits, where we found a sea answerable to the ocean.

On his first passage Davis had carefully made a chart of the strait, so in returning
he was able to navigate the winding channels and swift currents. Once inside,
the crew took on and dried the meat of 14,000 penguins. Davis reckoned that
the victuals might last six months – barely enough to reach England. He ordered
short rations. The allowance was 2.5oz of meal per day per man, this twice a
week, so that 5oz served for a week. Three days a week the crew had three spoon-
fuls of oil per man. Two days a week, peason (dried peas or lentils), a pint between
four men a day, and every day five penguins for four men, and six quarts of water
for four men per day. With this rationing, Jane writes, 'we lived, though weakly,
and very feeble'. On 22 December they shaped a course for Brazil.

On 30 January 1593 they reached Ilha de Placencia in Brazil. Landing a boat
at dawn, they were hoping to catch the Portuguese asleep and to steal their *cassava* meal. The settlement had been razed, the houses burned to the ground, and
that night, while the shore party was sleeping, Indians and Portuguese attacked
them. Only two English escaped. The next morning, crew from the ship found
them 'slain, and laid naked on a rank one by another, with their faces upward, and
a cross set by them'. Two pinnaces from Rio de Janeiro appeared. Davis quickly
weighed anchor and left.

It was now early February. Jane observes: 'Of seventy-six persons which
departed in our ship out of England, we were now left but twenty-seven, having
lost thirteen in this place, with their chief furniture, as muskets, calivers, powder,
and shot. Our cask was all in decay, so that we could not take in more water
than was in our ship, for want of cask, and that which we had was marvellous ill-
conditioned.' And now they were to face the return voyage. But 'to depart with
eight tons of water in such bad cask was to starve at sea, and in staying our case
was ruinous'.

At Cabo Frio the wind went contrary and remained so for three weeks, but
rain fortunately filled their casks.

But after we came near unto the sun, our dried penguins began to corrupt, and
there bred in them a most lothsome and ugly worm of an inch long [maggots].
This worm did so mightily increase, and devour our victuals, that there was in
reason no hope how we should avoid famine, but be devoured of these wicked
creatures: There was nothing that they did not devour, only iron excepted: Our

clothes, boots, shoes, hats, shirts, stockings: And for the ship they did eat the timbers, as that we greatly feared they would undo us, by gnawing through the ship's sides [the teredo worm]. Great was the care and diligence of our captain, master, and company to consume these vermin, but the more we laboured to kill them, the more they increased; so that at the last we could not sleep for them, but they would eat our flesh, and bite like mosquitoes.

The maggots were not the only plague of those aboard. The account continues:

In this woeful case, after we had passed the Equinoctial toward the north, our men began to fall sick of such a monstrous disease, as I think the like was never heard of: For in their ankles it began to swell; from thence in two days it would be in their breasts, so that they could not draw their breath, and then fell into their cods; and their cods and yards did swell most grievously, and most dread-fully to behold, so that they could neither stand, lie, nor go. Whereupon our men grew mad with grief. Our captain with extreme anguish of his soul, was in such woeful case, that he desired only a speedy end, and though he were scarce able to speak for sorrow, yet he persuaded them to patience, and to give God thanks, and like dutiful children to accept of his chastisement. For all this divers grew raging mad, and some died in most lothsome and furious pain.

According to Surgeon General Keevil, Davis' crew most likely had amoebic dys-entery, transmitted through contaminated drinking water.[2]

All the crew died, save sixteen, of which only five (Jane was one) were able to move about. Somehow, the captain and one boy were still in perfect health:

The captain and master, as occasion served, would take in, and heave out the topsails, the master only attended on the spritsail, and all of us at the capstan without sheets and tacks. In fine our misery and weakness was so great, that we could not take in, nor heave out a sail: So our topsail and spritsails were torn all in pieces by the weather. The master and captain taking their turns at the helm, were mightily distressed and monstrously grieved with the most woeful lamentation of our sick men. Thus as lost wanderers upon the sea, the 11 of June 1593, it pleased God that we arrived at Bear-haven in Ireland, and there ran the ship on shore: Where the Irish men helped us to take in our sails, and to moor our ship for floating.

For a certain substantial charge, that was. Davis left three or four to mind the ship and, with the others, in five days found passage on an English fishing boat bound for Padstow, Cornwall.

Purchas reports much the same story as Jane, but he is more critical of Davis.[3] In high-flown prose, editor-churchman Purchas sermonises:

The Sea is a waving wavering foundation, the winds' theatre both for comedies and tragedies. You have seen Drake acting both: And in both you here find Cavendish ... [S]ublunary things are like the moon their nearest planet, which never views the earth two days together with one face. God hath made our way to him so full of chances and changes, that our unsteady, slippery way on this earth, and calm-storm-voyage in these seas, may make us more to meditate and thirst after that haven of instability, and heaven of eternity. Some passionate speeches of Master Cavendish against some private persons not employed in this action, I have suppressed, some others I have let pass; not that I charge Captain Davis or others, but that it may appear what the general thought of them. Master Hakluyt hath published Master Jane's report of this voyage, which makes more favourable on Captain Davis his side. If he did deal treacherously, treachery found him out, as in his last voyage before is declared. If any think the captain here to conceive amiss, I shall be willing to have the most charitable conceit, and therefore remit the reader to Master Hakluyt's relation aforesaid, for his apology.

According to Purchas, Cavendish's vessels had reunited at Port Desire in March. They attempted the strait again on 8 April 1592. Inside, foul weather kept them at anchor from 21 April to 15 May. Men died. Supplies ran short. Cavendish, in the *Galleon Leicester*, had wanted to make the attempt again, but the crew had refused. The fleet turned back east. On 20 May off Port Desire, in yet another storm, the fleet separated. Davis in the *Desire* and Cotton in the *Daintie* had parted from Cavendish in the *Galleon* and Cooke in the *Roebuck*. Cavendish and Cooke had then sailed first for St Helena but, through poor navigation, missed it and made for Ascension Island. They missed that too. Cavendish was by then gravely ill. He made his will shortly before his death and was committed to the deep somewhere in the south Atlantic sometime in the latter part of May 1592, aged 31 or 32. Just four years earlier, this great mariner, the third captain (after the captain of Magellan's ship, and Drake) and the second Englishman to round the world, 1586–88, had struck it rich. *Sic transit gloria.* Cavendish's untimely and early demise shows the perils of the sea and of command.

Cumberland's Fifth Voyage, Takes *Madre de Dios*

The Earl of Cumberland set sail for the West Indies on 6 May 1592 from Plymouth.[4] He hired the *Tigre*, 600 tons, for £300 a month wages, used two of his own ships, the *Samson* and the *Golden Noble*, and two small vessels. Cumberland gave over command of the fleet to Captain Norton, with orders to make for the Azores. There Norton joined forces with Sir John Burroughs in the *Roebuck*, a heavily armed 200-ton merchantman belonging to Ralegh. The law and custom of the sea was that men-of-war joining together would share equally the tonnage taken. They set about pillaging a burned-out carrack while other English ships – the queen's *Foresight*, Robert Crosse, captain; the *Daintie*, one of John Hawkyns' ships, Tomson, captain; and the *Golden Dragon*, commanded by Christopher Newport – joined in the hunt for three or four other carracks. They spread out across the sea and waited five weeks for prey.

On 3 August the great carrack *Madre de Dios* came over the horizon. The *Daintie* fired a broadside, fell astern and fired again, until the rest of the fleet could come up and join the attack. Meanwhile, the carrack fired back. The *Golden Dragon* and Burroughs joined in about three in the afternoon and took a shot from a cannon perrier below the waterline, in the breadroom, forcing the *Dragon* to bear up to stop the leak. Crosse in the *Foresight* fired a broadside, but was so close that his sails were blanketed and he lost way. He reluctantly lashed the Spaniard by the shrouds and sailed away with her. Cumberland's ships, the 'worst of sail', came up last, about eleven at night, not intending to board. But hearing the *Foresight* call to Norton, 'And you be men, save the Queen's ship', Norton ordered the *Samson* to grapple the Spaniard on one side and the *Tigre* on the other. The *Tigre*, 'running stemling aboard, broke her beak-head to the huddings; the *Samson* laid the *Foresight* aboard, and entered through her into the carrack, whereby the *Foresight* without entering any one man, took opportunity to free herself'.

Both ships' companies boarded by the forechain, but the carrack's forecastle was so high that some men fell overboard in the attempt to climb it. The assault continued for an hour and a half, against stiff resistance. But once the English gained the deck, the Portuguese retreated to the hold. The English now went for the loot, each man with a candle. A cabin with 600 cartridges of powder caught fire, but Norton and others with buckets of water quenched the flames. Burroughs, pretending the queen's name, took command, repaired the carrack and sent her and her treasure off to Dartmouth. The English had taken one of the richest prizes in Elizabethan maritime history. Cumberland's portion would have been £2–3 million, but because he had relinquished his command to Norton, he had to be content with a gift of just £36,000. Once again, the Azores proved the centre of contention between England and Spain.

Privateers in the Caribbean

Thirteen English privateers were cruising off the coast of Cuba in June 1592, but despite their numbers, returned without profit.[5] Corporal John Twitt, aboard the admiral, tells the story of Christopher Newport's voyage in the *Golden Dragon*, 150 tons, nineteen cannon, smaller guns and muskets, and three other ships totalling some 300–350 tons, with a crew of 200.[6] This was a fairly powerful fleet, financed by eleven adventurers, most from London. It set out from London on

25 January 1592, and with favourable winds fetched Dominica on 4 April 1592. Newport's raid on a frigate south of Hispaniola brought in only twenty-two jars of copper money that was to have been spent on buying wine in San Juan. A land attack on a town in Hispaniola gained him some ransom: cattle and two wainloads of sugar.

At La Yaguana on Hispaniola's north coast, a centre known for illegal trade in slaves, sugar and hides for foreigners, a pre-dawn attack on 27 April was discovered and the alarm raised. The town's 150 horse and some snipers met the English on a 'fair green' before the town. The horses charged, but the English stood firm. The Spanish next stampeded a herd of 200 cattle towards the English, but the cattle turned back and charged the Spanish. The English killed the governor and many other colonials, deemed 'very hardy, and of great valure'. Writes Twitt: 'Being thus frustrated of our pretended voyage, we stood for the Bay of Honduras', where Newport took 5 or 6 tons of quicksilver, church bells, some money, linen, silk, cotton, a thousand hides, jars of balsamum and iron. In the Gulf of Florida he took a frigate's 'five and fifty hogs, and about some two hundred weight of excellent tobacco rolled up in seines [nets]. We lightened them of their hogs and tobacco, and sent the men away with their frigate.'

Newport had sacked four towns, seventeen frigates and two ships (eight of these in the Golfo de Honduras). He sailed for the Azores, and it was there that Newport met Burroughs, where together they and Cumberland took the *Madre de Dios*. It was this one prize that made his expedition so profitable, not the hogs or copper coin. Newport, with forty of his men from the *Dragon* and twelve from the *Prudence*, brought the prize into Dartmouth on 7 September 1592. The *Madre de Dios* was so large that she had to lie anchored in the middle of the River Dart, where eventually she was to rot away. Newport reached Dover about 10 November 1592.

Another voyage typifies the Caribbean corsairs.[7] William King's *Salomon* was a powerful ship, 200 tons, with twenty-six cannon and 100 crew. She was supported by another vessel, the *Jane Bonaventure*, 40 tons, with twenty-six crew. King provisioned for a year, which was unusual, as most cruises provisioned for only six months. The two set sail on 26 January 1592 for the Gulf of México. The commander was the experienced mariner William King of Ratcliffe, then 27, who was most likely the author of the account of the 1591 engagement off Cabo Corrientes and is most certainly the author of this 1592 account. King did take some prizes but missed the *flota*. The only really successful privateer in 1592 was the 'lone wolf' Christopher Newport, the same Newport who was to emerge later taking colonists to North America.

Between 1590 and 1597, Captain William Parker, gentleman, made eight voyages of reprisal.[8] From 1592 six of those eight voyages were to the West Indies, concentrating on Puerto de Caballos and the Golfo Dulce. Andrews writes about Parker's two voyages made in 1592 and 1593. Parker was from Plymouth, a sometime servant to Ralegh who later was to attend the Lord Admiral. It was he who passed on vague information about El Dorado to Ralegh and, more usefully, gave Ralegh a Spanish rutter for the West Indies. Parker, like Drake before him, liked surprise attacks by small raiding parties. Parker's *Richard* took 800 hides from a 20-ton Spanish frigate from La Havana.

The Earl of Cumberland in 1593 assembled seven ships for his sixth voyage for the Azores[9]: the *Royall*; the *Golden Lion* as admiral and commanded by himself; the *Bonaventure* as vice-admiral; the *Blacke Chaldon*, *Pilgrime*, *Anthonie* and *Discoverie*. He sailed to the Azores, where he found a Spanish fleet three times the size of his. Cumberland came down with illness, possibly scurvy. Nevertheless, his ships took a substantial prize, making this voyage his most profitable one.

Sir John Burgh was a younger son of William, 4th Lord Burgh of Gainsborough, and brother of Thomas, 5th Lord Burgh, Lord-Deputy in Ireland. Born 1562, Sir John Burgh was associated with Ralegh, who in 1592 had appointed him to command land forces that fought in taking the great carrack *Madre de Dios*. This venture with four vessels to Guiana was Ralegh's own. It was probably financed from the profits of the earlier taking of the *Madre de Dios*, since Ralegh, Burgh, Newport and Newport's backers had shared in the profits from that prize.

Burgh sailed to Guiana, Trinidad and La Margarita in 1593 as captain of Ralegh's *Roebuck*, 300 tons, John Bedford, master; with the *Golden Dragon*, 150 tons, Christopher Newport, captain, and Andrew Shillinge, master; the *Prudence*, 100 tons, Thomas Wally, captain, and Thomas Warne, master; and the *Virgin*, 50 tons, Henry Kedgell, captain, and Cuthbert Grippe, master.

The Spanish account of the *Golden Dragon*'s attack on La Margarita records that in September, three English galleons appeared at the port of Pueblo del Mar, and before daybreak landed 400 men to sack the city of Asunción. They were turned back by Spanish defenders along the road to the city, though the English seized more than 100 black men and pearls worth 5,000 pesos. They exchanged the prisoners for ransom and then left the island. The *Golden Dragon* arrived home before 10 December 1593, severely battered from battle and damaged by storms. Early in 1594 Sir John was to be killed in a duel with John Gilbert, eldest son of Sir Humphrey Gilbert.

James Langton, as general commander, sailed for the Earl of Cumberland on the earl's seventh voyage, with the *Anthony*, 120 tons, the *Pilgrim*, 100 tons, and the pinnace *Discovery*, 12 tons.[10] The three-vessel expedition, well-manned and outfitted, was a success. Cumberland trusted Langton and later chose him to lead his 1595 and 1598 expeditions. Andrews notes that the Spanish respected him. He was a good leader in a fight and was equally able to write to the Spanish commander in chivalric terms and bargain with traders in the language of the street. A Spaniard described Langton as 'a good-sized, reddish man, with hair long in the old fashion, some thirty-five years of age', and added: 'Captain Langton is the leader to whom regard must be paid.'

The fleet sailed to the Pearl Coast and raided La Margarita, then sailed on to Cumaná and to Río de la Hacha. Writes Andrews: 'The lesson was one which emerges again and again from the activities of the English in the Caribbean in the nineties: that places like Cumaná and Río de la Hacha were quite capable of defending themselves against privateers, unless they were taken by surprise.'

Langton's next objective was Hispaniola. He worked his way around the island, accumulating ransom and loot until the end of January, as a Spanish report says, 'loitering along that shore as safely as though it were his own country, because the very inhabitants there, whom he was despoiling, afforded him protection'. He blockaded Santo Domingo for six weeks and captured nine ships but little loot. Sailing for Honduras, he again did well in taking seven more vessels. The cargo was not particularly rich, but it was large. The *Anthony* brought back a prize worth £5,340; the *Pilgrim* £570.

Newport's *Golden Dragon* underwent quick repair in a matter of weeks. In January 1594 she was off to the Caribbean once more, with Newport again as captain, Henry Ravens as master, and once more accompanied by the *Prudence*, John Brough, captain.[11] By 15 April at Puerto de Caballos, Honduras, he had burned two ships and taken away two others. The town was empty, since Langton had raided it two weeks earlier.

On the day of Newport's raid the governor and captain-general of Honduras, Gerónimo Sánchez de Carranza, wrote to Don Francisco Colona:

> As I lay in bed ill with fever, having been bled not five days before, the lookout made the smoke signal meaning large ships sighted. When they came in view, they seemed to be English. I dressed at once and ordered that I should be carried to the beach in a chair. I caused many mules to be fetched and in good order with great haste caused the residents and merchants to remove their money and valuable merchandise from the town. I then ordered the crier to bid them, on penalty of death, to come to the defence of the place. Only twenty men, unarmed, responded. The five harquebuses they brought had neither powder nor shot.[12]

Though the governor's fever was rising and the English were bombarding the town, he directed the defence from the beach so that his few men would seem to be many. Governor Carranza was to write to the Crown: 'By stratagem and ruse I, alone and unaided, drove from the harbour Captain Christopher Newport, who landed with some 200 muskets. He went away again without taking anything of your majesty's royal treasury.' As for the general state of things in the Caribbean, he writes that those with military experience should judge 'what I accomplished in Puerto de Caballos, sick, without troops, a fortress or artillery, deserted by all and left alone at the post of danger. Being myself a man who understands war, I know that they would find no remissness to reprimand, but so much foresight to praise, that your majesty might show me favour.'

After Langton and Newport, William Parker in the *Richard* was the next to sack Puerto de Caballos.[13] He raided the town in May that year, then again in 1597. With its long, open beach that could not be defended, the place was an easy job for corsairs. Parker, with forty-five crew, attacked at midnight, catching the Spanish sleeping. Again the governor and colonists fled into the bush, and for a fortnight Parker and a French corsair held the town, plundering the bullion, hides and indigo that had been brought back into town once Newport had left.

Another Caribbean privateer was Michael Geare, who by 1590 was master of the *John*, a Watts vessel that made another voyage there in 1591.[14] Geare was a tough fighter, but 'none too scrupulous' in taking more than his fair share of loot. In 1594–95 he commanded and was part-owner of the *Michael and John* of London, 100–120 tons. He was to make at least three more voyages to the Caribbean: 1596, 1601–02 and 1602–03. In his 1594–95 voyage, he had success off Puerto Rico and Santo Domingo, but off La Havana in May 1595 he barely escaped being captured by a Spanish galleon.

Admiral Don Sebastián de Arencibia set out with a galleon and three shallops from La Havana and on 4 May 1595 engaged Geare. The *Michael and John* and the Spanish galleon were only 300 paces apart but, writes the Spanish admiral:

> because he was a good sailer he broke out three in addition to his regular sails, whereas my flagship had not even its usual number and those it had were old. I tried to get new sails, but they were not to be procured in this city, for Don Francisco Coloma carried off everything when he went. So the enemy flagship got away from me, abandoning to me her vice-admiral and another shallop, with a couple of dozen living prisoners including the vice-admiral. We had killed about fifty others. I lost sixteen or eighteen men killed.

Don Luis Fajardo, commander of the La Havana fleet, wrote to the Crown that 'the incident appeared important to the residents of this city, because this is the first prize the armada has made and because this corsair is the one who was doing the most damage along this coast; and because it was a hard-fought affair'. Geare smuggled his ransom and substantial plunder into England.

The *Rose Lion* was a powerfully armed merchantman that, besides trading, undertook privateering voyages.[15] In late September to early October 1594 she was fitted out in Plymouth by her captain, Thomas West. One of the merchants underwriting the enterprise was Thomas Myddleton, owner of one of the largest sugar refineries in London, with sugar interests in Antwerp. Sugar, the major item that figures in the prize manifests of the period, accounted for Myddleton's great wealth. The 1594–95 voyage of the *Rose Lion* was profitable, bringing home ginger, sugar and other cargo from a prize taken off Santo Domingo.

The same year Richard Hawkyns left on his fateful voyage, 1593, the Earl of Cumberland set out from England bound for the Caribbean on the sixth (and seventh) of his voyages of trade, pillage and plunder.[16] The seventh voyage, so called by Purchas, is actually part of the sixth: Cumberland split his fleet and sent three vessels to the West Indies. The *Anthonie*, 120 tons, the *Pilgrime*, 100 tons, and the pinnace *Discoverie*, tonnage unknown, accompanied by two Spanish pilots, steered for the Antilles and Saint Lucia. They first attacked La Margarita, took some £2,000 in pearls and ransomed a town for 2,000 ducats. At Santo Domingo the vessels found food and ransomed the estates, leaving then for Jamaica and Cuba, and more booty. The ships returned to Plymouth on 14 May 1594.

seven

⋘⋙

A *DAINTIE* AT DEAR COST, 1593–95

As false as air, as water, wind, or sandy earth.

Shakespeare, *Troilus and Cressida*, 1601–02

In 1593–94 yet another Elizabethan set out for the South Sea via the Strait of Magellan. Richard Hawkyns, son of Sir John Hawkyns, had in mind to trade with Japan, the Philippines, Moluccas, China and the East Indies.[1] Richard Hawkyns was a sailor's sailor, careful with his ship, having the loyalty of his crew, and though like his grandfather and father essentially a merchant mariner, he would, like his father, fight when necessary. Like the rest of the family, he knew the West Indies. He had commanded the galliot *Duck* in Francis Drake's 1585 voyage. As a writer, he shows a facility and adroitness in style that approaches Sir Walter Ralegh's race-built lean prose.

Returning from the Armada campaign of 1588, Hawkyns set out to build a 300 to 400-ton vessel, the *Repentance*, 'finished in that perfection as could be required. For she was pleasing to the eye, profitable for stowage, good of sail and well-conditioned.' Riding at Deptford, 'the Queen's Majesty passing by her, and to her Palace of Greenwich, commanded her barge-men to row round about her, and viewing her from post to stem, disliked nothing but her name, and said, that she would christen her anew, and that thenceforth she should be called the *Daintie*; which name she brooked as well for her proportion and grace, as for the many happy voyages she made in her Majesty's services'. The name *Repentence*, Purchas offers, was ominous ('celestial characters sort not to terrestrial fabrics') and lists the *Revenge*, the *Thunderbolt* and the *Jesus of Lubeck*, all of whom came to bad ends. Hawkyns laid aboard victuals, munitions, stores and cargoes for traffic, and began to 'wage men'. He left the provisioning of beef, pork, biscuit and cider for the West Country, as these items were cheaper there than in London.

The *Daintie* cast off from Blackwall on 8 April 1593. Hawkyns ordered the pilot to make for Gravesend. *Daintie* was deeply laden, and her ports were open. Still in the Thames, she heeled and began to take on water. The more she heeled, the more she listed. In danger of capsizing, Hawkyns immediately ordered the sheets flown to right the ship. She slowly, and after great effort, righted herself. Hawkyns warns mariners to 'have an eye to their ports, and to see those shut and caulked, which may cause danger' and cites infamous capsizes.

On 26 April he reached Plymouth, where he took on provisions. It took Hawkyns and Plymouth's justices two days of searching 'all lodgings, taverns, and ale-houses' to round up these 'vagabonds', soon drunk or in debt to landlords, publicans and others. He paid off their debts and brought them back to the fleet, observing '*impunitas peccandi illecebra*' (the impunity of illicit sin). Hawkyns hired a third more men than he needed to sail the ship.

With much pomp and circumstance, on the evening of 12 June 1593, he set sail from Plymouth. The 30-year-old Hawkyns hoped to follow in the golden wakes of Drake and Cavendish and return rich. Trumpets and other musical instruments played fanfares, and the ships' cannon fired salutes that echoed off the Hoe, to which the fort replied in kind. Sir John Hawkyns, Richard's father, watched the three vessels sail off. It was to be the last time he would see his son. The fleet consisted of the *Daintie* (300–400 tons), the *Hawke* (100 tons) and the pinnace *Fancie* (60 tons) – all Hawkyns' ships. They directed their course for the Madeiras, then Guinea.

After four months at sea and contrary winds, the *Daintie* at last reached the coast of Brazil on 18 October 1593 'thwart of Cape Saint Augustine, which lies in six degrees to the Southwards of the Line'. Sickness (perhaps scurvy) had 'wasted' more than half the crew. With only twenty-four of the men in the fleet healthy, he made for the coast and fetched the port of Santos, 'alias nostra Señora de Victoria'. On 5 November Hawkyns anchored near Cabo Blanco. The sick were taken ashore and tended by the fleet's three surgeons.

The healthy crew fished, 'romeged' (rummaged, fumigated) the ship, filled the water butts, felled and cut wood. With not enough men to sail her, Hawkyns stripped the *Hawke* and burned her. Time on land revived most of the crew. On 10 December, when Hawkyns sailed for Cabo Frio, only six men were still sick. At about the height of Rio de la Plata the pinnace *Fancie* was separated at night from Hawkyns in a storm. That was the last Hawkyns saw of his pinnace, her crew and captain. He points out that her captain, Robert Tharlton, had earlier in these same waters deserted the fleet of Thomas Cavendish.

Hawkyns carried on to latitude 48° S. His chart showed no land there, but land there was, some 60 leagues off South America. The date was 2 February 1594. But without his pinnace, Hawkyns could not reconnoitre. 'This I have sorrowed for many times since for it had likelihood to be an excellent country. It hath great rivers of fresh waters; for the out-shoot of them colours the sea in many places, as we ran alongst it. It is not mountainous, but much of the disposition of England, and as temperate.' Hawkyns thought it the eastern part of Terra Australis Incognita. He had, in fact, come on to those same Falkland Islands that John Davis had discovered just a year and a half earlier.

With an eye to colonisation, Hawkyns too claimed the land for England and named it after Queen Elizabeth. In 'perpetual memory of her chastity, and remembrance of my endeavours, I gave it the name Hawkyns' Maidenland'. The winds were fair for the strait. Hawkyns and the *Daintie* set a course west and south, to latitude 52° 50' S, where on 10 February he sighted land, the headland to the strait. The *Daintie* threaded her way along in the narrow waters, bucking tidal currents, forced by adverse winds to anchor for some two or three days at a time. Hawkyns' men recaulked the *Daintie*'s deck, filled the water casks, cut wood, salted penguins, baked biscuit and gathered mussels.

The Southern Sea, Sharp Storms

After Drake and Cavendish, Hawkyns became the third Englishman to navigate successfully the full length of the Strait of Magellan. His passage was forty-six days (Drake, sixteen; Cavendish, fifty-one). Once in the Southern Sea, Hawkyns was hit by a storm that lasted ten days, 'one of the sharpest storms that ever I felt to endure so long'. After it had blown itself out at last, he could shape his course towards Concepción. Like Drake before him, Hawkyns knew he must maintain the element of surprise until he was past Callao, the port for Lima. But the crew persuaded Hawkyns to spoil and plunder. 'The mariner is ordinarily so carried away with the desire of pillage, as sometimes for very appearances of small moment, he loses his voyage.'

Hawkyns and the *Daintie* hauled the coast aboard and found Valparaíso. In the harbour were four ships. That evening the crew lowered boats and soon took the Spanish vessels. These yielded 500 *botozios* of wine (*botijos*, earthenware jugs), 200 or 300 hens, some bread, bacon, dried beef, wax, candles, planks, spars and timber, Indian mantles, tallow, *manteca de puerco* (lard) and many large new chests. Inside the chests the crew hoped for gold bullion but found only apples. At daybreak, while ransoming the vessels, another ship sailed in loaded with good bacon, bread, hens and gold. Hawkyns took the goods, returned the ship to the Spanish, and set her pilot-owner, Alonso Berezbuena, ashore, as he was married and had children. Now reprovisioned from his prizes, the *Daintie* was 'as well stored and victualled as the day we departed from England', writes Hawkyns. But in that week's time, the whole coast had learned of the English pirate and his crew of seventy-five.

More than the Spanish, Hawkyns feared Chilean wine, which despite 'all the diligence and prevention I could use day and night, overthrew many of my people. A foul fault, because too common amongst seamen, and deserves some rigorous punishment with severity to be executed.' From Valparaíso, Hawkyns sailed directly to Coquinbo, then to Arica, then left the kingdom of Chile for the Bay of Pisco, at latitude 15° 50' S. Along the way, he took a pinnace – essential, as he had lost his own earlier.

Spanish Hunt Down the *Daintie*

The Chileans had warned the viceroy of Perú, Don Garcia Huertado de Mendoca, Marqués of Cavete, that an English ship was in Spanish waters. He sent six ships and some 2,000 men to seek out and destroy the *Daintie*. The force was under the command of the viceroy's wife's brother, Admiral Don Beltrán de Castro Ydelluca. At daybreak the morning after Hawkyns left Chilca (it was mid-May), the Spanish and English sighted each other. About nine in the morning, the wind picked up, and the *Daintie* put out to sea, 'the Spaniards cheek by jowl with us, ever getting to the windwards upon us; for that the shipping of the South Sea is ever moulded sharp under water, and long; all their voyages depending upon turning to windwards, and the breeze blowing ever southerly'.

As the sun rose, the winds freshened, which with the

rowling sea, that ever beats upon this coast, coming out of the westernboard, caused a chopping sea, wherewith the admiral of the Spaniards snapped his main mast asunder, and so began to lag astern, and with him, two other ships. The vice-admiral split her mainsail, being come within shot of us upon our broadside, but to leewards: The rear-admiral cracked her main yard asunder in the middest, being ahead of us: One of the armada, which had gotten upon the broadside of us, to windwards, durst not assault us.

Night was then coming on. Hawkyns and his officers consulted on how to shake off the Spaniards. The Spanish admiral and two others were astern of the *Daintie* some 4 leagues, the vice-admiral was to leeward, a mile off, the rear-admiral was dead ahead by a culverin shot, and another was 'upon our loofe [luff, to windward], within shot also'. The moon was due to rise in two hours. Hawkyns bore up before the wind, and sailed between the admiral and the vice-admiral. Dawn found the *Daintie* clear of the Spanish. Hawkyns shaped his course for the bay of Atacames, where they planned to trim the pinnace, cut wood and fill the water casks; then get on as quickly as possible.

The Spanish fleet returned to Callao. There, they were mocked and scorned by the women, who reviled and called them cowards and *golnias* (*gollería*, a dainty, delicacy?), and threatened the marines with daggers and pistols. The sailors and marines vowed to recover their reputations. The viceroy commanded Admiral Beltrán to sea with two ships and a pinnace and 2,000 men (other sources, 1,300 men) to capture Hawkyns, the *Daintie*, and her crew of seventy-five. The odds were fifteen to one against the English.

Hawkyns was now some 50 leagues north of Lima. He notes that all along the west coast of South America, the ocean currents are strong, sometimes to the south, sometimes to the north. At latitude 6° 30' S, currents drove the *Daintie* into the bay formed by the Punta de Augussa and two islands. To double the point, they hoped to put about on a north-westerly course but instead found themselves being driven ashore. At evening the wind died, and the next morning 'the sun's rising manifested unto us our error and peril, by discovering unto us the land within two leagues right ahead. The current had carried us without any wind, at the least four leagues.'

They passed in sight of Puerto Vicjo, latitude 2° 10' S, and made for Cabo Passaos, just under the equinoctial line. Hawkyns doubled the cape and hauled in ENE to fetch the bay of Atacames, 7 leagues from the cape. There, on 10 June, the *Daintie* dropped anchor, and for five days the crew filled water casks, supplied themselves with wood, put the pinnace in order and left their Indians ashore with fish hooks, lines and bread. They had proved useless as sailors and only ate up food. Hawkyns had planned to set sail on the morning of 15 June, but on the evening before he sighted yet another sail, 3 leagues to seaward. The pinnace gave chase. Hawkyns ordered that if by evening they had not stood in again towards shore, the pinnace should rendezvous with the *Daintie* at Cabo San Francisco. He planned to set sail without delay the next morning.

At nine in the morning he weighed anchor and stood for the Cabo, where they beat off and on for two days, waiting for the pinnace. She appeared, but without her mainmast, and put into the bay of San Matthew, where Hawkyns repaired her. After two days, at dawn, the two vessels were about to weigh anchor and were a pike ready (peak halyard hoisted) to cut sail. At that moment one of the lookouts spied a Spanish armada coming around the cape. Thinking it was the treasure fleet, some wanted to give chase. But it was the wrong time of year for the Peruvian treasure fleet to be carrying it to Panamá.

At this point Hawkyns was still at anchor, and upwind of the Spaniard. He did not want to fight, but the crew felt otherwise. Hawkyns writes that the typical mariner is like a stiff-necked horse or a fast river current that will 'overthrow' both fence and bank:

Even so the common sort of seamen, apprehending a conceit in their imaginations, neither experiment, knowledge, examples, reasons nor authority, can alter or remove them for their conceited opinions. In this extremity, with reason I laboured to convince them, and to contradict their pretences: but they altogether without reason, or against reason, break out, some into vaunting and bragging, some into reproaches of want of courage, others into wishings, that they had never come out of their country, if we should refuse to fight with two ships whatsoever. And to mend the matter, the gunner (for his part) assured me that with the first tier of shot, he would lay the one of them in the suds: And our pinnace, that she would take the other to task. One promised, that he would cut down the main yard, another that he would take their flag; and all in general showed a great desire to come to trial with the enemy.

Spanish Engage the *Daintie*

Hawkyns agreed to have the captain reconnoitre in the pinnace but ordered him not to engage the enemy. So they did, but on coming about to return, the Spanish vice-admiral began chasing and firing on her. To gain sea room, Hawkyns and the *Daintie* weighed anchor and stood off to sea, all sails set, hoping to maintain the weather gauge. But the wind died and Hawkyns fell off to leeward. The Spanish admiral was soon to weather of Hawkyns and fell off to within a musket shot of the *Daintie*:

> [Hawkyns] hailed first with our noise of trumpets, then with our waits [musicians], and after with our artillery: Which they answered with artillery, two for one. For they had double the ordnance we had, and almost ten men for one. Immediately they came shoaring [shoring] aboard of us, upon our lee quarter contrary to our expectation, and the custom of men of war. And doubtless, had our gunner been the man he was reputed to be, and as the world sold him to me, she had received great hurt by that manner of boarding.

But the stern pieces were unprimed, as were nearly all those to leeward. By then there was 6ft of water in the hold.

'Hereby all men are to take warning by me, not to trust any man in such extremities', here, the gunner. Artillery must be ready. 'This was my oversight, this my overthrow', Hawkyns says. He and the other officers, he writes, were occupied in 'clearing our decks, lacing our nettings, making of bulwarks, arming our tops, fitting our waist-cloths, tallowing our pikes, slinging our yards, doubling our sheets and tacks, placing and ordering our people, and procuring that they should be well fitted and provided of all things'. The gunners had 500 cartridges ready, but during one hour of fighting Hawkyns had to assign three crew to making and filling more cartridges. But not 1 yard of the 500 ells of canvas and other cloth intended for the purpose could be found. Though dangerous, the gun crews had to charge and discharge with the ladle. The captain (and author) manned the guns as the Spanish admiral came close. Before going to sea, the gunner had laid in

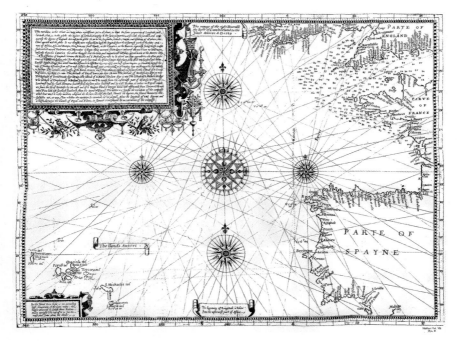

1. Map of Sir George Clifford, 3rd Earl of Cumberland's 1589 Voyage to the Azores, by Edward Wright. Wright was on the voyage, wrote the account and produced the map. In Wright's *Certain Errors in Navigation* (London, 1599).

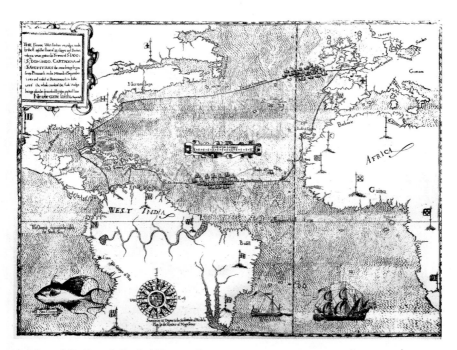

2. Map of Sir Francis Drake's West Indies voyage, 1585–86. Engraving by Baptista Boazio in Walter Bigges, *A Summarie and True Discourse of Sir Frances Drake's West Indian Voyage* (London: R. Field, 1589).

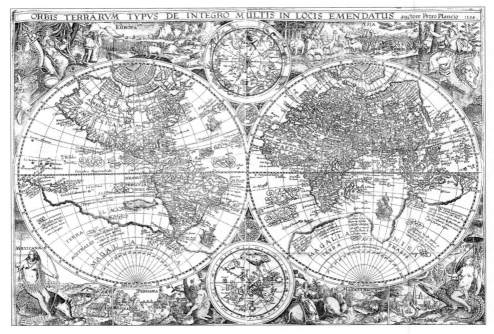

3. World map by Peter Plancius, 1594. Employs Mercator projection. 'Mexicana' is North America, 'Magallanica', the fabled southern continent. In Jan Huyghen van Linschoten, *Itinerario* (Amsterdam, 1604–05).

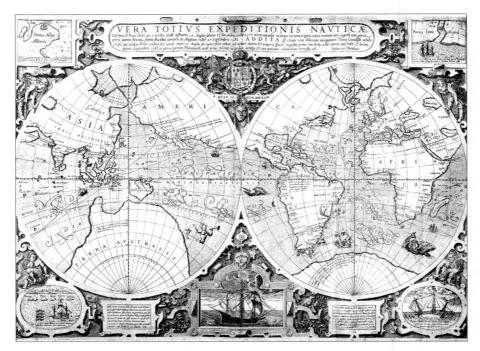

4. World map by Judocus Hondius, *c.* 1595. Shows circumnavigations by Drake and Cavendish. Drake's *Pelican* (*Golden Hinde*) in centre medallion. Grenville Library, British Library.

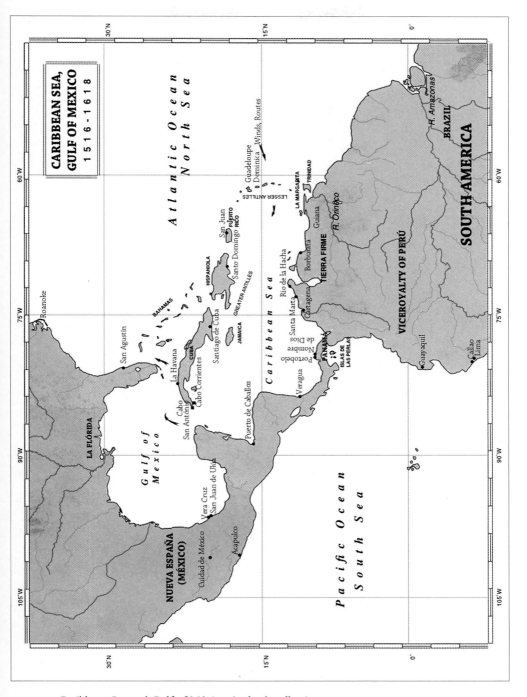

5. Caribbean Sea and Gulf of México. Author's collection.

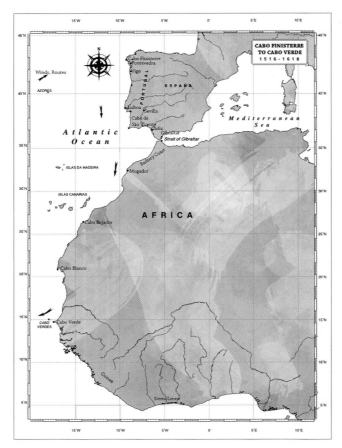

6. Cabo Finistere to Cabo Verde. Author's collection.

7. Map of Florida by James Le Moyne, 1594. Watercolour. Engraved by Theodor de Bry, *Grands Voyages* (Frankfurt, 1591).

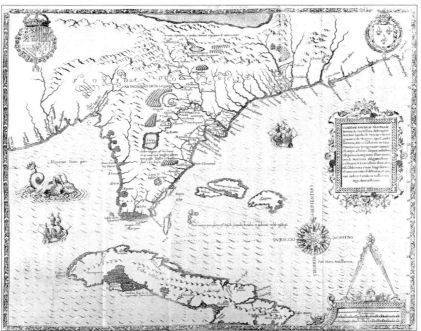

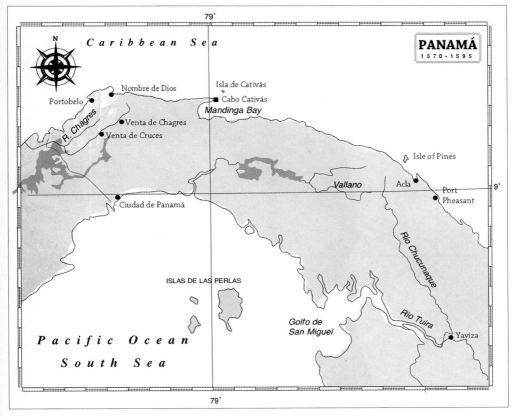

8. Panamá. Author's collection.

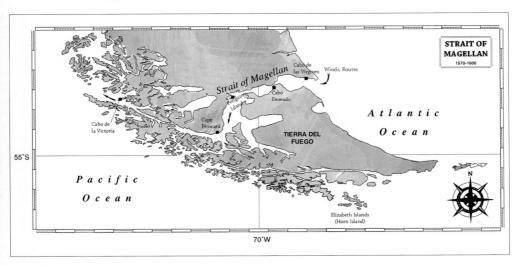

9. Strait of Magellan. Author's collection.

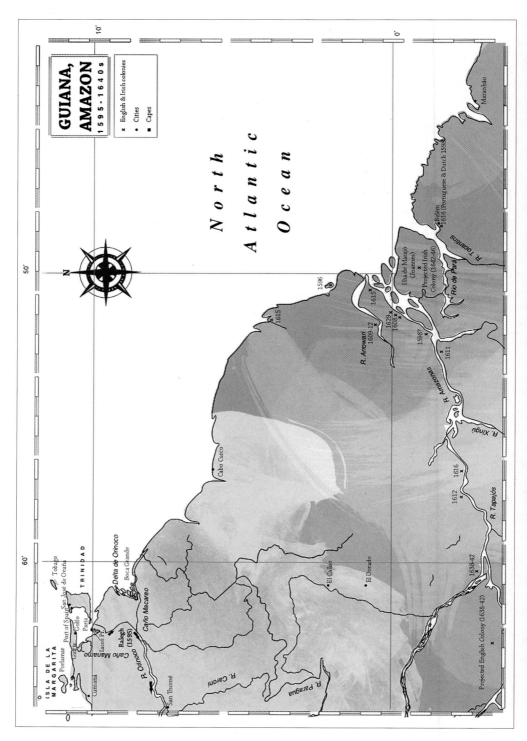

10. Guiana and the Amazon. Author's collection.

Caribbean Sea

Panamá

SPANISH MAIN

Trinidad

R. Orinoco   GUIANA

North

Atlantic

Ocean

Cabo San Francisco

Guayaquil

Callao
Lima

R. Amazonas

Maranhão
(São Luís)

Cabo
São Roque

SOUTH
AMERICA

BRAZIL

Recife

Salvador
(Pernambuco)

Arequipa
Arica

VICEROYALTY
OF PERÚ

Rio de Janeiro
São Vicente

Pacific

Ocean

Valparaíso

R. de la
Plata

South

Atlantic

Ocean

Buenos
Aires

Puerto Deseado (Port Desire)
Cabo Blanco

Port
St Julian

Falkland
Islands

N

Strait of Magellan

Tierra Del
Fuego

SOUTH
AMERICA
1516 - 1618

11. South America. Author's collection.

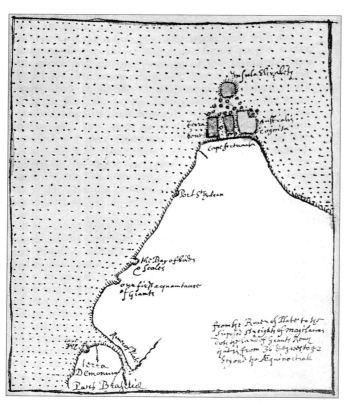

12. Sketch of Cape Horn, 1577. Copy drawn by Joseph Conyers, London, of original by Francis Fletcher, chaplain on Drake's circumnavigation. Shows part of Patagonia, the Strait of Magellan and the islands of Tierra del Fuego. North at bottom of the map. British Library (Hereafter: *BL*).

13. Map of Guiana by Sir Walter Ralegh, 1595. North at the bottom of the map. Manuscript Room, *BL*.

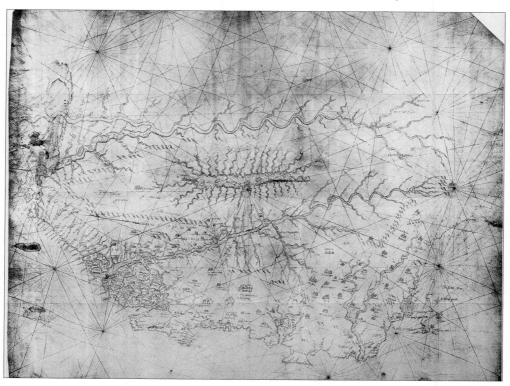

14. *Jesus of Lubeck.*
Bought by Henry VIII
in 1544 from Hanse
merchants of Lubeck.
Lost in battle to the
Spanish at San Juan de
Ulúa, 1568. Watercolour,
Anthony's Roll, Pepys
Library, Magdalene
College, Cambridge.

15. *Minion.* Heavily
damaged in battle at
San Juan de Ulúa, 1568.
Condemned 1570.
Anthony's Roll, Pepys
Library, Magdalene
College, Cambridge.

16. *Below: Elizabeth
Bonaventure.* Purchased
1567 as a merchantman,
rebuilt 1581 as a
galleon; broken up 1611.
Drake's admiral in his
1585 West Indies voyage,
at centre of fleet flying
the Cross of St George.
Grenville Library, *BL.*

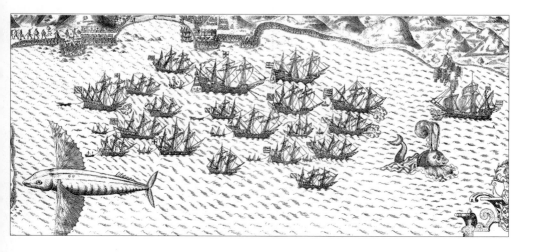

17. *Black Pinnace*. Carrying the body of Sir Philip Sidney back from Flushing to London, 1586. Engraving in *The Procession at the Obsequies of Sir Philip Sidney, Knight* (London, 1587). Anthony's Roll, Pepys Library, Magdalene College, Cambridge.

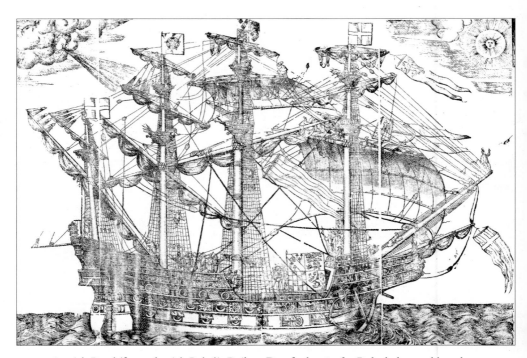

18. *Ark Royal* (formerly *Ark Ralegh*). Built at Deptford, 1587 for Ralegh, later sold to the Crown. Rebuilt 1608 as the *Anne Royal*. Print Department, *BL*.

19. Galleys were essential to Spanish tropical port and coastal defence. Engraving by Josef Furttenbach, *Architectura Navalis* (Ulm, 1629).

20. Spanish treasure frigate. Drawing by an English spy. The National Archives, London (Kew). Richard Hakluyt (ed.), *Principall Navigations … 1598–1600.*

21. Sir Francis Drake, from the map engraved by Judocus Hondius, c. 1595. *BL.*

22. Sir Thomas Cavendish, from the map engraved by Judocus Hondius, c. 1595. *BL.*

23. Sir Walter Ralegh, 1598, attributed to Federico Zuccaro (Zucchero). National Portrait Gallery of Ireland, Dublin.

24. Sir John Hawkyns, engraving by Henricus Hondius (Henry Holland), *Herwologia Anglica* (London, 1620).

25. Queen Elizabeth, 1595, engraving published by Joannes Woutnelius, 1596.

26. Sir George Clifford, 3rd Earl of Cumberland, 1588. Artist unknown. National Portrait Gallery, London.

27. Ralegh captures Don António de Berrío, governor of Trinidad, 1595. Engraving in Theodor de Bry, *Grands Voyages* (Frankfurt, 1599). Washington: Library of Congress.

28. Ralegh with Guianian *cassique* Topiawari, 1595. Engraving in Theodor de Bry, *Historica Americae* (Frankfurt, 1634). Washington: Library of Congress.

29. Fishing for pearls, Spanish Main. Engraving in Theodor de Bry, *Grands Voyages* (Frankfurt, 1594). Washington: Library of Congress.

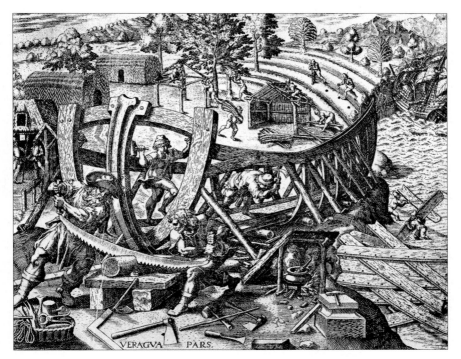

30. Shipbuilding in the Americas. Engraving in Theodor de Bry, *Grands Voyages* (Frankfurt, 1594). Washington: Library of Congress.

31. Amazons at war. Engraving in Levinus Hulsius, *Collections of Voyages* (Frankfurt, 1599–1649). Washington: Library of Congress.

32. Amazons frolicking. Engraving in Levinus Hulsius, *Collections of Voyages* (Frankfurt, 1599–1649). Washington: Library of Congress.

33. Refining gold in Guiana. Engraving in Theodor de Bry, *Historica Americae* (1634). Washington: Library of Congress.

brass balls of artificial fire (6 slurbows and 200 balls), but though stored in double barrels, all had been spoilt by salt water. And the gunner? Though English, he had spent some years in Portuguese Terceira as a gunner, and Hawkyns doubted his loyalty. Few of the cannon were prepared to fire when needed. Ineptly, some crew had even loaded shot before powder.

According to Hawkyns, the reason the Spanish admiral then came to leeward of the *Daintie* was that, as her artillery was long range and the wind fresh, and as they were on a beat, they could not use their artillery to weather of the English. It is indeed proper, writes Hawkyns, to have short ordnance, except in the stern or in the bow chasers. Reasons? Easier charging, easier recoil in protecting the ship's hull, and better for traversing and changing the elevation. The longer the piece is, the greater the danger of retaining fire. The Spanish fell off and went ahead, having destroyed the *Daintie*'s gallery. Then they came about, now to weather of the *Daintie*, within musket range. With musket and artillery the Spanish fired. The pinnace was cut off from the ship and was boarded by the Spanish vice-admiral.

Now aboard the Spanish admiral, according to Spanish sources, was the English gunner who had served at Terceira. He offered to sink the *Daintie* with the first shot. Traversing a piece in the bow to make his shot, the turncoat 'had his head carried away with the first or second shot, made out of our ship', writes Hawkyns, who moralises that such fate is 'a good warning for those which fight against their country'. The fight continued hot on both sides, with much artillery and musket fire. Three times the Spanish tried to board. That third time the plan was to lay the admiral on the weather bow, and the vice-admiral on the weather quarter. But the vice-admiral was greedy for prize money, and instead of co-ordinating with the admiral, came aboard to windward, on the broadside. But as she was longer than the *Daintie*, being 'rarely built' (race-built) and without defence works, the English muskets and fireworks cleared her decks in a moment, killing thirty-six Spaniards, including the pilot.

The vice-admiral called to the admiral for help. The two determined to batter the English with just artillery, either to sink the *Daintie* or to force her surrender. During the battle the ship's master had 'one of his eyes, his nose, and half his face shot away'. The ship's master and Henry Courton were both killed, says Hawkyns, and on these two he had 'principally relied for the prosecution of our voyage, if God by sickness, or otherwise should take me away'.

The Spanish kept firing on the English, now and then stopping to invite the English to surrender, '*a Buena Querra*' (*buena guerra*, fair conduct of war). The *Daintie*'s captain saw that many of the crew were wounded or killed, and that the few left could not defend the ship. As the Spanish had offered life and liberty and to send the crew home, the crew put to the captain that he should put out a flag of truce. Hawkyns writes that 'the great loss of blood had weakened me much. The torment of my wounds newly received made me faint, and I laboured for life, within short space expecting I should give up the ghost.' He moans: 'Great is the Cross, which almighty God hath suffered to come upon me.'

In a soliloquy he writes:

Hold they not this for a maxim; that, *nulla fides est servanda cum hereticis* [no faith is to be kept with heretics]. In which number they account us to be. Have you forgotten their faith violated with my father, in S. John de Ulúa ... Have you forgotten how they dealt with John Oxenham [Oxnam], and his company, in this sea, yielding upon composition? And how after a long imprisonment, and many miseries (being carried from Panamá to Lima) and there hanged with all his company, as pirates, by the justice? ... Came we into the South Sea to put out flags of truce? And left we our pleasant England, with all her contentments, with intention or purpose to avail ourselves of white rags?

For three days the English valiantly fought off the Spanish. Every morning an hour before dawn the Spanish would cease firing for a time to set the day's battle plan. In the lull, the English would quickly repair what they could. No one slept. There was little sustenance except bread and wine. On the second day, when the Spanish vice-admiral came upon the quarter, one of the master's mates, William Blanch, was lucky in carrying away the Spaniard's mainmast with one of the stern cannon. The English stayed close in on her weather, firing with great and small shot to prevent them from cutting all by the board. It was a mistake, writes the author, for by lying a-hull to leeward of Hawkyns, the English might, with a few shot, have sunk her. Though the Spanish in this case had artillery with greater range, the English had artillery pieces with greater bore and heavier shot that could do more damage. 'Besides (our ship being yare [nimble] and good of steerage) no doubt but we should have played better with our ordnance, and with more effect then did our enemies.'

The *Daintie* Undone

The Spanish general was not able to help his vice-admiral. He left him and pursued Hawkyns, firing with great and small shot. The vice-admiral had cut away the damaged mainmast and with just foresail and mizzen came on. Before sunset he was abeam of the English. Hawkyns writes:

Here I hold it necessary, to make mention of two things, which were most prejudicial unto us ... The one is to fight unarmed, where they may fight armed. The other, is in coming to fight, to drink themselves drunk. Yea, some are so mad, that they mingle powder with wine to give it the greater force, imagining that it gives spirit, strength and courage, and takes away all fear and doubt. The latter is, for the most part true, but the former is false and beastly, and altogether against reason. For though the nature of wine with moderation, is to comfort and revive the heart, and to fortify and strengthen the spirit; yet the immoderate use thereof works quite contrary effects.

Such was the case of Hawkyns' crew, besotted by potent Chilean wine.

Back to the battle. For three days this bloody sacrament continued, as day and night the English and Spanish fought. The Spanish ships were more weatherly, and throughout held the windward gauge. These were not the lumbering hulks out-sailed by the English in the Channel in 1588. Here, things were different. Spanish shot punished the English, and the English shot did little. On the afternoon of the third day, 22 June 1594, the *Daintie's* sails were in shreds, her masts ragged stumps, her pumps reduced to splinters, her hull holed below the waterline by fourteen shot, and she was wallowing with 7 or 8ft of water in the hold. Nearly all of her crew had been killed or were wounded. The Spanish still called out '*buena querra*' and suggestions of embarkation back to England upon surrender. 'Our captain, and those which remained of our company, were all of opinion that our best course was to surrender our selves before our ship sunk.' Hawkyns, sorely wounded and at this point 'in a manner void of sense, and out of hope to live or recover', reluctantly agreed to surrender.

The English lowered their ensign and hoisted a flag of truce. Hawkyns released Juan Gomes de Pineda, a Spanish pilot and prisoner shackled in the *Daintie's* hold, and told him to go to Admiral Beltrán de Castro Ydelluca for some pledge, and that done, they would surrender themselves and the ship. Otherwise, 'he should never enjoy of us, nor ours any thing, but a resolution every man to die fighting'. Meanwhile, the vice-admiral, not aware of the negotiations, had come onto the *Daintie's* quarter and fired her two chase pieces at the English, wounding the captain in the thigh and one of the master's mates in the arm, and laying the *Daintie* aboard. At the same time, Beltrán on the admiral, according to the Order of the Knights of Alcántara, promised the English their lives and return to England. As confirmation he sent his glove to Hawkyns. Beltrán sent Captain Pedro Álvares de Pulgar to bring Hawkyns to the Spanish ship. Hawkyns was received with great courtesy and compassion and, as Hawkyns tells it, Beltrán 'even with tears in his eyes, and words of great consolation commanded me to be accommodated in his own cabin, where he sought to cure and comfort me the best he could; the like he used with all our hurt men, six and thirty at least'. Chivalry was not quite dead in June 1594.

While the ships were lashed together, the mainmast of the *Daintie* fell by the board. The Spanish, ransacking the ship for booty, had neglected to man the pumps. The *Daintie* was taking on more and more water and was close to sink-ing. The Spanish quickly ordered sixty mariners and soldiers and any English left to man the pumps, and to put the *Daintie* in shape to sail for Perico, the port for Panamá. For thirty-six hours the Spanish and English worked together, pumping out the hold, fitting and mending the foresail. Beltrán then set course for the Islas de las Perlas. The *Daintie* sailed badly without her mainsail and had to be taken in tow. They needed twelve days to reach the islands, those same islands, writes Hawkyns, 'where not many years earlier, Drake's officer John Oxenham was sailing and pillaging, before he, his ship, and his crew were captured by the Spanish'.

The Spanish admiral looked after Hawkyns and his men, and the English surgeons treated both English and Spanish seamen. Under the care of the English surgeons, not one of the wounded English seamen died – many had eight, ten or twelve wounds, and some more – and all was done without surgical instruments or salves. The Spanish had many more wounded than the English. The English helped out, says Hawkyns, as the Spanish surgeons were ignorant and had no supplies.

Hawkyns notes that he knew no Spanish and that at the surrender he had to call on an interpreter or use Latin or French, and a 'little smattering I had of the Portugal'. Though Don Beltrán was magnanimous towards his prisoner, others said that the English were Lutherans and that no agreement with heretics should be honoured. Some said that as the English had fought as good soldiers, they deserved good quarter. Others called the English 'corsairs' or 'pirates'. But Don Beltrán owed his authority to the viceroy of Perú and said he was bound to send Hawkyns and crew to Lima. Hawkyns argued that they were not corsairs. Spain had started the war with England, and so, being at war, English ships sailed under official licence. Indeed, he argued, the English courts prosecuted any English pirate who sailed without a letter of marque. Don Beltrán assured Hawkyns that on his word as a knight, 'your ransom (if any shall be thought due) shall be but a couple of greyhounds for me; and other two for my brother, the Conde de Lemes, and this I swear to you by the habit of Alcántara. Provided always, that the King my Master leave you to my dispose, as of right you belong unto me'.

On 7 July they were within sight of Perico, a pair of small islands 2 leagues WNW off Ciudad de Panamá. The city had a pier for small barks, which at high tide had some 6 or 7ft of water, but at low tide was dry. The *Daintie* was safe near there. On 9 July they anchored, while bonfires greeted the victorious Spanish. With 'luminaries' in their houses and lights in the churches' windows and galleries, the English thought the city might be burning. At eight that evening, jubilant gunners at the fort fired salvos in celebration. Beltrán answered with broadsides.

On leaving, Admiral Beltrán de Castro offered to take unsealed letters from Hawkyns in the king's packet to his uncle, Don Rodrigo de Castro, cardinal and archbishop of Seville, and to other friends who would see that letters reached England. Hawkyns dictated letters to a servant and had three or four copies made of a letter to his father, recounting the events of the voyage. The *Daintie* was grounded, repaired and renamed the *Visitation* after the day of the visitation of the Virgin Mary. The ship had been shored to take the falling tide (tides there were 15 or 16ft), but during the solemnities she fell over on one side. As she was without masts and empty, there was little damage.

Hawkyns was first sent to Perú, then Spain. As for ransom, Beltrán let the viceroy know that he was content that Hawkyns be exchanged for two greyhounds for himself and two for his brother.

John Ellis, captain of the *Daintie*, adds to Hawkyns' account.[2] After three years in prison in Lima, the crew was released. Ellis was taken on to Cusco, 'which is a city about the bigness of Bristol'. Ellis mentions that he had two letters written by Thomas Sanders, servant of Hawkyns from the prison at Sanlúcar, which comment on one Master Lucas, condemned by the Holy House to the galleys and sent to Nombre de Dios, though he died during the voyage there. Ellis writes that the Spanish viceroy in Lima admired Hawkyns' valour and installed him in a 'princely house all richly hanged, the which he had to himself, with a great allowance from the King, besides many presents from the Queen: But within six or seven days he was carried by the Fathers to the Holy House, not as a man to be executed, but to rest there until they heard from the King what should be done with them'.

A deal was struck. In exchange for Hawkyns acknowledging Spain's exclusive right to trade in the Indies, Philip II would pardon him. Against Admiral Beltrán de Castro's wishes, Hawkyns was first held in Perú for three years, and then transported to prison in Madrid. Hawkyns tried to escape, was caught and was kept under even closer guard. Beltrán's family, especially his brother, the Conde de Lemes, protested Hawkyns' treatment. At length his release became a matter of ducats. Hawkyns' stepmother, Margaret Vaughan, could pay the £3,000 ransom but refused to do so. Only when Hawkyns wrote to Sir Robert Cecil to intervene did Vaughan relent and give up what was Hawkyns' money.

Six weeks before Christmas 1602, and after nearly ten years away, Richard Hawkyns was finally released. He stepped ashore on English soil on Monday 16 November 1609. His father had died fourteen years earlier, off Puerto Rico. Now at home, the son was head of the illustrious seafaring family. Shortly after James I's accession in 1603, Richard Hawkyns was knighted and made vice-admiral of Devon. He was elected mayor of Plymouth and served as a Member of Parliament in 1603–04. Twenty years later, on return from an expedition in 1622 to clear out a nest of Barbary pirates, he died of a 'vexation'. It was a reasonably peaceful end to the vagaries of outrageous fortunes.

Lancaster Sacks Olinda

Brazil, attractive since William Hawkyns' voyages there in the 1530s, became the objective of James Lancaster in 1594–95. He left Blackwall, London, in October 1594, bound there in charge of three of John Watts' ships: the *Consent*, 240 tons, admiral, commanded by Lancaster; the *Salomon*, 170 tons, vice-admiral, Edmund Barker, captain; and the *Virgin*, 60 tons, rear-admiral, John Audely, captain.[3] The crew consisted of men and boys, 275 in all. Storms forced the fleet into

Dartmouth. Lancaster set out again on 30 November. From a pilot, Lancaster learned that an East Indian carrack had been cast away in Pernambuco and her rich cargo had been stored in Olinda's warehouses in the lower town. Lancaster would have it. For three weeks on the island of Maio he constructed a galley-frigate, brought out in pieces from England. Captain Venner and his fleet sailed into Maio and joined Lancaster.

Together they crossed over and fetched Olinda about midnight on 29 March. Three Dutch vessels were in the harbour. About two the next afternoon, with tide at the flood, Lancaster attacked. The Portuguese fled into the bush. 'This day of our arrival was their Good Friday, when by custom they usually whip themselves: But God sent us now for a general scourge to them all, whereby that labour among them might be well spared.' It was another Lenten coincidence. Oxnam had scourged the Spanish in the Pacific off the Perlas on Ash Wednesday, 1577.

The warehouses contained an oriental treasure: 'As brazilwood, sugars, calico cloth, pepper, cinnamon, mace, nutmegs, with diverse other good things, to the great comfort of us all.' For the next two days Lancaster fortified the town with a 9ft palisade, built a fort and armed it with five cannon. The Dutch were at first stubbornly neutral, 'as that nation is in these causes', but eventually joined Lancaster against the Portuguese. Like the English, their business too was profit.

Three or four days later three French men-of-war and two pinnaces sailed into the harbour. One of the captains was John Noyer from Dieppe. Lancaster knew him, for just the year before he had taken the Frenchman's ship. They joined forces. On the third day the Portuguese sent the bishop and three or four prominent citizens to bargain with Lancaster. Lancaster stalled. He left them waiting from nine in the morning until two in the afternoon. 'Are they not gone yet?' he asked. Lancaster's gentlemen marvelled that he would not talk to the Portuguese. Lancaster replied:

> Sirs, I have been brought up among this people, I have lived among them as a gentleman, served with them as a soldier, and lived among them as a merchant, so that I should have some understanding of their demeanours and nature; and I know when they cannot prevail with the sword by force, then they deal with their deceivable tongues; for faith and truth they have none, neither will use any, unless it be to their own advantage. And this I give you warning, that if you give them parle, they will betray us ... I warrant you they understand me better then you think they do.

He ordered that if more emissaries were to come, they would be hanged. Three or four nights later two did come. They were hanged.

A ship sailed into the harbour with 10 Portuguese women and 100 men, 60 of them black. Lancaster turned the women and black men out of town, but hitched up the Portuguese men to draw the heavily laden carts, 'which to us was a very great ease. For the country is very hot and ill for our nation to take any great travel [travel, travail (work)] in'. The Portuguese tried fire ships and fire rafts to drive out the English, Dutch and French, to no avail.

Lancaster's ships were by this time fully laden. It was the thirty-first day of occupation, and he planned to sail that night. But in the morning, when Lancaster saw that on the point the Portuguese had been laying planks to support cannon, he sent thirty-five English and French in to stop them. They broke rank in their pursuit, and all were killed.

At eleven that night, with a fair wind, the combined fleet of fifteen set sail from Olinda: three Hollanders (450, 350 and 300 tons each), four French, a ship Lancaster gave the French, Venner's three sail and Lancaster's four, all laden with 'merchandises, and that of good worth', much sugar, brazilwood and cotton. A storm separated the fleet. In July Lancaster's remaining fleet reached England at the Downs. In all, Lancaster had taken twenty-nine ships and frigates, sacked and held Olinda for over a month, and taken an East Indian carrack's rich cargazon (cargo). Fifteen ships and barks taken as prizes brought the haul up the Thames to Blackwall. It had been a most successful voyage for Lancaster, Watts and the other investors.

Cumberland's Eighth Voyage, 'ruinous'

In 1594 the Earl of Cumberland set forth from Plymouth on 6 April on his eighth voyage, once again for the Azores.[4] His ships were the *Royal Exchange*, 250 tons, admiral, commanded by Captain George Cave; the *May Floure*, 250 tons, vice-admiral, commanded by Captain William Antonie; the *Samson*, rear-admiral, commanded by Captain Nicholas Downton; plus a caravel and a small pinnace. The voyage is recounted by several sources, including three of the captains.[5]

About mid-June, west of Faial, Cumberland's fleet came onto a carrack, *Cinco Chagas*, a huge vessel of 2,000 tons, sailing eastward. The plan was for the admiral to lay the carrack aboard in the prow, the vice-admiral in the waist, and the rear-admiral in the quarter. But as it fell out, the admiral laid her aboard at the loof (the after part of the bow), recoiled astern, and being so close the vice-admiral was forced to run with her bolt sprit between the two quarters. This forced the rear-admiral to lay her aboard on the bow. Both sides used 'fireworks' (incendiary bombs) and soon both English and Spanish were attempting to put out fires aboard their ships. Cumberland's admiral and vice-admiral had to fall off. The rear-admiral was fouled by the carrack's spritsail yard, but the ships' boats got her free.

The crew tried to convince the commander of the carrack, Don Francisco de Melo, to put out a flag of truce. The ship's carpenter said he could quench the fire, but Melo cried out: '*Coraje*, I will never yield.' To no avail. The burning carrack and her treasure quickly sank, and many hundreds drowned: soldiers, sailors and 'many of their bravest Spanish gallants, men and women goodly personages gorgeously apparelled, yea, and decked with rich chains of gold, jewels, pearls, and precious stones of great price'. Some threw off their chains and jewels, and 'naked as they were born, cast themselves into the sea to adventure upon English mercy'. Just two survived. One was the former governor of the province of Sofala in Mozambique, and the other was the captain of another carrack. Both were taken to England to Cumberland's London home and after nine months were ransomed. Off the Cape of Good Hope, the crew and passengers had numbered more than 1,100 before infection killed most of them. The carrack's burden, freighted with pearls, jewels, drugs, silks and pepper, had exceeded that of the *Madre de Dios*. English casualties were just twenty.

On 29 June another large carrack appeared on the horizon. She was the Spanish man-of-war *San Felipe*, 1,500 tons. Cumberland ordered her to strike or suffer the fate of the *Cinco Chagas*. Her commander, Don Lewys de Costinio, replied that the English should be aware and beware, as he had been one of those who had taken Grenville's *Revenge*. The carrack and the English fleet fired away at each other all day, then on Tuesday 2 July a gale separated the English fleet and the *San Felipe* escaped 'with large spread sails wind convenient and sea room at will'. Cumberland's vessels had been seriously damaged. With little cargo, they returned mostly in ballast to England by August and September, 'having done much harm to the enemy, and little good to themselves'. It had been a ruinous voyage for Cumberland.

Dudley to West Indies

Sir Robert Dudley, the recently knighted bastard son of another of Elizabeth's favourites, Robert Dudley, 1st Earl of Leicester, sailed from Southampton on 6 November 1594 to seek his own fortune on the high seas.[6] He left Plymouth on 17 November. Dudley's ship and admiral was the *Beare*, 200 tons; the vice-admiral was the *Beares Whelpe*, Captain Munck commanding. Dudley also sailed with two small pinnaces, the *Frisking* and the *Earewig*. In a storm he lost the *Beares Whelpe* and one of the pinnaces, though off the Canaries for twelve days he took caravels. His fleet now numbered three, his crew 140. Dudley then sailed to Cabo Blanco, the place known for having the 'most infectious serenas or dews that fall all along these coasts of Africa'. From there he sailed west. After twenty-two days he reached Trinidad on 1 February 1595. His numbers were now down to fifty men. He ordered the two caravels on 17 February to plunder the Indies, then return directly to England.

For himself, Guianan gold was his objective. He learned from the Indians of Guiana that in Yguiri there was a metal called *arara*, copper or base gold, that in the highlands of Paria there was silver and 'most excellent cane-tobacco', and that at Waliame there was a gold mine. Dudley sent a party into the mainland to investigate. When the men returned sixteen days later, they had explored the Orocoa upstream some 150 miles. They returned half-starved, not having had water for the previous three days. If he wanted to go out again, the company of explorers assured Dudley he would have to go out on his own.

During the exploration a pinnace from Plymouth arrived, under Captain Popham. Together, Dudley and Popham waited nearly two months for Ralegh, their plan being to explore Guiana together. To that end, 'by our intelligence and his boats we might have done some good: But it seemed he came not in six or eight weeks after. So Captain Popham and I held it not convenient to stay any longer.' Dudley and Popham watered their ships at Paracoa and set sail from Trinidad on 12 March, hoping to intercept the Spanish *flota*. 'The fleet I found not, but foul weather enough to scatter many fleets; which companion left me not in greatest extremity, till I came to the isles of Flores and Corvo.' His victuals were nearly gone. His crew numbered a third of the original number. His fleet was just the 200-ton *Beare*, when returning home he met a 'well-appointed' 600-ton Spaniard in the Azores. He engaged the enemy for two days, until he had spent all his powder. He left the Spaniard there, a hulk without sails or masts. Dudley's great ordnance had shot her hull through 'between wind and water' so often that 300 leagues from land she could not escape sinking. Dudley made for England, and arrived at St Ives in Cornwall at the end of May 1595, 'scaping most dangerously in a great fog the rocks of Scilly'. There he learned that the Spaniard had gone to the bottom. In all, Dudley had sunk and burned nine Spaniards, a 'loss to them, though I got nothing'.

Cumberland's Ninth Voyage: Hot Fight, No Profit

Cumberland's ninth voyage was once again to the Azores.[7] 'The Earl not liking his ill partage in the *Madre de Dios*, nor this unhappier loss of two carracks for want of sufficient strength to take them, built a ship of his own of 900 tons at Deptford, which the Queen at her launching named the *Scourge of Malice*, the best ship that ever before had been built by any subject.' Better even, it was to be understood, than Ralegh's *Ark Ralegh*. Cumberland took the *Scourge* (*Malice Scourge*, 600–900 tons) on three voyages. She was later sold to the East India Company, where she proved herself successful against the Portuguese. On this ninth voyage she and two other vessels sailed to the Azores, took a caravel and her lading of sugar, then in a fog spotted the outline of a carrack. She was the *San Tomás*, vice-admiral of the Spanish fleet. They closed, and in a bit of bravado, Cumberland writes, they 'fell in so hot a fight that she was glad to bear up to recover herself amongst the rest of her consorts'. Off the Spanish coast, Cumberland seized three Dutch ships with provisions for the Spanish. But with victuals gone, Cumberland's fine man-of-war returned to England, again to no profit.

The years 1593–95 had largely been disastrous for the English. True, Lancaster had scored great success in Brazil and, moreover, had drawn in the aid of both the Dutch and French in attacking the Portuguese. But Richard Hawkyns, hoping to make a killing like Drake and Cavendish by circumnavigating the globe, was instead taken prisoner and held for nine years before being ransomed. As for Cumberland in these years, seeking fortune at sea once again proved hopeless.

eight

COMMITTED TO THE DEEP, 1595–96

The waters were his winding sheet, the sea was made for his tomb;
Yet for his fame the ocean sea, was not sufficient room.
                    Richard Barnfield, *Epitaph on Hawkins*, 1595

The years 1595 and 1596 were no doubt the most important ones for English tropical America. Sir Walter Ralegh made his first passage to America. Sir John Hawkyns and Sir Francis Drake made their last. It was to be the end of an era and the start of another. Eleven years earlier Ralegh had sent out an expedition under Lane to colonise Virginia. After less than a year that 1584 enterprise had failed when Drake brought home the discouraged colonists. In 1595, Ralegh himself set out across the Atlantic to undertake another western planting, this time in the tropics, in fabled Guiana.[1] He was not alone in that dream of a paradise in the tropics. Along the Portuguese-Spanish Main, the Amazon and the Orinoco rivers were to prove excellent sites for settlements by English, Irish, French and Dutch colonisers, as Lorimer has shown.[2] In the River Amazon alone, so strong was the drive to plant an England in the tropics that between 1598 and 1646 there were some dozen English and Irish settlements, with two other large ones planned as late as the 1630s and 1640s.

Ralegh hoped that new investors would join his enterprise, to be one of the first to take Guiana's yet-unravished maidenhead. Once his Virginia hopes had soured, spurred by the Spanish accounts of El Dorado, Ralegh, as early as 1587, had thought Guiana might provide him with wealth and a pardon from Queen Elizabeth. He had fallen from her grace in 1592 when he secretly married Elizabeth Throckmorton, one of the queen's virginal ladies-in-waiting. Elizabeth had banished them both from court. Exiles from that Eden, Ralegh sought another. At court, Ralegh for some time had been caught between two factions:

on one side William Cecil, Lord Burghley, and on the other Robert Devereux, Earl of Essex.

Ralegh's patent from the queen? He was to annoy the king of Spain, raid the Spanish Main and the Caribbean, and as in his earlier patent for Virginia, could possess any land unoccupied by a Christian king. Guiana was thus fair game. He had money and backing from Cecil and had Indian interpreters and a Spanish rutter for the Golfo de Paria between Trinidad and the Main. At the queen's prompting, the 20-year-old Robert Dudley (bastard son of Robert Dudley, 1st Earl of Leicester, Elizabeth's favourite) was part of the expedition. (At about 43, Ralegh was more than twice the age of this new rival.) Dudley sailed with a good captain, an experienced navigator and 140 men. Dudley, George Popham, Amyas (Amias) Preston and George Somers were expected to join Ralegh off Trinidad to engage in privateering. Plunder would pay for planting tobacco and cotton.

After numerous delays and desertions, Ralegh left Plymouth on Thursday 6 February 1595. His fleet included his admiral (ship's name unknown). Her captain was Jacob Whiddon, and John Douglas was master. The vice-admiral was the 90-ton *Lyons Whelpe*, owned by the Lord Admiral, Charles, Lord Howard. George Clifford, Ralegh's nephew, was captain (this was not George Clifford, Earl of Cumberland). There was a small bark commanded by Captain Cross, and a gallego under Lawrence Keymis' command. Keymis had left Balliol College and mathematics to seek his fortune with Ralegh as his chief lieutenant. Three hundred men, half of them soldiers and half gentlemen adventurers, sailed with Ralegh. He expected that Dudley and his 140 men, Amyas Preston and George Somers would join his expedition at Trinidad. On Sunday 9 February, with prosperous winds, the fleet reached Cabo Finisterre. Somewhere off the coast of Spain, the fleet lost Keymis and his gallego, but they continued on to the Canaries, arriving there on 17 February. For two or three days Ralegh revictualled. For a week he waited in vain at Tenerife for Captain Amyas Preston and Clifford with the *Lyons Whelpe*, then Ralegh in the admiral and Cross in the bark set out on their own for the Spanish Main.

Preston and Somers to the Caribbean

Where were Preston and Somers? The 1595 voyage of Amyas Preston and George Somers is intertwined with Ralegh's Guiana expedition.[3] The author of the Preston-Somers expedition is Robert Davie. He is probably, observes Andrews, the Robert Davis who was master of the *Bark Ralegh* in Gilbert's 1585 voyage ten years earlier, and the same as Robert Davies of Lyme, who delivered his prizes to Ralegh in 1591. He is the same Captain Davies (Davie) on whose behalf Ralegh had interceded with Sir Robert Cecil in 1594.

Preston was ready to leave for the Caribbean in February, about the time Ralegh set sail, but lay in Plymouth until 12 March. Ralegh was by then five weeks along on his voyage. Preston's expedition contained a large number of soldiers as well as seamen and a complement of gentlemen. It was a force intended principally for land operations and, had it met up with Ralegh, might have accomplished something. But the two fleets did not connect, and Preston's depredations in any case had little effect on the Spanish.

The account of Preston's voyage, written by Robert Davie, seaman and captain, notes that the venture was unco-ordinated in leaving England and, once at sea, the vessels went their own ways. Just two weeks into the passage, on 31 March, Preston set off after a sail and was separated from Somers and his pinnace. In the Madeiras Davie's ship rejoined the others, and on 13 April these set their course for the West Indies, arriving at Dominica on 8 May. After a week they sailed south, calling at the Testigos, passing by La Margarita and proceeding to the Main, where their plunderings were met by strong Spanish resistance. Preston and Davie sailed to Lago Maracaibo, where they rejoined Somers. From there they sailed north to Hispaniola on 16 June, arriving four days later and anchoring under Cabo Tiburón on the 21st. On the 25th they were at sea again, and in the words of Robert Davie, 'a great sickness fell among our fleet, and there died about eighty men of the same. This sickness was the flux of the belly, which is a common disease in that country.' Surgeon Commander J.J. Keevil finds that it was most likely amoebic dysentery.[4]

At the beginning of July Preston and Somers reached Jamaica, and on the 12th were off Cabo Corrientes. They watered and that night set sail for Cabo San António, arriving the next morning. Preston, Somers and author Davie at last met Ralegh, but it was too late to aid his mission. Ralegh was already returning from his 'painful, and happy discovery of Guiana'. Preston kept company with Ralegh and his three ships until the night of the 20th, when the fleet separated. On 28 July Preston and the others entered the Gulf of Bahama and set course homeward. On 10 September Somers and Preston sailed into Milford Haven. Theirs was a voyage noteworthy for accomplishing little.

Ralegh's Landfall, Trinidad

Ralegh and his two vessels reached Trinidad on 22 March, ten days after Preston and Somers had finally left England. Ralegh cast anchor at Point Curiapan, 'which the Spaniards call Punto de Gallo ... situate in eight degrees or thereabouts'. (The correct latitude is 10° 2' 30" N. Ralegh's latitudes are consistently low by 2–4°.)[5] Spaniards came aboard to buy linen. He feasted them 'after our manner', and 'those poor soldiers having been many years without wine, a few draughts made them merry, in which mood they vaunted of Guiana and of the riches thereof, and all what they knew of the ways and passages'. Ralegh let out that he was there only to relieve his Englishmen planted in Virginia but that weather had forced him to Trinidad.

The year before, Ralegh had sent Captain Whiddon to reconnoitre Guiana, but Whiddon's information proved to be well off the mark. Ralegh writes: 'For the country is situate above 600 English miles further from the sea, than I was made believe it had been.'[6] Ralegh kept this information from his men. He anchored his ships at sea.

Ralegh directed George Clifford to take the *Lyons Whelpe* and Captain Calfield in his bark and to sail east against the wind to find the mouth of the River Capuri. The Orinoco delta has some 20,000km² of swamp, and of the fifty or so channels, only seven are navigable, and these only by small vessels, except for one usable by a larger ship. At the bar Whiddon and Douglas found just 5ft at low tide and 9 at high in those seven channels. The mouth of the River Amana (Caño Manamo) proved equally impassable. From May to October the Equatorial Current sets WNW, making it impossible to beat out from the southern part of the Golfo de Paria across to Jacos Point on Trinidad.

Ralegh had an old *cassique* (chief) from Trinidad as a pilot, who with John Douglas went to search out branches issuing into the eastern end of the bay. He found four (the *caños* Vagre, Manamitos, Manamo and Pedernales), one of them as broad as the Thames at Woolwich, but the bay there was a shoal 6ft, too shallow for the ships to enter. Ralegh took sixty men in the gallego (which as a galley now drew 5ft), and with the *Lyons Whelpe*'s boat and Captain Calfield's wherry each carrying twenty men, and with another ten in Ralegh's barge (a galley), they went up the Orinoco. Ralegh had not been able to learn from Don Berrío of any other way in, save by an entrance far to windward, which, given the winds and currents, they could not do. 'We had as much sea to cross in our wherries as between Dover and Calais, and in a great billow, the wind and current being both very strong, so as we were driven to go in those small boats directly before the wind into the bottom of the bay of Guanipa [about a five-hour sail], and from thence to enter the mouth of some one of those rivers, which John Douglas had last discovered.' Once off the bay and into the river delta, neither sun nor compass was of help in guiding Ralegh, given the multitude of twisting branches. Tall trees prevented seeing any distance. As late as the nineteenth century, sailing directions for the Orinoco delta note that even locals still got lost there.

Ralegh describes the Orinoco as having sixteen branches spread over 373 miles (much wider than the delta of the Amazon, some 149 miles wide). In these branches there are islands as big as the Isle of Wight. Three days into the expedition the galley grounded, but the next morning, throwing all the ballast overboard, and with 'tugging and hauling to and fro', Ralegh's crew got her afloat again. It was easy to run aground. Even the main *caños* have dark brown silty water, and the lesser ones are black, stained by decaying trees and plants. On the fourth day of hard rowing upstream, Ralegh writes that they fell into 'as goodly a river as ever I beheld, which was called the great Amana [Manamo], which ran more directly without windings and turnings than the other'.

Ralegh continues:

[The men were] all driven to lie in the rain and weather, in the open air, in the burning sun, and upon the hard boards, and to dress our meat, and to carry all manner of furniture in them, wherewith they were so pestered and unsavoury, that what with victuals being most fish, with the wet clothes of so many men thrust together and the heat of the sun, I will undertake there was never any prison in England, that could be found more unsavoury and lothsome, especially to myself, who had for many years before been dieted and cared for in a sort far differing.

They took on an old Indian guide, who led them upstream deep into the heart of the jungle. Ralegh writes in his *Discoverie* that as the rainy season was upon him, waiting ten days for Captain Preston in Trinidad had cost him the chance of finding the city of Manoa.

Guiana, 'a country that hath yet her maidenhead'

Ralegh observes that the women of the Amazon are not the Amazons of classical mythology. These American Amazons come together with men once a year, in April, when they choose a male:

[For a full month] they feast, dance and drink of their wines in abundance, and the moon being done, they all depart to their own provinces. If they conceive, and be delivered of a son, they return him to the father, if of a daughter they nourish it, and retain it, and as many as have daughters send unto the begetters a present, all being desirous to increase their own sex and kind, but that they cut off the right dug of the breast I do not find to be true.

Ralegh reports that for three or four hatchets, the Indians will 'sell the sons and daughters of their own bretheren and sisters, and for somewhat more even their own daughters: Hereof the Spaniards make great profit, for buying a maid of twelve or thirteen years for three or four hatchets, they sell them again at Margarita in the West Indies for fifty and one hundred pesos, which is so many crowns'.

Though mornings and evenings were clearer and cooler, every day between noon and four in the afternoon it rained heavily. Mosquitoes were thick, requiring anchoring at night in the middle of the lagoons where there was a breeze.

Between May and September the Orinoco floods to a height of 30ft above its banks, covering islands and the surrounding land. In winter the Warau Indians live above the water in tree houses and get about in canoes. At the time Ralegh was there, the waters of the Orinoco were on the rise. 'All the branches and small rivers which fall into the Orinoco were raised with such speed as, if we waded them over the shoes in the morning outward, we were covered to the shoulders homeward the very same day.'

The party had been away from the fleet for two weeks, at which point: 'On the fifteenth day we discovered afar off the mountains of Guiana to our great joy.' There they met more friendly Indians, who fed them. An Indian pilot took them further upstream, where Ralegh estimates the Orinoco was 30 miles wide. The banks had 'a blue metalline colour, like unto the best steel ore, which I assuredly take it to be'. Precious ore was foremost in the mind of most of these English and Spanish voyagers. The expedition split into smaller parties to reconnoitre. Ralegh found the march tiring, he 'being a very ill footman'. Prospecting revealed spar, a crystalline 'kind of stone like sapphires' that gave promise of gold. A Spaniard had told Ralegh that his samples were '*el madre del oro*', the mother of gold, a sign that ore was there but deeper in the ground.

Once upstream beyond the tidal flow, Ralegh's crew had to row constantly against the river's strong current. Oarsmen were relieved every hour. Gentlemen were made to pull as well as the ordinary seamen. The weather was stiflingly hot and the high trees cut off any breeze. As the expedition inched its way upstream, the river current grew still stronger. Victuals were running short and there was nothing to drink. Ralegh's party was now within 5° of the equinoctial line (his journal has latitude 9° N). He drove the men on, saying that another day's rowing would get them to help and food. Turn back, he said, and they would surely starve. The men stayed alive off the fruits of the land.

The old Indian pilot directed Ralegh to anchor the galley and take the barge and wherries up a branch to the right, where he said they would find a town of the Arawaks and an ample store of bread, fish and wine. Since they had left the galley that day, they had rowed 40 miles, and evening was coming on. At last, at one in the morning, they saw a light, and then heard dogs barking. Arriving there, they found the village nearly empty. In one house Ralegh and crew found a 'good store of bread, fish, hens, and Indian drink, and so rested that night'. The next day, reprovisioned, they returned downstream to the galley.

Ralegh was enthusiastic about Guiana, and provides a rich description of the upper reaches of the Orinoco:

> The most beautiful country that ever mine eyes beheld … plains of twenty miles in length, the grass short and green, and in diverse parts groves of trees by themselves, as if they had been by all the art and labour in the world so made of purpose: And still as we rowed, the deer came down feeding by the water's

side, as if they had been used to a keeper's call. Upon this river there were great store of fowl, and of many sorts: We saw in it diverse sorts of strange fishes, and of marvelous bigness, but for lagartos [alligator (*jacaré*), or cayman] it exceeded, for there were thousands of those ugly serpents, and the people call it for the abundance of them the River of Lagartos, in their language. I had a Negro, a very proper young fellow, that leaping out of the galley to swim in the mouth of this river, was in all our sights taken and devoured with one of those lagartos.

During the expedition Ralegh saw evidence of gold: 'As I was creeping through the bushes, I saw an Indian basket hidden, which was the refiner's basket, for I found in it, his quicksilver, saltpeter, and diverse things for the trial of metals, and also the dust of such ore as he had refined, but in those canoas which escaped there was a good quantity of ore and gold.' Ralegh offered a £500 reward to the soldier who could take one of the three Spanish prospectors they suspected were in the bush nearby, but to no avail. That basket and a few quoits of gold were as close as Ralegh came to the fabled riches.

Ralegh continued on to the land of another *cassique*, Toparimaca, where three rivers meet (near the present site of Barrancas). The sailors feasted with Toparimaca and two other *cassiques*. They all drank Indian wine, relaxed in cotton *hamacas* (Brazil beds), with 'two women attending them with six cups and a little ladle to fill them, out of an earthen pitcher of wine'. Each drank three cups at a time, 'and in this sort they drink drunk at their feasts and meetings'. Ralegh was much taken by the *cassique*'s wife:

> In all my life I have seldom seen a better favoured woman: She was of good stature, with black eyes, fat of body, of an excellent countenance, her hair almost as long as herself, tied up again in pretty knots, and it seemed she stood not in that awe of her husband, as the rest, for she spoke and discoursed, and drank among the gentlemen and captains, and was very pleasant, knowing her own comeliness, and taking great pride therein. I have seen a lady in England so like her, as but for the difference of colour I would have sworn might have been the same.

Ralegh had heard of a great silver mine further along the Orinoco's banks, but as the river had already risen 4 or 5ft and the current was growing still stronger, the English could not row against it, much less dig for silver along its banks. He nevertheless praises Guiana as a land of promise:[7]

> For health, good air, pleasure and riches, I am resolved it cannot be equalled by any region in the east or west. Moreover the country is so healthful, as one hundred persons and more, which lay without shift most sluttishly, and were every day almost melted with heat in rowing and marching, and suddenly wet

again with great showers, and did eat of all sorts of corrupt fruits, and made meals of fresh fish without seasoning, of tortugas, of logartos, and of all sorts good and bad, without either order or measure, and besides lodged in the open air every night, we lost not any one, nor had one ill disposed to my knowledge, nor found any calentura, or other of the pestilent diseases which dwell in all hot regions; and so near the Equinoctial Line.

Ralegh expands on Guiana's merits:

I never saw a more beautiful country, nor more lively prospects, hills so raised here and there over the valleys, the river winding into diverse branches, the plains adjoining without bush or stubble, all fair green grass, the ground of hard sand easy to march on, either for horse or foot, the deer crossing in every path, the birds towards the evening singing on every tree with a thousand several tunes, cranes and herons of white, crimson, and carnation perching on the river's side, the air fresh with a gentle easterly wind, and every stone that we stopped to take up, promised either gold or silver by his complexion. Your Lordship [Robert Cecil] shall see of many sorts, and I hope some of them cannot be bettered under the sun, and yet we had no means but with our daggers and fingers to tear them out here and there, the rocks being most hard of that mineral spar aforesaid, and is like a flint, and is altogether as hard or harder, and besides the veins lie a fathom or two deep in the rocks.

Here was prose crafted to bend an investor's ear.

It was now time for Ralegh to start back. The expedition had been away from the ships for a month:

While we lay at anchor on the coast of Canuri … I thought it time lost to linger any longer in that place, especially for that the fury of the Orenoque began daily to threaten us with dangers in our return, for no half day passed, but the river began to rage and overflow very fearfully, and the rains came down in terrible showers, and gusts in great abundance: And withall, our men began to cry out for want of shift, for no man had place to bestow any other apparel than that which he wore on his back, and that was thoroughly washed on his body for the most part ten times in one day: And we had now been well near a month, every day passing to the westward, farther and farther from our ships. We therefore turned towards the east, and spent the rest of the time in discovering the river towards the sea.

Ralegh again met the old chief Topiawari, who gave his son to Ralegh to return to England. To learn the Indian language, Ralegh left behind with Topiawari a servant, Francis Sparrey, and his cabin boy, Hugh Godwin, aged 16.

Retracing their way, the English had to stay close to the riverbanks in their small boats, 'being all heartily afraid both of the billow, and terrible current of the river'. At the mouth of the River Cumaca Ralegh met up with Keymis, who had been exploring by land. The Orinoco was running still faster and they could not linger. Once in the bay, Ralegh had to make his way with the boats back to Trinidad, across rough open water:

> I protest before God, that we were in a most desperate estate: For the same night which we anchored in the mouth of the river of Capuri, where it falls into the sea, there arose a mighty storm, and the river's mouth was at least a league broad, so as we ran before night close under the land with our small boats, and brought the galley as near as we could, but she had as much ado to live as could be, and there wanted little of her sinking, and all those in her: For mine own part, I confess, I was very doubtful which way to take, either to go over in the pestered galley, there being but six foot water over the sands, for two leagues together, and that also in the channel, and she drew five: Or to adventure in so great a billow, and in so doubtful weather, to cross the seas in my barge.
>
> The longer we tarried the worse it was, and therefore I took Captain Gifford, Captain Calfield, and my cousin Grenville, into my barge, and after it cleared up, about midnight we put ourselves to God's keeping, and thrust out into the sea, leaving the galley at anchor, who durst not adventure but by daylight. And so being all very sober, and melancholy, one faintly cheering another to show courage, it pleased God that the next day about nine of the clock, we descried the island of Trinidado, and steering for the nearest part of it, we kept the shore till we came to Curiapan, where we found our ships at anchor, than which, there was never to us a more joyful sight.

Ralegh (as edited by Cecil) summarises the advantages of an English Orinoco settlement: Common soldiers here will be able to fight not for lesser metals but only for gold. In Guiana will be found more temples with golden images and sepulchres filled with treasure than Cortez found in Nueva España or Pizarro found in Perú. The conquest of the Orinoco, he says, will eclipse all those made by the Spanish. Moreover, the country is healthy, despite sleeping outdoors 'without shift most sluttishly' and nearly melting from the heat, being drenched with showers, eating all sorts of 'corrupt fruits' and making meals of fresh fish 'without seasoning'. Ralegh underscores that he lost not one man on the expedition. The land promises silver and gold and already yields cotton, silk, balsamum, sugar and ginger.

Ralegh finds still more advantages. A ship can sail from England to Guiana and back in twelve weeks, without winter, storms, lee shores, enemy coasts, rocks or the shoals that plague most voyages to the West Indies.

To conclude, Guiana is a country that hath yet her maidenhead, never sacked, turned, nor wrought, the face of the earth hath not been torn, nor the virtue and salt of the soil spent by manurance, the graves have not been opened for gold, the mines not broken with sledges, nor their images pulled down out of their temples. It has never been entered by any army of strength, and never conquered or possessed by any Christian prince. It is besides so defensible, that if two forts be built in one of the provinces which I have seen, the flood sets in so near the bank, where the channel also lies, that no ship can pass up, but within a pike's length of the artillery, first of the one, and afterwards of the other: Which two forts will be a sufficient guard both to the empire of Inca, and to an hundred other several kingdoms, lying within the said river, even to the city of Quito in Perú.

Should the enemy come in wherries or barges or canoes, he adds, the woods along the rivers are so thick for 200 miles that 'a mouse cannot sit in a boat unhit from the bank'.

Once back aboard, Ralegh raided several other settlements on the Spanish Main. Heavy losses to Spanish muskets and Indian poisoned arrows convinced him to give up any thoughts of plundering Río de la Hacha and Santa Marta. Though others made their voyages profitable through pillage and plunder, Ralegh disdained 'picory' (thievery) and so on return had little to show for his efforts. His cargo would not cover even half the expenses of his voyage. He hoped that in joining Preston and Somers off Cuba, their combined fleets could remedy that. But unknown to Ralegh, the treasure *flota* had safely anchored in the harbour of La Havana. Ralegh, Preston and Somers stayed together for a week before Ralegh set course back to England on his own. He had some thought of calling at Virginia but gave over that idea. Captain and crew wanted to head directly for home.

Ralegh Returns, No 'auracular proof'

Ralegh reached England on 5 September, neither burnished nor ballasted by gold but only burned dark by the heat of the sun. At his estate, Sherborne Castle, in Dorset, at least his wife Bess was glad to have him home. Many at court believed he had not even made a voyage to Guiana. With little to show for his efforts, he was still in disgrace. Like Frobisher's rocks in the 1570s, Ralegh's ore and gem samples were considered worthless. A scruple of promise was not enough. Yet Ralegh's geology was not off the mark. There were indeed diamonds and gold in Guiana, for in the nineteenth century the world's largest gold deposits were to be found at El Callao. Not able to provide 'auracular proof', Ralegh countered by writing his *Discoverie* as seductive propaganda to woo money to his cause.

Readers included Shakespeare, Chapman and later Milton. It was translated into Dutch, Latin, German and French.

Perhaps Ralegh's Guiana, in protecting the natives from the Spanish, might indeed prosper. Here was what historian Stephen Coote calls the start of an 'imperialist role for England based on self-interested benevolence'.[8] But what Ralegh most hoped for he did not get – the support of his sometime mistress, the virgin Queen Elizabeth. He recalled her own verse, written about this time, in reflecting on her many suitors: 'Go, go, go, seek some other ware, importune me no more.'

A year after Ralegh's expedition, on 13 April 1596, Licentiate Pedro de Liaño wrote to the Crown from La Margarita that 'the Englishman Gualterral was coming with a large force, with the purpose of burning and destroying all the ports on the coast'.[9] In response to Ralegh's Guiana expedition, the Spanish established at the Río Caroní their first post there at the end of 1595, as Keymis was to discover when he returned the next year. Ripeness was all. The Elizabethans well knew the proverb, 'you must seize Occasion by the forelock, for she is bald behind'.

Ralegh hoped the publication of his *Discoverie* would gain him support. His untitled manuscript, in twenty-two numbered folios, is written in his small secretary hand.[10] It begins with dedicatory lines to the Lord Admiral, Charles, Lord Howard and to Sir Robert Cecil. Ralegh probably began his manuscript on the homebound voyage, likely finishing it by 15 October, when Burghley wanted to see it. It was circulating by 7 November. As on William Hawkyns' Brazilian voyage in the 1530s and Frobisher's Arctic ventures in the 1570s, Ralegh too had brought back his own 'occular proof' from the New World: a 'supposed prince' (the son of an Indian *cassique*) he left in the queen's care. Such a token and the prospect of gold, Ralegh hoped, would gain him favour with his queen.

Even more than Ralegh, his friend and protector Burghley appreciated that the investors were attracted to gold. To that end Cecil edited Ralegh's manuscript for publication. Cecil deflated Ralegh's claims and did not like Ralegh's description of Guiana as an Eden of pleasures, a land where, as Ralegh writes, one could 'find store of pot companions' who drink pineapple wine, a drink 'fitter for Princes, then for *borachos*', who can buy themselves as many women as they wanted and smoke tobacco 'till they become bacon'. Cecil was especially wary of Ralegh's sketches of the comely native women. All were well aware that Elizabeth in the 1590s was an elderly yet still vain queen. Ralegh's account speaks of unbridled youth, of coming onto many hundreds of women 'stark naked', and 'not inferior in shape and favour to any of Europe, colour excepted'.

Ralegh's *Discoverie* (Quinn suggests the author may in fact have been Keymis or Thomas Hariot, as Ralegh was then very busy with matters of colonisation abroad and politics at home) should be viewed next to another anonymous contemporary document on Guiana, one that argues that in lieu of Spain's policy of violent and cruel imperialism, Guiana could flourish under benevolent Protestant rule.[11] In 1595, though, Elizabeth's prime concern was protecting England. She knew that another armada attack was quite likely. Her economy had bottomed and her coffers were empty. The expense of keeping armies in France, Ireland and the Netherlands and the cost of Drake's last expedition had drained away any royal support for Ralegh's Guiana. On his return, Ralegh was impatient and despondent. Delay, he wrote, meant 'farewell Guiana forever'. In sum, any Guiana venture would have to be his private undertaking.

On his return to England Ralegh was soon in touch with Cecil and others. He wrote to Cecil on 12 November 1595: 'I assure myself that there are not more diamonds in the East Indies than are to be found in Guiana, which you see also verified by the relation of the Spanish letters.' Two weeks later, in another letter to Cecil dated 26 November 1595, Ralegh writes: 'Sir: I beseech you let us know whether we shall be travellers or tinkers, conquerours or crounes [imbeciles], for if the winter pass without making provision there can be no victualling in the summer, and if it be now furloughed *farewell Guiana* forever. Then must I determine to beg or run away: Honour and gold and all good forever hopeless.'

Ralegh sent Keymis out to Guiana in January 1596, knowing that Berrío would have quickly built forts along the lower Orinoco. Keymis was directed to survey the entire coastline from the Amazon to the Orinoco to find a river route to Manoa. Though he returned without finding it, Ralegh persisted, sending out a third voyage in late 1596. The small pinnace, the *Watte*, named after Ralegh's son, went to sea under Captain Leonard Berry and Master William Downe from Limehouse. Again, their object was to find alternative river routes to Manoa. The pinnace returned in late June 1597 with no route found.

During the voyage Downe had encountered Captain John Ley in the bark *John of London*. Ley had left Dartmouth on Shrove Tuesday 1597 to sail for this 'untraded place', Guiana, and in all would make three voyages to Guiana and the Amazon, in 1597, 1598 and 1601. On the first he went to the River Wiapoco, where he assembled a prefabricated shallop and with her explored up to the fall line of the river. Ley had already explored the lower reaches of nearly every river from there to the Maroni when he encountered Berry and the *Watte*. They concluded it would take too much work to go beyond the falls to the fabled city of Manoa. Ley's next voyage there, made in the *Black Ley* in June 1598, found him exploring up the Amazon some 80 leagues. He was to make a third voyage in October 1601.

Meanwhile, Ralegh was occupied in the summer and autumn of 1597 with preparing West Country defences against an imminent Spanish attack. Spain was on a war footing and England, not Guiana, was at stake. Still, Ralegh attempted to counter his critics and gain supporters for his enterprise. He writes that he wandered 400 miles into Guiana by land and river, that the country has more gold than the best of the Indies or Perú, and that the Indians willingly accept

English sovereignty over them. He writes that the minerals he himself found are signs of gold. The samples showed that there was gold, though it would be difficult to extract. His timing was unfortunate, but time was to prove Ralegh's claim right.

Ralegh, in charge of the Western defences, argued that since the defeat of the Armada in 1588, Spain was now stronger than ever. Her renewed strength, he observed, comes not 'from the trades of sacks, and Seville oranges, nor from ought else that either Spain, Portugal, or any of his other provinces produce: It is his Indian gold that endangers and disturbs all the nations of Europe, it purchases intelligence, creeps into councils, and sets bound loyalty at liberty, in the greatest monarchies of Europe'. To defend England, the fight against Spain is best fought in the Americas.

Hawkyns and Drake for West Indies

Whitehall took note of Ralegh's idea, for it fit neatly with a plan that Drake and Hawkyns had been putting forward since the 1570s: to attack Spain at her source of wealth in the Americas. Hawkyns and Drake's 1595–96 West Indies voyage was intended to do just that. Thomas Maynarde's onboard account of the voyage provides details.[12]

It is probable that Hawkyns and Drake first aimed to sack and then hold the area of Panamá, but by the time the fleet sailed, the plan was limited to raiding Puerto Rico and Panamá to interrupt the flow of Spanish treasure from the Americas. The joint stock organisation's motive, which was profit, dovetailed with the Crown's political one, was to curtail Spain's gold pipeline. It was a cheap way for the Crown to put a navy to sea, but by dividing command between Hawkyns and Drake, the Crown effectively had two fleets, split by organisation and the different temperaments of its commanders. In 1595 both men were old, with Hawkyns the slower and elder of the two. Andrews sketches their ways of thinking, 'their set habits of thought, which in Hawkins produced a plodding caution, in Drake a careless and eventually wild opportunism' as they sailed for their primary objective: Panamá.

The Spanish, as usual, had advance notice of the English plans. António de Berrío in Trinidad and Pedro de Salazar, governor of La Margarita, were forewarned. The voyage in 1595 was to pre-empt another armada attack on England planned for the summer of 1596. The queen wrote on 11 August 1595 to Drake, Hawkyns, Sir Thomas Gorges and Sir Thomas Baskerville that the '96 armada in ships and soldiers would be far greater than the one in '88. Hence she wanted the '95 expedition limited to six months, with the objectives being to attack on land and at sea to intercept the annual *flota*. Drake and Hawkyns replied to the queen on 13 August, the day they received her letter, objecting that the provisions, land forces and twenty pinnaces all 'very much encumber our ships and are utterly unfit for that purpose'. Six months, moreover, was too short a time.

Elizabeth was annoyed with Hawkyns and Drake for questioning her orders. On 16 August 1595 Drake and Hawkyns wrote back to the queen with news that a 350-ton Spanish ship, with 2.5 million in treasure, had lost her mast and had needed to put into San Juan. The ship was unrigged, her ordnance taken ashore. She was utterly vulnerable. Here, they argued, was treasure for the picking. Such a chance tipped the balance, and the Crown gave orders that the fleet could sail for Puerto Rico. The commanders were instructed 'with God's favour to take that place with all speed'. But the weather in Plymouth was too foul and tempestuous for immediate departure.

The English armada numbered twenty-seven vessels. The admiral, commanded by Hawkyns, was the *Garland*, 660 tons. Drake commanded the vice-admiral, *Defiance*, 550 tons. The other Crown vessels were the *Hope*, the *Foresight*, the *Bonaventure* and the *Adventure*. In all, it was some 6,000 tons of shipping and 2,500 men, a conservative manning by the guideline of one man for each 2 tons of ship. Many of the captains and masters knew the Caribbean. Hawkyns and Drake each recruited the men (and their allegiances) for their respective squadrons; Baskerville's soldiers were loyal to Essex, as the sailors were loyal either to Hawkyns or to Drake.

The voyage was organised as a joint stock venture but flying the royal standard. The queen supplied six ships and paid two-thirds of the other costs, including hiring twelve merchantmen and paying the 2,500 men. The remaining one-third of the costs was paid for by Hawkyns, Drake and the shareholders. The fitting-out cost was £31,000, of which the queen paid £20,000. The total investment was above £50,000. After the voyage, about £12,000 went to wages and other expenses, of which the queen paid £8,000. Andrews notes that the real cost of the voyage was well over £43,000, since the royal ships were contributed without charge. Hawkyns spent more on fitting out than Drake did, but the tonnage of Hawkyns' fleet was much greater than Drake's.

Victualling included various grains such as wheat, malt, rye and barley, beer, wine, fish, oatmeal, butter, cheese, salted pork, Italian macaroni, couscous, mustard seed and raisins. Drugs included *electuarium contra scorbutum* (probably Dr Stephens' elixir), *diaphenicon* (a purgative for fevers) and *electuarium de suco rosarum* (for tertian ague). There was Brittany linen, plus a lute, oboes, sackbutts, cornets, orpharions, bandora, 'and such like' musical instruments, muskets, powder, books, a Bible, psalters, service books. The *Richard* carried prefabricated pinnaces to be assembled once in the Indies. Two ketches carried sheathing and other commissioning provisions, masts for fifteen pinnaces, iron shot and salt. Provisioning in itself was a major undertaking, underscoring the voyage's importance.

Thomas Maynarde, from Devon and related to Drake and one of Drake's young protégés, provides a perceptive account with his sketches of Drake and Hawkyns.

In 1595 Drake was then about 56, his red beard gone grey. Maynarde writes that Drake was 'a man of great spirit and fit to undertake matters, in my poor opinion better able to conduct forces and discreetly to govern in conducting them to places where service was to be done, than to command in the execution thereof. But assuredly his very name was a great terror to the enemy.' As for the other commander, Hawkyns, at age 63, was 'old and wary entering into matters with so laden a foot, that the others' meat would be eaten before his spit could come before the fire'. Drake's peremptory manner and Hawkyns' caution did not make for a coherent joint command, despite both commanders' vow to serve the queen 'to good purpose'.

Twenty-Seven Sail for West Indies

This English armada, a fleet of twenty-seven sail, set out from Plymouth on Thursday 28 August – 1,500 sailors (loyal to either Hawkyns or Drake) and 1,000 soldiers (loyal to Sir Thomas Baskerville, his own loyalties with Essex). On 2 or 3 September, off Cabo São Vicente, Hawkyns announced the places to be attacked. First was San Juan de Puerto Rico (for the treasure ship), then directly to Nombre de Dios, then overland to raid Ciudad de Panamá. The plan promised great riches as long as the English were quick about it and as long as the Spanish did not get wind of the fleet. But seven or eight days later, Drake called the officers aboard the *Defiance* to ask whether they should first make for the Canaries or the Madeiras to get the provisions they lacked and to take the opportunity to plunder. Hawkyns objected. The fleet should sail directly for the Indies, according to plan, or surprise would be lost. Baskerville pacified them. At dinner the next day, it was agreed that they would shape their course for the Canaries. The English fleet was in the Canaries when the *Salomon*'s surgeon was captured and, under torture, revealed the plans. The local viceroy quickly despatched an *adviso* to Puerto Rico and Panamá warning that the English were coming.

On 28 September the English fleet left, taking with them two Azorean pilots who had local knowledge of Caribbean waters. It was a four-week crossing. On the night of 26 October Drake's squadron was hit by a storm that separated four or five ships from the rest of the fleet. One was the bark *Francis*, soon taken by five Spanish frigates commanded by Don Pedro Tello de Guzmán. Now knowing surprise was gone, Drake wanted to take out after the Spanish, but Hawkyns prevailed, arguing the need to trim the ships, mount ordnance (stored below for the crossing), take on water and set up some of the pinnaces that would attack Puerto Rico. To chase Guzmán, Hawkyns argued, would only divert the English from their objective. On 27 October Drake sighted Martinique. The plan had been to water at Dominica, but 'being inhabited by Indians our men straggling some would have their throats cut'. Instead, Drake anchored at Guadeloupe, arriving first. Hawkyns arrived on the 29th. Hawkyns was ill as the English captains prepared for the attack, mounting cannon, drilling soldiers and putting together the pinnaces.

On 5 November they set sail north-west, past Montserrat, Redonda, Nevis, Saint Christopher's (St Kitts) and Saba, towards the Virgins, which they reached on the afternoon of 8 November. The fleet felt its way through the islands towards San Juan de Puerto Rico, and on the morning of 11 November anchored off San Juan. The Spanish defences had been forewarned and were ready. For ten days they had protected the city by sinking two vessels, one the treasure galleon *Bergona*.

By this time Hawkyns was keeping to his cabin below. He was gravely ill as the English prepared to attack. At about three in the afternoon of 12 November, he died. Drake was now in sole command. There at anchor, the accurate Spanish cannon, 150 by the English account but 70 by the Spanish, fired on the English who lost 40 or 50 men, or a total of 140; or, according to Baskerville, '200 hurt and slain men'. That night Drake sailed into the harbour with thirty pinnaces and soldiers. One Spanish ship caught fire, but by the light of the flames the Spanish could direct their fire even more effectively. The English were soon driven out. Maynarde records Drake's speech to the men: 'I will bring thee to twenty places far more wealthy and easier to be gotten.'

Hawkyns was buried at sea off San Juan before Drake and the two squadrons sailed away. On the 19th they anchored in the Bahía San Germán at the south-western end of Puerto Rico, where they set up four more pinnaces and distributed victuals from the *John Trelawney* or the *Pulpit* to the rest of the fleet. On 24 November the fleet sailed south for Curaçao. After four days Drake fell in with the island but, deceived by current and westerly drift, thought his landfall was Aruba. The next morning, seeing his error, he made for Cabo de la Vela, anchoring in its lee. On 1 December he sailed into Río de la Hacha. The soldiers went ashore in pinnaces and with little resistance took the village. It was empty of people and valuables, all safely in the woods.

Drake this time planned to bypass Cartagena and go directly for Nombre de Dios. He told the men that it was 'folly for us to gather our harvest grain by grain being so likely at Panamá to thrust our hands into the whole in heaps'. On 29 December Baskerville, Maynarde and the soldiers set out from Nombre de Dios across the San Blas Mountains of Panamá. The soldiers were the 'strongest and lustiest of our army', 600 men marching under seven colours. The first day they made 3 leagues, the next day 6, already halfway across the isthmus. They came to the charred ruin of a lodging house, large enough to accommodate 500 horses. Less than a league further on they were ambushed. The soldiers' powder and match had been spoiled by rain and there was not enough bread for even one day's ration. The Spanish killed or wounded between twenty and seventy of Baskerville's men. On 2 January the party staggered back to Nombre de Dios, 'wearied with illness of the way surbaited for the want of shoes and weak with their diet'. They had only a little biscuit and cheese in the sleeves of their doublets and nothing else, according to one of the English taken prisoner by the Spanish. Maynarde writes: 'This march hath made many swear that he will never venture to buy gold at such a price again. I confess noble spirits desirous to do service to their Prince and country may be soon persuaded to all hardness and danger, but having once made trial thereof would be very loth (as I suppose) to carry any force that way again.'

'We must have gold before we see England'

A new plan was needed. On 4 January 1596 Drake called the commanders together, being at this point, writes Maynarde, at his wits' end:

> Like as upon the coming of the sun, dews and mists begin to vanish, so our blinded eyes began now to open and we found that the glorious speeches of an hundred places that they knew in the Indies to make us rich was but a bait to draw her Majesty to give them honourable employments and us to adventure our lives for their glory, for now cards and maps must be our chiefest directors, he [Drake] being in these parts at the furthest limit of his knowledge.

The English thus left on 5 January for Nicaragua. On the 10th they reached Escudos and anchored off the island, where they took an *adviso*. The area, notes Maynarde, 'is counted the sickliest place of the Indies, and here died many of our men'. On 22 January Captain Plott, Captain Edgerton and others were buried. With too few crew to man the ships, Drake ordered the *Delight* and Captain Eden's frigate scuttled.

Aside, Maynarde asked Drake why he had 'conjured' him out of England to stay in those parts as long as himself. Maynarde writes:

> He answered with grief protesting that he was as ignorant of the Indies as myself, and that he never thought any place could be so changed, as it were from a delicious and pleasant arbour, into a waste land desert wilderness, besides the variableness of the wind and weather so stormy and blusterous as he never saw it before, but he most wondered that since his coming out of England he never saw sail worthy the giving chase unto, yet in the greatness of his mind he would in the end conclude with these words. 'It matters not man, God hath many things in store for us, and I know many means to do her Majesty good service and to make us rich, for we must have gold before we see England,' when, good gentleman (in my conceit), it fared with him as with some careless living man who prodigally consumes his time fondly persuading himself that the nurse that fed him in his childhood will likewise nourish him in his old

age and finding the dug dried and withered enforced then to behold his folly tormented in mind dieth with starved body.

Since Panamá, Maynarde writes, Drake 'never carried mirth nor joy in his face, yet no man he loved must conjecture that he took thought thereof. But here he began to grow sickly.' Drake sank a caravel brought from England, transferred her victuals into a prize frigate, and sailed for Portobelo, 9 leagues from Nombre de Dios. From there he could launch an attack on the Spanish.

Portobelo's harbour, says Maynarde, 'was the best harbour we came unto since we left Plymouth', but the crew continued to battle sickness. Captain Josias of the *Delight* and fleet surgeon James Wood both died. Drake had been below in his cabin for some days, 'having been extremely sick of a flux'. On 27 January Drake added a codicil to his will, naming Thomas Drake as his executor, and expressed his wish to be buried ashore, were he to die.

In the early morning hours of 28 January, Drake rose from his berth delirious. He ordered his servant to prepare him for engagement and to dress him in his armour. He 'used some speeches', and then in full battledress returned to bed. At four in the morning Drake died. Baskerville wrote that 'Sir Francis fell sick as I think through grief'. Maynarde thought Drake died of depression. Drake was buried at sea, against his will. 'His internment was after this manner; his corpse being laid in a coffin of lead, he was let down into the sea, the trumpets in doleful manner echoing out this lamentation for great a loss, and all the cannons in the fleet were discharged according to the custom of all sea funeral obsequies.' Hawkyns had been wrapped and sewn in canvas, then eased into the waters off San Juan. Drake's lead coffin sank quickly into the harbour of Portobelo. The two greatest heroes of 1588 were gone.

What killed Hawkyns and Drake? A dozen and more diseases then flourished among sailors in the American tropics. The main causes for death were acute toxaemia from victuals and water; then dysentery; scurvy (vitamin C deficiency); and malaria. Amoebic dysentery thrives in the tropics, and given the contaminated food and water aboard ships at that time, this is a reasonable guess at the cause of death. Most find amoebic dysentery to be the likely cause of Drake's death, though malaria is a possibility.[13]

With Drake now dead, Maynarde continues, 'most men's hearts were bent to hasten for England, as soon as they might'. Baskerville, a landsman, was now in charge. He had the *Delight*, the *Elizabeth* and three Spanish frigates sunk, and had many of the black and Spanish prisoners put ashore. On Sunday 8 February the English set sail, the crew on short rations:

Very hard allowance. For men each morning one quart of beer and two cakes of biscuit and one cake of biscuit for dinner and for supper one quart of beer and two cakes of biscuit and two cans of water with a pint of pease or half a pint of rice or somewhat more of oatmeal. This was our allowance being at Portobelo and six weeks before, but that we had some time stockfish.

On Monday 15 March they passed out of the Caribbean Sea into the Gulf of México, then sailed east. Once in the Atlantic they ran with the 'most foul weather and contrary winds' until 1 May, when the sounding lead found 90 fathoms as they neared the English Channel. On 3 May they sighted the Isles of Scilly, and that same day came to anchor there. Maynarde sums up the voyage: 'I verily think that filtching men of war shall do more good than such a fleet if they have any forwarning of their coming', and that to dispossess Spain of Puerto Rico, Hispaniola and Cuba would be more costly than any profit gained, for with just a few days' warning, the towns can convey their valuables to safety. He calls his account one of 'many idle words and ill compared sentences, it was done on the sea which I think can alter any disposition'.

Hawkyns' and Drake's 1595–96 voyage made strategic sense, but was from the start ill-executed. England's aims were split between profit and politics. The Spanish were well aware of every move by the English, so harbours were defended, cannon loaded, matches lit. In 1595 Hawkyns and Drake, moreover, were two old men of very different temperaments, unwillingly yoked together by their aged queen.

Purchas, writing thirty years later, adds a passage by one 'R.M.' who had served with both Hawkyns and Drake:

Sir, I have according to your request, and my own plainness sent you here the comparison between those two commanders Sir Francis Drake and Sir John Hawkyns. They were both much given to travel in their youth and age, attempting many honourable voyages alike; as that of Sir John Hawkyns to Guinea, to the isles of America, to Saint John de Ulúa. So likewise Sir Francis Drake after many discoveries of the West Indies, and other parts, was the first Englishman that did ever compass the world; wherein, as also in his deep judgement in sea causes, he did far exceed not Sir John Hawkyns alone, but all others whomsoever.

In their own natures and disposition they did as much differ; as in the managing matters of wars, Sir Francis being of a lively spirit, resolute, quick, and sufficiently valiant: The other slow, jealous, and hardly brought to resolution. In counsel Sir John Hawkyns did often differ from the judgement of others, seeing thereby to know more in doubtful things, than he would utter. Sir Francis was a willing hearer of every man's opinion, but commonly a follower of his own: He never attempted any action, wherein he was an absolute commander, but he performed the same with great reputation, and did easily dispatch great matters; contrarywise Sir John Hawkyns did only give the bare attempt of things, for the most part without any fortune or good success therein.

Sir John Hawkyns did naturally hate the land-soldier, and though he were very popular, yet he affected more the common sort, than his equals; Sir Francis contrarily did much love the land-soldier, and greatly advanced good parts, wheresoever he found them. He was also affable to all men and of easy access. They were both of many virtues, and agreeing in some. As patience in enduring labours and hardness, observation and memory of things past, and great discretion in sudden dangers, in which, neither of them was much distempered, and in some other virtues they differed. Sir John Hawkyns had in him mercy and aptness to forgive, and true of word; Sir Francis hard in reconciliation, and constancy in friendship; he was withall severe and courteous, magnanimous, and liberal.

They were both faulty in ambition, but more the one than the other; for in Sir Francis was an insatiable desire of honour, indeed beyond reason. He was infinite in promises, and more temperate in adversity, than in better fortune. He had also other imperfections, as aptness to anger, and bitterness in disgracing, and too much pleased with open flattery: Sir John Hawkins had in him malice with dissimulation, rudeness in behaviour, and passing sparing, indeed miserable.

They were both happy alike in being great commanders, but not of equal success, and grew great and famous by one means, rising through their own virtues, and the fortune of the sea. There was no comparison to be made between their well deserving and good parts, for therein Sir Francis Drake did far exceed. This is all I have observed in the voyages, wherein I have served with them. R.M.

Bloody Flux and Battle

The voyage had lost 500 to battle or disease. The remains of the fleet returned to Plymouth in early May 1596, its ranks emaciated. The Virgin Islands, Puerto Rico and Panamá had proven sickly places. In 1597, Dr Layfield, chaplain to the Earl of Cumberland, was to describe the sicknesses of Puerto Rico and the dysentery that most likely killed Hawkyns and Drake in 1595:

It was an extreme looseness of the body, which within few days would grow into a flux of blood, sometimes in the beginning accompanied with a hot ague, but always in the end attended by an extreme debility and waste of spirits: So that some two days before death, the arms and legs of the sick would be wonderful cold. And that was held for a certain sign of near departure. This sickness usually within few days (for it was very extreme to the number of sixty, eighty, and an hundred stools [in a] day) brought a languishing weakness over all the body.[14]

In today's terms, this is dysentery, brought on by contaminated food and polluted water, with an infection of the large intestine causing abdominal cramps and painful diarrhoea with blood: the 'bloody flux'. The amoebic form, caused by a protozoan, is common in the tropics. As for Hawkyns and Drake, what Spanish musket and cannon could not do, disease did.

In less than a year – just eleven months – Ralegh 'discovered' Guiana, and Hawkyns and Drake died. It was an extraordinary time marking both the quick and the dead.

nine

———— ∞∞∞ ————

Taken at the Flood, 1596–1603

All that glisters is not gold.

Shakespeare, *The Merchant of Venice*, 1596–98

*J*anuary 1596 found both Hawkyns and Drake dead and Ralegh out of favour at the court of an aged Elizabeth. For the years 1596 to 1603, the threat of another Spanish armada kept most of the English fleet in home waters. The era of privateering voyages to the Caribbean was largely over, but colonising voyages were getting under way.

At the end of this period came a crucial transition: Elizabeth died and James assumed the throne. Under James as king, England's foreign policy was to sue for peace with Spain. Ralegh, already out of favour and with political enemies, lost property and position almost at once. Under suspicion of treason, he was committed to the Tower, but Ralegh continued his years of considerable effort to make the Guiana colony successful.

One of the two boys who had stayed on in Guiana in 1595, Ralegh's 16-year-old cabin boy Hugh Godwin, met a nasty end when he was eaten alive by four jaguars. Francis Sparrey, the other one of the pair, began to explore the area but was captured by the Spanish. He managed to buy his freedom, was transported to Madrid for interrogation, and wrote an account of his experiences.[1] When he returned to England in 1602 he was in his early twenties, toughened by the heat of the tropics and Jesuit interrogators.

Sherley to the West Indies

The well-connected and well-supported Sir Anthony Sherley, knight, sailed in 1596 to La Margarita, and from there along the Spanish Main to Jamaica and Honduras, and homeward via Newfoundland.[2] His fleet of seven vessels was provisioned for ten months. Sickness and storm plagued Sherley and his crew as they sailed first to the Cabo Verdes, then to Dominica, which they reached on 17 October: 'With all our men sick and feeble, we found there two hot baths, and kind Indians.' Most recovered, and plundering as they went, the fleet sailed for La Margarita, Bonaire, Santa Marta, and then north to Jamaica, where on 2 March 1597 Sherley joined with Captain William Parker, gentleman, of Plymouth.

Together they sailed to Honduras, hoping in vain for Spanish treasure. On 10 April they entered the Río Dolce, where they assembled a pinnace brought out from England in six parts 'to be set together with screws', in which they planned to embark on the South Sea to try their fortune. Thirty leagues up the river they found the mountains too high, the path too long and the town too poor to plunder, so they returned downstream to their ships. All they came away with was the tantalising knowledge that the South Sea was just 20 leagues further on. The two captains went separate ways off La Havana on 13 May. In just the *Bevice*, with little to show for his travails, Sherley returned to England.

As for Parker, he and his men raided the coast for five weeks more, taking Campeche on Easter Day 1597. During the attack, he writes, he was 'shot under the left breast with a bullet, which bullet lies still in the chin of my back'. He seized a frigate in the harbour laden with £5,000, the king's tribute intended for shipment from San Juan de Ulúa. Parker made for La Havana, then home. He fell in with the Isles of Scilly about 1 July and within two days arrived at Plymouth, where, he writes, 'we found the Right Honourable the Earl of Essex setting forth with a great fleet for the Isles of the Azores'.

Guiana, 'opportunity at the flood'

Ralegh lost no time in his plan to settle Guiana. In January 1596 he sent off Lawrence Keymis with two ships to lead the second expedition.[3] His narrative begins on Sunday 2 January 1596, when he left Portland road in the *Darling* of London, along with a small pinnace, the *Discoverer*, William Downe, master. Just four days later, on the following Thursday, the *Discoverer* was lost from sight in a storm. On Friday 13 February the *Darling* fell in with the Canaries. After some 550 leagues, on 14 March, towards night and still about 6 leagues from shore, Keymis sighted low land. It was the mouth of the River Arrowari.

They coasted westward to the River Wiapoco. The Indians had been hoping for the return of the English so that together they might drive the Spaniards from their land. A *cassique* guided them to the River Orinoco. Anchoring there on 6 April, they learned the Spanish had already established a village of twenty to thirty houses but still numbered fewer than fifty-five men and were as yet without cannon. The pinnace *Discoverer*, separated four days out of England, unexpectedly rejoined Keymis, and it was time to return home. Keymis took the victuals from the pinnace and, as her rudder was broken, burned her. The *Darling* made for St Lucia, Grenada and then St Vincent (with fierce cannibals but good tobacco).

Keymis writes to Ralegh of the riches of Guiana, saying in his explorations he has discovered some forty navigable rivers and heard of a large lake at the head of the River Essequibo: 'Thus I have emptied your purse, spending my time and travail in following your Lordship's directions for the full discovery of this coast and the rivers thereof; concerning the not making of a voyage for your private profit, I pretend nothing. Sorry I am, that where I sought no excuse, by the Spaniards being there I found my defect remediless.' Keymis is captivated by the Orinoco: 'Myself, and the remain of my few years, I have bequeathed wholly to Raleana, and all my thoughts live only in that action.' Guiana is easy to reach and dangerless, he writes, and the country is free from infectious sickness. The cause is profitable, as gold and other items of value can be had there. The cause too is just – freeing the Indians from the Spaniards, who 'must hold by tyranny that which they get by the sword'. Do not 'leave all unto the Spaniard', he urges. The English have more ships, people and means than the Spanish, 'and yet do nothing'. The cause is also necessary, being 'the only help to put a bitt in the mouth of the unbridled Spaniard'. The opportunity is at the flood, for 'like occasion seldom happens in many ages'.

Later in 1596 Ralegh sent a third expedition to Guiana.[4] The author of the account was Thomas Masham, gentleman. The pinnace *Watte* sailed from Weymouth, and off the Barbary Coast was joined by Benjamin Wood's *Beare*, *Beares Whelpe* and the *Benjamin*, bound for China via the Strait of Magellan. The four vessels made their Atlantic crossing together. On 27 February 1597 they sighted land low on the horizon. They were near the Amazon at about latitude 2° 30' N. The *Watte* worked her way north-west along the coast towards Cape Cecil and the mouth of the River Cassiporé, 'with much ado making many boards [tacks]' and anchoring as tides required, until she reached the River Wiapoco.[5] In the pinnace the crew rowed 16 leagues up to the river's fall line, getting a warm reception from the Caribes. In the River Coritine the *Watte* encountered the bark *John of London*, Charles Leigh, captain.[6] On learning that the Spanish were gathering to attack them, the two vessels sailed off for the Caribbean islands.

Thomas Masham finds Guiana to be temperate, though it 'stand within the Tropic, and something near to the Equinoctial, so that the sun is twice a year over their heads and never far from them'.[7] It was a healthy place:

We lost not a man upon the coast, one that was sick before he came there, was nothing sicker for being there, but came home safe, thanks be to God. And for mine own part, I was never better in body in all my life, and in like sort fared it with the rest of the company: For indeed it is not so extreme hot as many imagine. The people in all the lower parts of the country go naked, both men and women, being of several languages, very tractable, and ingenious, and very loving and kind to Englishmen generally.

Masham reports that there is 'great store of gold, as we are certainly informed by the lower Indians, of whom we had some gold'. Food was so plentiful and tasty that the English had no need to draw on their own stores. Around the rivers, there were various fowl, and 'great store of as good fish in the rivers, as any is in the world'. Tortoise flesh was plentiful, and tortoise eggs innumerable. Deer, swine, connies, hares, cocks and hens, and potatoes were abundant, and all times of the year one could have the 'rarest fruits of the world'. As for commodities, he says, there is a long hemp, fine cotton wool, plus a great store of pitch, various sweet gums, West Indian pepper, balsamum, parrots and monkeys.

The *Watte* and the *John of London* sailed north past St Vincent, St Lucia and Martinique, and on 13 May parted ways. Masham reached the Azores on 9 June. On 28 June 1597 the *Watte* was off the Lizard, and that night she 'came all safe to Plymouth, blessed be God'.

Following the publication of Ralegh's *Discoverie* in 1596, the Dutch, among others, developed an increased interest in exploiting Guiana.[8] Adrian Cabeliau sailed on the *Zeeridder*, Jacob Cornelisz alias Oom, captain, arriving in Guiana on 9 February 1598. On 13 October between St Lucia and Grenada, Cabeliau's vessel encountered 'the galley of Sir Walter Ralegh, of London, of about twenty-five tons, and coming from the coast of Barbary'. This was the 37-ton *Darling* of Southampton, which had indeed been sent out privateering in 1598 by Ralegh, Sir Robert Cecil, and Richard and Francis Burley.

Cumberland's Twelfth and Last Voyage, Sacks San Juan

While Sparrey was in the Orinoco, George Clifford, Earl of Cumberland, set out on the last of his twelve voyages, this one to the West Indies in 1598.[9] Three of the twelve were to Latin America – those in 1586, 1593 and 1598. The author of the account of this voyage is John Layfield, DD, who sailed as chaplain. Editor Purchas notes that the earl wrote his own account for part of it and that others were also writing their own accounts.

Cumberland's was to be the last major voyage of plunder and occupation by the English in the Caribbean. The fleet of sixteen ships, two pinnaces and two barges – in all, 4,600 tons – was, after Drake's 1585–86 West Indies raid and the

Hawkyns–Drake voyage of 1595–96, the third-largest English fleet to sail the Caribbean that century. Six of the vessels were Cumberland's own, another six John Watts', and the rest were supplied by William Garraway, Thomas Cordell and others. The captains and masters were all seasoned seamen: John Watts, James Langton, Gerard Middleton, John Ley, William Wynter and others. The largest vessels were the *Scourge of Malice*, 900 tons; followed by the *Ascension* and the *Prosperous*, both 400 tons; the *Galleon Constance*, the *Consent* and the *Merchant Royal*, 350 tons; and the *Sampson* and *Centurion*, each 300 tons. Among the others was one borrowed from Ralegh, the *Guiana*, 200 tons. Crew numbered about 1,000 sailors and 700 soldiers, with gentlemen, surgeons and two Portuguese pilots. To Chaplain Layfield's eye, the soldiers were 'very raw and unpractised'.

Cumberland commanded the admiral, the *Scourge of Malice*, and Sir John Berkeley in the *Merchant Royal* was vice-admiral as well as colonel-general of the soldiers. Money for the voyage came from London merchants and merchant-privateers (for Cumberland's vessels), and it was a well-provisioned fleet. Cumberland's plan for the seven-month voyage was to take him first to Spain, then the Canaries, and then across to the Caribbean (Dominica, the Virgins and Puerto Rico), before a return via the Azores (Flores). Like Drake three years earlier, his main objective was to sack San Juan de Puerto Rico.

After paying the queen upon return, the voyage's profits were to be divided into ten shares and based on the tonnage of his ships; Cumberland was probably to receive at least a quarter of the expected profits. His royal patent for the voyage was issued on 14 January. Two days later Cumberland made a new will, naming, among others, Burghley and Essex as executors. Being a courtier to Elizabeth had proven an expensive proposition for the earl. Though his was the eighth most important earldom in England at that time, his purse was empty, so he staked nearly all his estates and fortunes on the uncertainty of going to sea.

Cumberland's fleet was down the Thames by mid-February and left Portsmouth on 6 March 1598. On 10 March they were off Plymouth, and despite 'the wind being prosperous though much', Cumberland continued on. Three days out, Chaplain Layfield glanced up while conducting the prayer service to find a gentleman reading Lodovico Ariosto's *Orlando Furioso*, a secular, sexy and popular epic of the time. Layfield warned the man after the service that he must serve God better and that if caught reading such trash again, Layfield would throw the book overboard and have the gentleman removed from the ship. This was the Layfield who in a few years would be named by King James to the committee charged by him to produce the Authorised Bible.

Off Tenerife, Cumberland called his officers together and informed them that their destination would be Puerto Rico, 'the very key of the West Indies, which locks and shuts all the gold and silver in the continent of America and Brasilia', and all of them except John Ley in the pinnace *Bark Ley*, who parted from them and made for the Río Orinoco, were filled 'with greedy desire, and hopeful expectation'. With two other vessels and two prizes, Cumberland made landfall on Dominica on 23 May. The rest of the fleet arrived the next day. The men rested and recovered in a hot spring there (as hot as the waters in Bath, writes Layfield) and were welcomed by the Indians with food and tobacco in trade for swords, clothes and trifles. A local *cassique* prepared a banquet, and Chaplin Layfield solemnly reports that the gentlemen danced with the chief's naked daughters. Layfield describes Dominica as having very fat soil, 'matching the garden-plots in England for a rich black mould', and so heavily wooded it is 'marvellous how those naked souls can be able to pull themselves through them, without renting their natural clothes'. Even the hills were wooded, and the trees grow 'so like good children of some happy civil body, without envy or oppression, as that they look like a proud meadow about Oxford, when after some eruption, Thames is again couched low within his own banks'.

At dawn on Tuesday 6 June Cumberland and Berkeley arrived at the bay of Cangrejos, 3 leagues east of San Juan, and Cumberland ordered the men into the boats, promising them the maidenhead of this, the second city of the Indies for its harbour. The harbour at San Juan, called El Tejar and second only to Cartagena's, was protected by several forts, the principal one being El Morro at the harbour entrance. Construction on El Morro had begun nine years earlier, in 1589, and had proved its worth in 1595 by driving off Drake's attack. San Juan, by 1598, had eighty brass cannon and 334 infantry.

For both Drake and Cumberland there had been no advantage of surprise. Cumberland knew how Drake had been driven away and formed a different plan of attack. The Spanish expected Cumberland to attack at the harbour as Drake had, but he planned to approach instead from Cangrejos Bay. Berkeley had nearly 1,000 men divided into seven companies, well equipped with muskets, harquebusiers and pikes. At El Boquerón inlet, upon meeting Spanish fire, the men diverted several miles through thick woods in the sweltering heat. Once at the Aguilar bridge, they found the barricade shut and defended, but a slave told them that the causeway could be waded through at low tide and that the next low tide was at two the following morning. Two hours before dawn, Sir John Berkeley's regiment led the attack.

The English were dressed in full armour. By daybreak as the tide was rising, the soldiers were caught wading heavily alongside the causeway:

Here his Lordship [Cumberland] was (by the stumbling of him that bore his target) overthrown, even to the danger of drowning; for his armour so over-burdened him, that the sergeant major that by chance was next had much ado at the first and second time to get him from under the water: When he was up, he had received so much salt water that it drove him to so great extremity of present sickness, that he was forced to lie down in the very place upon the causeway; till being somewhat recovered, he was able to be led to a place of some more safety and ease; in which place the bullets made him threatening music on every side.

It was by then mid-tide. The current was running fast, and the water rose rapidly from their knees to their middles as the Spanish raked the English and the causeway with gunfire. The English retreated and Cumberland returned to the *Scourge*.

To this point Cumberland had been the account's author, but now Layfield takes up his pen:

> Thus far the same honourable hand hath been our actor and author: But here when he comes to doing, breaks off speaking, and (*tam Marte quam Mercurio*) exchangeth words for swords, and mercurial arts into martial acts; of which we have another relator, as of the rest of this voyage: A man near in attendance to his honourable master.

Purchas prints Layfield's manuscript 'very much abbreviated'.

The next plan was to capture the El Boquerón fort at the inlet, either by having Berkeley land his men there or by renewing the attack on the San António fort. The English ran a Flemish vessel aground to a place where it could fire on both the fort and the bridge. At five in the afternoon Cumberland's five pinnaces landed 200 men. The Spanish forces withdrew, and Thursday at dawn, unopposed, the English entered San Juan. The people had retreated into the mangrove swamps and melted into the surrounding country. Cumberland fortified the city and prepared to storm the fort El Morro at the harbour's mouth. For a full week he brought in cannon from the *Malice*, then began the siege. Inside the fort were 400 men who had – unknown to Cumberland – only one day's food and no water. They soon surrendered. On the morning of 21 June, while dining at the bishop's palace, the two sides worked out the terms of surrender. The Cross of St George was raised from the ramparts of El Morro, and the English fleet entered El Tejar harbour. During the two-week campaign only two English had been lost – a remarkable achievement.

During the negotiations, the city's leaders dined daily with the English. Though the earl allowed the Spanish to retain their weapons, he ordered they be transported elsewhere. The English understood the strategic importance of taking and holding San Juan, knowing it controlled the sea route back to Spain. Here at San Juan de Puerto Rico, Cumberland had gained the victory denied the veteran mariners Drake and Hawkyns. It was the privateering Earl of Cumberland's well-deserved moment of glory, earned in his last of twelve voyages.

Cumberland next strengthened the island's defences, for he intended to hold the island with 500–600 soldiers while awaiting Queen Elizabeth's orders. He maintained strict discipline and punished those who pillaged and plundered, handing down swift justice on any men who committed outrages against the Spanish. He publicly disarmed a very good soldier 'for over-violent spoiling a gentlewoman of her jewels'. Cumberland seized six empty vessels in the harbour and a 200-ton vessel laden with victuals bound for Brazil. Cumberland took the cargo and, with two other vessels, sent off 300 prisoners escorted by two English ships to Cartagena, arriving there on 26 July.

But amoebic dysentery (if it were that) struck them hard. By July 200 were dead and another 400 were suffering from it. Sir John Berkeley was gravely ill. 'For within a while that his Lordship had been in Puerto Rico, many of our men fell sick, and at the very first not very many died. The Spanish as well as the English were both sick and died of the sickness, as besides *seralta* was seen in diverse others. Others suspected their bodily labours to have procured it, and both seem to have concurred.' The disease killed in only a few days from the onset of symptoms to the finish. Meanwhile, it kept the healthy fully preoccupied with ministering to the sick: 'And this was it, which rather than the number already dead, made his Lordship first think of quitting the place.' By the end of July, more than 400 of Cumberland's men were dead and another 400 ill.

Cumberland feared he would not have enough sailors to man the ships and return home. He soon recognised that the English could not hold Puerto Rico and set about having the island and city ransomed. But the Spanish delayed. Cumberland prepared the fleet for a 'happy, and by many, much desired return', as Layfield writes, 'since it was clear that it was not God's pleasure, that yet this island should be inhabited by the English'. The crew loaded aboard all the hides, ginger, sugar, munitions and ordnance – some fourscore cast pieces that Chaplain Layfield judged to be 'some of them the goodliest that ever I saw'.

On 14 August Cumberland set sail for the Azores with the *Malice*, the *Sampson* and seven other vessels, leaving Berkeley and others behind to hold the city. West of the Azores, Cumberland was hit by an intense storm with waves, writes Layfield, 'higher than our main-top'. At Flores, the Portuguese gave the earl supplies, but when he learned from them that he would not be encountering the Spanish *flota*, he left the Azores on 16 September for England. Fifteen ships, a bark, a pinnace and 1,000 men sailed up the Thames and arrived at Blackwall on 1 October 1598.

In this voyage Cumberland lost 700 men in all, 600 of them to what was probably amoebic dysentery. His twelfth and last expedition was nevertheless a success. In Lisbon, one writer observed that 'the small forces of an English Earl can shut in both the East and West India Fleet'. By stopping the Spanish fleets from sailing to both the East and West Indies that year, he had for a time prevented New World treasure from reaching Spain. Cumberland argued for a fleet to keep Spain on the defensive, but the Crown thought otherwise. There were other matters that needed attention: There were rebellions at home; there was the continued threat of another attempted Spanish invasion; it was the fourth year of bad harvests; there was inflation; and the plague was infecting the country. Though Cumberland brought back eighty brass cannon, ginger, hides and sugar, these brought a return of only 8 per cent on principal for the investors. True, his voyage was effective politically, but financially it was yet another failure. Cumberland was once again unlucky and all the poorer for his efforts, even if to the Spanish, with Drake now lying 'full fathom five' off Portobelo, he now held the title of 'archpirate Earl of Cumberland'. Elizabeth received him in October, greatly appreciative of her privateering earl.

Ley for Guiana

When Cumberland had set out on his twelfth voyage to the Spanish West Indies, determined to take San Juan de Puerto Rico, one vessel among his fleet was the pinnace *Bark Ley*. She had left Cumberland and instead sailed for the Orinoco. This was John Ley, a third son and for a brief time a student at Oxford before migrating to Clements Inn, London, 'being nothing affected to study the law'. One of his brothers was Sir James Ley, the Balliol, Brasenose and Lincoln's Inn lawyer who, among his many later appointments, became one of the chief justices in Wales. Later, James Ley was Chief Justice of the King's Bench in Ireland and member of the Privy Council there.

John Ley, like many other younger sons lacking an inheritance, was lured by the call of the sea. He had sailed in Sir Martin Frobisher's second voyage to America, and as captain he commanded soldiers in the Low Countries for the Protestant cause. He went to Ireland with Sir William Russell, Lord Deputy in Dublin, from August 1595 to the spring of 1597, and he was at sea various times on voyages of reprisal, both as captain and as owner, commanding the *John Young* from Southampton. He was captain of the *Alcedo*, one of Watts' ships in the Frobisher squadron that went to the Azores, and had sailed to the Caribbean with Cumberland. He would sail there three times at his own expense. [10]

Ley's second voyage left Plymouth on Friday 10 March 1598. Cumberland had made him captain of the *Alcedo* in the flotilla assembled for Puerto Rico, but when the earl's fleet reached the Canaries, Ley transferred to his prize frigate, which he named the *Black Ley*. From the Cabo Verdes he set a south-westerly course for Guiana, and after thirty days reached the mouth of the River Amazon. The crew put together a shallop carried in pieces in the hold. Three hundred Indians watched, ready to attack, but were perhaps deterred at the sight of the ship's cannon. Ley took the frigate and shallop up the Amazon four score leagues to a spot near the confluence of the River Xingu and the Canal do Gurupá, anchored the *Black Ley*, and carried on further upstream in the shallop. The Indians were not friendly. Running out of food, he returned downstream. Ley went on to visit the rivers he had explored the year before, then made for St Vincent. On an island near Nevis, while taking on wood and water, he found two hot springs so extreme that they 'did boil a piece of salt beef in a quarter of an hour'. Ley returned to England about All Hallowstide, 1 November 1598.

If Ley's voyages did little to further English political and financial interests in the tropics, his adventures touched the imaginations of readers of the classics. He had experienced 'terrible tempests of winds rain lightning and thunder' with water-spouts that overturned the Indians' canoes. He found Indians with long fingernails with which they could catch fish and writes that these *caboclo d'agua* (Indian water devils) 'have the voice, and language of men, the Indians are much afeared to come near them, in their canoes, for these swimmers will overthrow the canoes, and drown the Indians'. The fabled men without heads and with eyes, noses and mouths in their chests seem to be the Esparicur people. Ley supports Ralegh's observation that the tropical Amazons have two breasts, not one cut off, as in Greek mythology, for these women shoot bows and arrows by holding the arrow away from their bodies. He notes that the Indians navigate by the Southern Cross, called 'Acunowmo', and that to them Orion is 'Petycaio' and the Pleiades, 'Topoimono'. With the seven stars of the Pleiades, he said, the Indians were able to forecast weather.

John Ley sailed from Plymouth on 30 October, on a third voyage to the Caribbean.[11] He reached the Canaries and from there, on 21 December, wrote home to say that he had two good carpenters and, once in the Indies, would set them to building a boat. That was the last word from John Ley. He was to die later on the voyage.

Parker takes Portobelo

Captain William Parker of Plymouth, who had joined forces with Sir Anthony Sherley several years before, departed England again for the West Indies.[12] This time he sailed in early November 1601 with two ships, one pinnace and two shallops in quarter, stowed in pieces in the hold. The admiral was the *Prudence*, 100 tons, commanded by Parker and manned by 130 'tall men'. The second ship was the vice-admiral *Pearle*, 60 tons, commanded by Robert Rawlin, and 'accompanied with sixty lusty fellows'. The pinnace, 20 tons, was manned by eighteen crew. In this consort were Edward Giles and Philip Ward, both gentlemen and captains by land, with other gentlemen 'of much towardliness and valour'.

From the Cabo Verdes Parker made for the Caribbean. His landfall was La Margarita, where he met Spanish resistance but took the place 'with diverse of the stoutest of our enemy's prisoners, and thirteen pirogues and canoes, which are barks and boats of the country: For ransom of all which I received £500 in pearl'. At Cabo de la Vela, he took a Portuguese ship bound for Cartagena, 250 tons burden, laden with 370 slaves brought from the Congo or Angola. He went into Las Cabeças, where he embarked 150 men in two small pinnaces and two shallops to raid Portobelo.

His ships anchored 'somewhat to the eastward of the castle of Saint Philip, under the rock where Sir Francis Drake his coffin was thrown overboard'. At two in the morning of 7 February, Parker entered the mouth of the river, 'the moon shining very brightly'. The English marched into Portobelo and went directly to the king's treasure house, 'very fair and large' and guarded by a squadron of soldiers and 'two brass pieces of field ordnance well-mounted on their carriages, which we presently possessed, and fiercely set upon the soldiers'. In taking the governor, Parker was shot through both thighs, but carried on, and after four or five hours, captured the king's *scrivano*. In the king's treasure house, Parker found only 9,000–10,000 ducats, bad luck since the treasury one week earlier had been filled with 120,000 ducats. That treasure had left on two frigates bound for Cartagena. Parker had his own surgeon treat the governor's wounds, then released the prisoner without ransom, which was far better treatment, writes Parker, than that used by the governor's great-uncle on John Ribault, Laudonière, and other French in Terra Florida, whom they had 'most cruelly murdered and massacred'.

On 9 February, Parker set sail and stood off to sea eastward towards Cartagena, anchoring in the bay of Sambo. For nearly two weeks they rested there, watering and taking on wood, before leaving for Jamaica and on to Cabo San António, disembognuing from the Gulf of Bahama into the Atlantic on 31 March 1602. Parker had good weather for his crossing. He victualled the vice-admiral and two pinnaces in the Azores, ordering them to stay at sea for further depredations. He set course for Plymouth, and arrived on 6 May 1602, ending a successful cruise.

Leigh at Guiana

Charles Leigh sailed to Guiana in 1602. At the Wiapoco he met a factor left there by John Ley. Charles Leigh was one of a small group of adventurers who had begun to explore and trade along the Guiana coast, generally attracting no publicity or official reports while they catalogued the names of rivers and the tribes on the lower reaches of those rivers. He notes that the Spanish now held Trinidad and the Orinoco, and that to avoid the Spanish the English would have to settle south of the River Essequibo. With the backing of Cecil and the Lord Admiral, he established a short-lived colony along the banks of the Wiapoco from 1604 to 1606 – short-lived because under the terms of the Anglo-Spanish treaty of 1604, England had conceded any sovereignty in the region to Spain.

Virgin Queen Dies

'Her Majesty departed this life, mildly like a lamb, easily like a ripe apple from the tree', wrote John Manningham in his diary in March 1603.[13] Queen Elizabeth, age 69 and in the forty-fifth year of her reign, had died at three in the morning of 24 March 1603, ending the era that had brought England from the periphery of European politics to its centre. With her death much was about to change. Her successor, James Stuart, wanted peace with Spain. This and other matters put him at odds with Sir Walter Ralegh.

Ralegh, though enmeshed in politics, was hardly ever politic and was seen by many as an ambitious upstart courtier who through flattery had gained the favours of the late queen. Eleven years earlier Ralegh, then in his forties, had bedded Bess Throckmorton, a 19-year-old lady-in-waiting to the queen, made her pregnant and secretly married her. Elizabeth had had him arrested. She expected the two to sue for pardon, but when the couple made no such plea, the Raleghs found themselves in disgrace for the next five years. The Cádiz raid of 1596 and the islands voyage of 1597 saw both Ralegh and the queen's young favourite, Robert Devereux, 2nd Earl of Essex, vying for victory and favour. When the Cádiz raid failed, each blamed the other.

James VI of Scotland acceded to the English throne in the spring of 1603. Matters grew worse for Ralegh. Earlier, he had openly questioned James Stuart's suitability for the Crown of England. Furthermore, many disliked Ralegh intensely. Lord Henry Howard, Earl of Northampton, Ralegh's enemy for more than twenty years, was now able to turn the newly crowned James I against him, insinuating that Ralegh was a traitor and a suspected atheist, along with Henry Brooke Lord Cobham, and Henry Percy, 9th Earl of Northumberland. Robert Cecil, though interested in Ralegh's Guiana, did not trust the man.

By May 1603, just a few weeks after he took the throne, James I had recalled all the monopolies Elizabeth had issued to Ralegh and granted them instead to his own people. Ralegh lost his positions as Captain of the Guard and governor of Jersey, and the occupancy of his residence, Durham House, in London. Henry Percy, Earl of Northumberland, had written to King James defending Ralegh, but to no avail.[14] Northumberland admitted that Ralegh was indeed 'insolent, extremely heated' but would prove no threat to James, adding that there are 'excellent good parts of nature in him, a man who is disadvantageous to me in some sort, which I cherish rather out of constancy than policy, and one whom I wish your Majesty not to lose, because I would wish that not one hair of a man's head should be against you that might be for you'.

Ralegh, though, was thought to be an obstacle to making peace with Spain, and peace was a cornerstone of James' foreign policy. On meeting Ralegh, the king exclaimed: 'Ralegh, Ralegh, O my soul, mon, I have heard rawly of thee.' John Aubrey was later to write in his *Brief Lives* that Ralegh was by princes 'rather to be afraid of than ashamed of. He had that awfulness and ascendancy in his aspect over other mortals.'[15]

Between 12 and 16 July 1603 Ralegh went to Windsor to join the king on a hunting party. Cecil approached him; Ralegh was to remain to answer some questions. By 20 July he was in the Tower of London suspected of treason as part of the Bye and Main plots to unseat James and put Lady Arabella Stuart on the throne. Ralegh's subsequent trial was a notorious miscarriage of justice in which he was convicted on hearsay rather than real evidence. Also convicted, but later pardoned, were Henry Brooke Lord Cobham, Lord Grey of Wilton, and Sir Griffin Markham. These three were to be executed on 10 December 1604, but before he signed their death warrants, James had already ordered a stay of execution for them. On the morning Ralegh was to be executed, he learned he had been reprieved, though not pardoned. By 16 December he was again imprisoned in the Tower. He was to remain there for the next thirteen years.

In the years 1596–1603 England had a real chance to plant a tropical England. The time was still ripe, and Ralegh and others did their best. Cumberland brilliantly took San Juan, thus gaining a base for England in the Caribbean. Having and holding the port was quite another matter, though, as disease turned success into failure; disease had notably killed off Hawkyns and Drake. If taken at this flood, the English might have gone on to greatness. But such labour was to be lost, undone by politics at home.

ten

No Scallop Shell of Quiet, 1604–10

El oro y amores eran malos de encubrir.
(Gold and love are hard to hide.)

Seventeenth-century Spanish proverb

After Ralegh sailed to Guiana in 1595 and publicised it as another Eden, many others sought it. Captain Charles Leigh again set sail for Guiana on 21 March 1604, this time from Woolwich in the 50-ton bark *Olive Plant*, with a crew of forty-six men and boys.[1] He reached the Barbary Coast in April, then sailed to the Cabo Verdes and on to the Caribbean. On 10 May he noticed a change in the colour of the sea, from clear blue-green to opaque and white. Two days later, about five in the morning, the ship reached two islands in the mouth of the River Amazon and anchored in 3 fathoms. Leigh and eight of his best men took the ship's boat towards shore, where Indians approached them to trade maize and blue-headed parrots for hatchets, knives, glasses and beads.

Leigh then made for the River Wiapoco, latitude 3° 30' N, anchoring there on 22 May 1604. Leigh took possession of the land in the name of King James. Two of the Indians had been to England and let Leigh know that the English were welcome to settle there. In exchange for a site on high ground on the north side of the river, Leigh agreed to help the local Indians against the Caribes and other hostile tribes. Leigh and thirty-five men and boys stayed on when the *Olive Plant* sailed back to England in June, taking 'five salvages' (savages) and letters to Leigh's brother, Sir Olave Leigh, reporting their success and a request that he send supplies to the colonists. Sir Olave soon sent out two ships.

Meanwhile, Charles Leigh and others explored 120 miles up the River Aracawa, trading cotton yarn and raw cotton wool for tobacco as they went. They were well received by the mainland Indians, who fed the party dried tiger's flesh, dried hog's flesh and small fish. Leigh asked about gold, and an old man pointed further up into the country. Too far to travel for the present, Leigh turned downstream and returned to the ship. The party had been away six days. But while Leigh had been exploring upriver for minerals, his servant at the settlement had been stirring up mutiny among the other settlers. All had hoped for easy riches. On returning, Leigh faced rebellion. The mutineers had eaten the victuals that were to have sustained the colonists until they had harvested their crops. 'Our potatoes which should have lasted us two months, were wholly spent hereupon being far distant from the Indians, who inhabit at the mouth of the river, forty miles from the falls, how we should be furnished with victuals from them in our extremity.' The mutineers, he writes, 'stood in defiance of the voyage, and told me plainly they would not stay, do what I would or could'. Somehow Leigh defused things, 'what by fair means and what by foul, I brought them all to consent to stay one whole year, through all extremities, if it were possible to make a full trial both of people and country, and to plant upon Mount Huntley, according to their promise'.

Leigh continued to take orders from the Indians for their wax, long white feathers, flax, tobacco, parrots, green and black monkeys, cotton yarn and raw cotton wool from the bolls, sweet gum, red pepper, urapo and ariepo woods, spleen stones, matite stones, roots and berries thought to be medicinal.

Leigh had planned to stay in Guiana seven or eight months to seek out mines and to assay minerals. In a letter dated May 1604 to his brother he writes that he intends to settle at the head of the River Caroleigh (Wiapoco), on the high ground he calls Mount Oliphe that overlooks a bay. There he will build houses, plant vegetable gardens, construct a shallop, and send twenty men in her to help the local Indians fight the Caribes. On 14 June Leigh had purchased for 'a few hatchets', houses and gardens

> planted with cassava, and potatoes sufficient for all my company: The situation of our houses is in the pleasantest and most fruitful place of all their habitations. And because it is a small village of six or seven houses; and the first place of our settled abode I have named it Principium: The hill on which it stands being part of the mountain on the west side of the entrance of the river, I have named Mount Howard, to honour the remembrance of my Lord Admiral, of whom heretofore I have received many favours [Charles Howard, 1st Earl of Nottingham].

With work, writes Leigh, the country could be made to yield sugar cane, cotton, fine flax, long pepper ('if there might be vent for it in England'), woods, dyes and gums, especially one sort of gum, 'which I am persuaded will prove very rich'.

Leigh also mentions that he has sent along 'a piece of a stone taken out of a mana-tee or sea cow. I am given to understand that a little thereof beaten into powder, and drunk in wine or ale, will in few hours cure any man that is troubled with the stone [gallstones?].'

Two Dutch ships have bought up all the available flax (over 10 tons), paying such high prices for it that Leigh can get none. But he does not doubt that next year he should be able to fill a ship with flax and other commodities. The Dutch have told him that in Holland flax fetches sixpence per pound, though some report that it fetches sixteen pence, which Leigh believes,

> for my weavers tell me that they will warrant it to dress exceeding well, and then it must need be excellent fine grounds for any stuff; for cotton here is little, not worth the speaking of, yet the country will yield abundance, and in six weeks the seed will yield cotton, and it bears continually and plentifully. I pray you sir send me more weavers, for I know not how to get anything spun for them, for the [Indian] women here are put to that extreme labour, that they have no time to spin, for they only fetch water, cut wood to burn, and bring it home upon their backs. They gather all their roots, and bring them out of their gardens, they make all their bread which is very laboursome, they dress all the victuals, make all the drink, attend upon the men while they are at meat, and besides, they dress up their houses in their kind, and nurse their own children: so as they are always toiled with labour, and have little or no time to spin. For sugar canes the world does not yield better soil for their increase, and whereas in Barbary it is fifteen or sixteen months before they come to perfection, here they grow up in ten months.

He needs more hatchets, beads, knives and looking-glasses for the Indians. These items had gone for buying victuals, but mostly 'to stop the mouths of my mutineers and monstrous sailors; to whom also I have promised two third parts of my iron'.

Leigh asks for 100 men sent out as soon as possible:

> to abide here, all labouring men and gardeners, for such are the fittest here for a time, with a few carpenters; and with them three or four good pieces of ord-nance with shot and powder; also fifty calivers for the men that stay here: If you can send these men in two ships, I doubt not but to lade one of them back in three months after arrival, and the other which I wish may be the *Olive Plant*, I would keep here and fit her for a frigate to keep and command the river.

In a few years, Leigh writes, the country will yield satisfaction beyond expecta-tion. He writes to his brother that he has contacted King James, the Privy Council and the Lord Admiral:

I pray you procure Sir Walter Ralegh's Indian or my Lord Admiral's, for I want an interpreter exceedingly, here is but one, and he understands but little to any purpose. I pray forget not to send preachers, sober and discrete men, and such as are well-persuaded of the Church government in England, &c. From Principium, or Mount Howard this second of July 1604.

By September, three months since the departure of the *Olive Plant*, Leigh and the colonists were growing weak from poor diet, disease and the tropical climate. And the promises of the Indians were proving merely air. The account continues:

Before and after the sickness of our captain, many of our men fell sick, some of agues, some of fluxes, some of giddiness in their heads, whereby they would often fall down: Such grew chiefly of the excessive heat of the sun in the day, and of the extreme damp of the earth, which would so moisten our *hamacas*, or cotton beds, wherein we lay a yard from the ground, that we were fain to imitate the Indians in making fires on both sides under them. And for all that we could do, some nine of our company were dead before our ship's arrival [sent by Leigh's brother].

Besides we were mightily vexed with a kind of worm, which at first was like to a flea, and would creep into the feet especially, and under the nails, and would exceedingly torment us, the time it was in, and more in the pulling out with a pin or needle, if they were few. But one of our men having his feet overgrown with them, for want of hose and shoes, was fain to submit himself to the Indians' cure, who tying one of his legs first with his feet upward, poured hot melted wax which is black upon it, and letting it lie upon it till it was thoroughly cold, they forcibly pulled it off; and therewithal the worms came out sticking in the same, seven or eight hundred in number. This man was named John Nettleton a dyer of London, which afterward was drowned.

As Leigh was tending to his fledgling colony on the banks of the Wiapoco, on 28 August 1604 the English and Spanish signed the Treaty of London at the old Somerset House. The long and undeclared war between England and Spain was officially over. It had been smouldering in the West Indies since the 1520s, and had burst into flame in 1585 when Elizabeth signed the Treaty of Nonsuch to aid Dutch Protestants against the Spanish, and had become an inferno when the Armada attacked in 1588.

The terms of the Treaty of London clearly favoured the Spanish. The English agreed to end their support of Dutch Protestants. The English would end attacks on Spain's overseas trade, especially in the Americas. In return, the Spanish would recognise England as Protestant. By 1604 things had changed. Hawkyns and Drake had died in 1595–96. England had had little success in high-seas depredations, had failed in the attack on Cádiz in 1596, and had failed to take the

Azores in 1597. Spain's attempts to mount another armada had come to nothing; Philip II had died in 1598 and had been followed by Philip III. Queen Elizabeth had died in 1603, succeeded by James Stuart as James I. Within months, the new monarch saw Ralegh tried, convicted of treason and committed to the Tower. Both countries were exhausted by the cost of war. Both wanted peace. The treaty addressed that aim, at least in Europe. But in the tropical Americas, the old enmities remained. The Spanish insisted on their hegemony, the English their right to trade and settle unclaimed land.

Castaways, Guiana-bound

In response to his brother Charles' request, Olave Leigh despatched more men and supplies to the fledgling colony on the banks of the Wiapoco. The *Oliph Blossome* cast off from Woolwich on 14 April 1605 under the command of Captain Cataline and young Captain Nicholas Saint John. The author of this account is John Nicol, a gentleman 'being desirous to see the world'.[2]

Contrary winds and currents put them well off course for Guiana, and with just four or five months' victuals. Sixty-seven men and Captain Saint John went ashore on 23 August 1605 at St Lucia, an island fierce with cannibalistic Caribes. For five or six weeks there was peace, the English and Caribes trading trinkets for victuals and 'drinking of tobacco and *aquavitae*'. One day though, the Caribes attacked, drove the English into the surf, and with their 'great Brazil swords they struck out our men's brains'. John Nicol survived: 'I only with three arrows in me, by running into the wood and swimming over a standing lake escaped.' The battle continued for seven or eight days. Only nineteen English survived, 'sore wounded with their arrows'. In what seemed like a miracle, these same Indians then brought the wounded English cassava, potatoes and plantains.

One traded a *piragua* for hatchets, knives and beads. The crew fashioned a mast and sail for the canoe. On Thursday 26 September at one in the morning, with just one *arrico* of water and one small firkin of rice, the survivors set out to sea. Nichol relates that there was 'not one having skill in the mariner's art', and that they were 'without card or compass' to direct them:

> We sailed by the sun in the daytime, and by the stars in the night, going always betwixt southwest and by west. The victuals that we had were not sufficient to serve that company for three days. For we had not above twenty biscuits, three cassavi cakes, a dozen plantains, and some thirty potatoes, and some four or five gallons of water, and a little barrel half full of rice.

The victuals were gone in two days, the water in three. Master Garret had given each two men a dish of rice twice a day, washed in salt water and eaten raw.

During the next week, a storm refilled their water casks. Sea birds that perched on the gunwale provided flesh. These, dried in the sun and salted with a touch of gunpowder, were then eaten. Writes Nicol:

> our boat's brim was so near the water, that every wave came over it, ready to sink us, but that four of us continually did lade the water forth by courses. Now, on the tenth day one Thomas Morgan died, not being able to live of that small allowance, and at noon we threw him overboard. Within an hour after it pleased God to glad us (who were likewise ready to follow our fellow) with a joyful sight of land, unto the nearest part whereof we made as fast as we could.

But the wind went dead calm and night fell before they could reach shore. In the dark the *piragua* drifted onto the rocks and split up.

Next morning Nicol and another hauled the damaged boat onto the shore, and with their swords made a bulkhead in the middle, fastening it with daggers, knives and bodkins, and stopping the leaks with their shirts. For four or five days they hauled the *piragua* along the coast until they were rescued by a party of Spaniards, Indians and 'Negroes'. The English were nursed back to health, and then were brought before the governor. Some thought the English were devils; some thought they should be canonised 'but that we were Lutherans'. The priests told them that the Spanish would gladly bestow their daughters and goods on them if they would stay. Nicol and three others embarked about 20 April for Cartagena, where they were imprisoned and then transported to Spain. From there Nicol found his way back to England, arriving on 2 February 1606. He had been away nearly a year. He never did reach Guiana.

The Guiana Colony

John Wilson of Wansted, Essex, lived for two years in Guiana and was 'one of the last ten to return into England from Wiapoco' in 1606.[3] Captain Charles Leigh and Sir Olave Leigh had sent him out with fifty others who arrived on 20 May 1604. Wilson observes that the colony might have thrived had not the company mutinied. Captain Prinx and his crew on the *Phoenix* were discontented as well, and Prinx jumped ship and took homeward passage in a Dutch vessel. When the *Phoenix* left Wiapoco for England about 1 July 1605, she brought back many of the settlers and what meagre bits the colony had produced.

In England Sir Olave quickly resupplied the ship and sent out 'thirty men of sundry trades'. The *Phoenix* left Woolage and arrived at the Wiapoco colony on 15 January 1606. The colonists had believed the ship would not be returning to them. Despondent, they had not stirred from their houses since the *Phoenix* had left for England the previous July. They were 'for the most part extreme sick, and some of them dead', writes Wilson. With no commodities that would bring a profit, the soldiers became disgruntled, 'insomuch they wished themselves in England again'.

Leigh in a letter recounted what had happened to the colony since the ship had left them. Sickness had been so severe that the colonists were too weak to travel inland for trade goods, but on about 14 March he and others nevertheless joined with the Wiapoco Indians to fight the Caribes. Some died not in fighting but of the bloody flux. The weather was foul. Once back at the ship, Leigh resolved to return to England for provisions. Aboard the ship, Leigh himself came down with the flux before they could sail. Captain Huntly secretly buried him ashore on 20 March before setting sail on 2 April 1605, promising those left at the colony that a ship would return within seven months with provisions.

Sir Olave Leigh had indeed provisioned a great flyboat, 170 tons, to go to Wiapoco. But the vessel never reached the colony, now just thirty-five settlers. Olave Leigh arranged for a Dutch vessel from Middlesborough to take the new governor, Richard Sacksie, fourteen settlers and some slaves to the colony. The vessel arrived at the River Wiapoco on about 1 May 1605, a month after the *Phoenix* had departed. After three weeks there, the Dutchman had sold the slaves in exchange for commodities, and on 21 May took aboard colonists who wanted to return to England. That same day a Frenchman sailed in, and on leaving, after two months of trading, took off ten more settlers.

As of mid-July 1605 the colony of Wiapoco consisted of just ten men, but those ten, surprisingly, were in good health. Wilson tells that their weeks passed 'spending our time in planting of carow called flax, whereof we planted about twenty English acres of land, and some tobacco'. The Indians supplied the English with food, so that the colonists 'lived very good cheap'. Wilson admits that the colonists would have been more diligent in procuring commodities from the Indians had it been English vessels that called in at Wiapoco. But the Dutch and French had come instead, buying local manite stone and flax. Now there were just nine English left, and these were soon packing to leave. They embarked on the Dutch vessel *Hope* on 31 May 1606. From Amsterdam, John Wilson and eight others crossed to England. Wilson praises the Dutch for the 'great kindness they showed myself and others of our nation'.

Guiana yet continued to attract still more English adventurers, despite its problems. Just four months after the last of Charles Leigh's colonists left, another Englishman staked his fortune on the site. William Turner, son of a London physician, sailed to Guiana in 1606.[4] He arrived in early September. Turner's account begins on 14 August 1606, when at about two in the afternoon, his ship's lookout sighted Barbados to the SSW. His ship sailed on to St Lucia, where 'the people go naked, having very long hair, and are very honest, kind-hearted people'. But in reality the Caribes there stole the ship's boat and kidnapped three sailors. At Guiana, Turner finds it 'monstrous hot all the day long till it be noon, and then there blows a cool breeze: And at noon you shall always have thundering and lightning without any rain for the most part'. He did not stay long. By 9 November he was at Puerto Rico, and on 22 December at the Azores, where his journal ends.

Fat Cow for Spanish Friar

Master Henry Challons, gentleman, writes that on Tuesday 12 August 1606, he set out from Plymouth for the Indies as captain of a small 55-ton vessel, the *Richard of Plimouth*.[5] Aboard were twenty-nine Englishmen and two Indians. His aim was to explore and, if conditions were right, to leave colonists to settle. The *Richard* was victualled for eleven or twelve months. The pilot of the *Richard of Plimouth* and author of the account was John Stoneman of Plymouth. The year before, Stoneman had been in Virginia with George Waymouth. The *Richard*'s master, Nicholas Hine of Cockington, near Dartmouth, made first for Madeira, then the Canaries. After a transatlantic passage of six weeks Captain Challons' landfall was St Lucia, latitude 14° 20' N. Loading wood and water there, the crew encountered forty or fifty Caribes, the same ones, writes Stoneman, who just the year before had slaughtered Captain Nicholas Saint John's company. Off Dominica, Stoneman saw a white flag being waved from the shore. He rescued a Spaniard, Franciscan Friar Blasius, held as a slave by the Indians. Two others had been killed, but Blasius was spared because he showed the Indians how to rig a sail for their canoes. The captain put the friar ashore at Puerto Rico, and in thanks, herdsmen brought the English a fat cow.

The small English ship was later taken by a fleet of eight sail. The Spanish put a crew aboard the *Richard*, but when they could not make her sail well they recruited two English crew to help them. Nor could the Spanish fleet stay in formation, writes pilot Stoneman. In early December the Spanish pilot could not find the Azores. After ten days Stoneman was asked to show his skill and find them. He did so, and more. With obvious satisfaction Stoneman writes: 'The pilot himself brought me his instruments, and besought me most earnestly to assist him, and to appease the company. Whereunto by their much importunity I yielded. And [later] by God's assistance on Christmas Eve, after our English account, I brought them safe to the bar of Saint Lucas, being the first ship of the whole fleet that arrived there.'

The English were imprisoned. One, Robert Cooke of London, died of the flux:

[The Spanish] caused his body to be drawn up and down the prison by the heels, naked, in most contemptible manner, crying, 'behold the Lutheran', as five others of our company being then in prison beheld: And so laid him under the conduit, and poured water into his dead body. This done, they cut off his ears, nose and members, as the Spaniards themselves confessed unto us, and so conveyed his body we could never learn whither, although we proffered them money to have his dead corpse to bury it.

After three months in prison, Stoneman bribed his guards to have liberty to go into the city by day and report back to the prison at night. Outside, Stoneman learned from a Dutch merchant living there that as the pilot had been in Virginia and would not provide details, the Spanish had 'resolved to bring to the rack and torment me, whereby to draw some further knowledge by confession from me, before any discharge might come for us'. On the next morning, 23 October, Stoneman and others fled from Seville. They made it to Lisbon and on 14 November, the winds being fair, they took passage in a small vessel from Bideford, the *Marget*. They landed at St Ives, Cornwall, on 24 November 1606.

> This I had rather noted to the end that it may be the better considered what numbers of ships and men have gone out of England, since the conclusion of peace between England and Spain [the 1604 Treaty of London], in the way of honest trade and traffic, and how many of them have miserably miscarried. Having been slain, drowned, hanged or pitifully captived, and thrust out of their ships and all their goods.

Beyond the line and even within it, the Treaty of London did not always apply.

Virginia, Once Again

While Ralegh was directing his Guiana enterprise from the Tower of London, others had taken up the seed of his first dream: the short-lived Virginia settlement of 1584. Twenty-two years later, other Englishmen were to try again. In December 1606 three ships set out from London to settle up the River James in the Chesapeake Bay: the *Susan Constant*, Christopher Newport, captain, 120 tons, 116ft, 17 crew, 54 passengers; the *Godspeed*, 68ft, 13 crew, 39 passengers; and the *Discovery*, 49ft, 9 crew, 11 passengers. It was a long, five-month passage. Newport's three ships dropped anchor up the River James off a low marshy island in May 1607. Later, on the mainland, the colonists would call their settlement Jamestown. It was the nineteenth attempt at planting a colony in North America.

Jamestown was to be the second permanent English settlement in North America. Far to the north, but along the sailing route homebound, was St John's, Newfoundland – the first one. Throughout the sixteenth century, St John's had long been the last port for provisioning and victualling before sailing eastward for England and Europe. It was also the base for English, French, Portuguese and others fishing for Grand Banks cod. Humphrey Gilbert sailed into the port in 1583 to reprovision. By virtue of his royal charter, on 5 August he declared it English. Ralegh's Guiana came twelve years later, in 1595. Later still was Jamestown in 1607, and again later, Plimouth in 1620. By the time of the Plimouth settlement in the 1620s, St John's, after some forty years, was indisputably English.

In 1607, to investors or second sons, the prospects of an English Guiana looked rather better than an English Virginia. However tenuous, the settlement along the Wiapoco had at least already sent back to England cargoes of flax, dyes, woods, tobacco and linen, and there was the ever-seductive prospect of striking gold. But Virginia? It was, in 1607, a fractious, mutinous, sickly venture that was to take another twenty years to show any permanence and profit from sot-weed, tobacco. More promising, in strong contrast within North America, were the efforts of Frenchman Samuel de Champlain, who had planted settlements in Acadia in Nova Scotia as early as 1604–07. Well up the St Lawrence River he was to found Quebec City in 1608 and later would become the first European to explore the Great Lakes. More promising, still to come were the Dutch fur-trading posts to be built in Albany and Manhattan in 1613–14.

English Separatists had been migrating to Holland for some years, most in autumn 1607, some six months after Newport had landed his settlers in the Chesapeake. For thirteen years these Separatists had lived first in Amsterdam and then in Leyden. They too wanted a new life and initially considered settling in Ralegh's celebrated Guiana, but they were put off by Theodor de Bry's depictions of cannibals so graphically pictured in Dutch books. Later, in September 1620, 100 colonists (later to be called Pilgrims, and founders of the Congregational Church) were to sail in the *Mayflower*, 160 tons, from Plymouth, and after a long passage, to anchor in Cape Cod Bay and step ashore on 21 December. They would set about building the houses and fortifications of the Plimouth plantation. Half that colony would die from starvation, cold and disease before the spring came.

In Guiana, 'gold good cheap'

Return now to 1607. During the summer Ralegh wrote from the Tower of London to Robert Cecil, Earl of Salisbury.[6] In that letter Ralegh writes that considering his advanced years, if given a ship, or two or three, he would hardly 'become a runnegate [runaway] and live from my wife, children and friends in a strange country'. Ralegh writes that he is now in his mid-fifties, an old man: 'My times are not long in the world and I shall not be able hereafter (if now) to perform such a journey. Your Lordship may have gold good cheap and may join others of your honourable friends in the matter if you please, for there is enough.'

About the time Ralegh wrote to Cecil, he also wrote to John Ramsay, one of James' Scottish favourites.[7] Ramsey, created Viscount Haddington in June 1606, was one of the many 'night-grown mushrumps' knighted by James soon after he took the throne, to the disdain of the English. Ralegh wanted Ramsay to raise money for the undertaking. If he were to stray from the plan, he tells him, 'let them cast me into the sea'. If he does not guide them to a mountain covered with gold and silver ore near a navigable river, he writes, let the commander have commission 'to cut off my head there'. Ralegh says he will post a £40,000 bond to this effect, difficult to do, as Lorimer points out, since Ralegh's Sherborne estate was worth only half that sum.

As well as settling in the Orinoco, English settlers had been colonising the River Amazon. William Davies, barber and surgeon, spent ten weeks there in 1608. In his account he explains that the Amazon has continual tempests of lightning, thunder and rain, commonly for sixteen or eighteen hours a day.[8] Its waters are full of alligators, water serpents, 'great store of fresh fish, of strange fashions' and 'muskitas' (mosquitoes), 'a small fly, which much offends a stranger coming newly into the country'. Both men and women go naked, but to keep the mosquitoes away 'they do use to anoint their bodies, both men and women, with a kind of red earth, because the muskitas, or flies shall not offend them'.

Regarding their nakedness, he says, though they have 'not so much as one thread about them to cover any part of their nakedness, the man takes a round cane as big as a penny candle, and two inches in length, through the which he pulls the foreskin of his yard, tying the skin with a piece of the rind of a tree about the bigness of a small pack-thread, thus making of it fast about his middle, he continues thus till he have occasion to use him'. In each ear is a reed or cane, about the size of a swan's quill, half an inch long, that is bored through the lobe of the ear. At the bridge of the nose 'he hangs in a reed a small glass bead or button which swings two and fro when he speaks'. The women observe no fashion, but are 'stark naked as they were born, with hair long of their heads, also their breasts hang very low, by reason they are never laced or braced up'.

Davies and his party could find neither gold nor silver ore in the Amazon, just 'great store of hens'. When the Indians turned down ten shillings in coin as payment for some hens, Davies bought a couple for a Jew's harp.

Harcourt's Guiana, Tobacco & Topazes

An Oxfordshire man of Stanton Harcourt, Robert Harcourt, set out for Guiana on 23 March 1608.[9] He addresses his account to Prince Charles. His fleet included the *Rose*, 80 tons; the pinnace *Patience*, 36 tons; and a shallop built at Dartmouth, the *Lilly*, 9 tons. Harcourt sailed in the *Rose* with Captain Edward Fisher, Captain Edward Harvey, Master Edward Gifford and Harcourt's cousin, Thomas Harcourt. Besides them, he had thirty-one landsmen (gentlemen and others), two Indians and twenty-three mariners. Harcourt's brother was captain of the *Patience*, with twenty landsmen and eleven mariners. In the *Lilly*, Jasper Lilly was master and had with him one landsman and two sailors. In all, says Harcourt, there were ninety-seven people, of which sixty were landsmen, a number 'too great for so few ships of no greater burden'.

The fleet sailed from Dartmouth on 23 March 1608, put back because of a wind shift, then set out again the next morning. The small fleet reached Tenerife on 7 April, where it reprovisioned before setting off across the Atlantic. From there, he stood for the Wiapoco in Guiana, having 'a prosperous wind, fair weather, and a smooth sea'. His was a quick passage of just four weeks. He reached the River Amazon on 9 May. The river 'puts out into the sea such a violent and mighty stream of fresh water, that being thirty leagues from land, we drank thereof, and found it as fresh and good as in a spring or pool'. On 11 May the vessels made landfall at eight in the morning and anchored in 5-fathom water. Harcourt's three vessels explored the wide mouth of the Amazon, then sailed to the River Wiapoco, where on 17 May they anchored. Indians came out in two or three canoes. One had been in England and had served Sir John Gilbert for many years. The Indians brought hens, fish, potatoes and more, all of it, writes Harcourt, 'heartily welcome to my hungrie companie. In recompence whereof, I gave them knives, beads, Jew's trumps, and such toys, which well-contented them.' Harcourt writes:

[I] brought to their remembrance the exploits performed by Sir Walter Ralegh in their country, in the reign of our late sovereign Queen Elizabeth, when (to free them from servitude) he most worthily vanquished the Spaniards at Trinidado: Burned their town, took their governor Don António de Berrío prisoner; delivered five of the Indian kings imprisoned, and bound by the neck with collars of iron; and with great labour and peril discovered the River of Orenoque, and the countries adjoining.

The Orenoqueponi had willingly become subjects of the 'late Queen; all which they well remembered, and said that Sir Walter Ralegh promised to have returned again unto them long since'.

Harcourt replied that Ralegh had not returned because the queen had given him employments of great importance, but that in his stead he had sent Captain Keymis. In the intervening thirteen years, he said, the queen had died, Ralegh had been committed to the Tower, and the present king has been busy ordering the affairs of the kingdom. The king now lets his subjects travel abroad, and Harcourt and his company have come to find a place to settle among the Indians. The Indians replied that they were pleased the English had come but counting the numbers of the English, there were too many mouths for them to feed. They had no provision for feeding so many strangers. They could furnish the English with houses, but in exchange, would like help in defending themselves against their enemies. This, they reminded Harcourt, was something promised by Ralegh and Leigh but not yet delivered. Harcourt replied he would leave his brother there to live with them, as well as some of the company, until more men could be sent from England to defend them. This satisfied the Indians. More aqua vitae, more festivities.

Harcourt surveyed the area for defence. The best site was a great rocky mountain, nearly inaccessible behind woods and rocks but a perfect harbour and site for a fort. Prospectors in Guiana had searched for gold, diamonds and semi-precious stones. They found topazes. These, Harcourt observes, if well cut and set in gold by a 'cunning workman', would 'make as fair a show, and give a lustre as any diamond'. Harcourt notes that sugar is a major crop in Guiana. Tobacco too is profitable, 'which albeit some dislike, yet the generality of men in this kingdom doth with great affection entertain it. It is not only in request in this our country of England, but also in Ireland, the Netherlands, in all the easterly countries, and Germany, and most of all amongst the Turks, and in Barbary.' It holds its price, is profitable for merchants and custom paid on it enriches the Crown. In 1610 tobacco imported into England was worth £60,000, a substantial sum. Tobacco, claims Harcourt, will 'bring as great a benefit and profit to the undertakers, as ever the Spaniards gained by the best and richest silver mine in all their Indies, considering the charge of both'.

In exchange for local commodities, goods to be traded were many and varied: axes, hatchets, bill-hooks, knives, tools, nails, large fish hooks, Jew's trumps, harping irons, looking-glasses, blue and white beads, crystal beads, hats, pins, needles, salt, shirts, bands, linen and wool clothes, swords, muskets, calivers, powder and shot. And gold? The reports of abundant gold, writes Harcourt, were false, and have generated mutinous anger amongst the company 'almost to the confusion and ruin of us all', though white spar found suggested that there was also gold and silver to be mined.

At the ship there was a problem. The hot sun was drying out her water casks, and the master told Harcourt that if he stayed longer in Guiana, the ships would not be in shape to return:

> All my company would starve at sea for want of beer, cider, and water, for all my cask was spoiled, because it was not iron-bound; the wooden hoops flew off, by reason of the heat of the climate; and our beer, and cider (whereof we had good store) did leak about the ship, that we could hardly save sufficient to relieve us, if we made a longer stay upon the coast.

Robert Harcourt appointed his brother, Captain Michael Harcourt, to stay behind and run the Wiapoco colony. When Harcourt at last reached the ships, he sailed for Trinidad, then for Nevis, where he enjoyed 'an hot Bath … one of the best and most sovereign in the world. I have heard that diverse of our nation have there been cured of the leprosy.' Harcourt left Nevis on the afternoon of 16 October. His ships passed Saint Christopher's, St Maarten and Anguilla. From there the course was homeward, past the Azores and through storms, until reaching Cape Clear at the south-west tip of Ireland, 'where against our wills we arrived at Crooke Haven the twenty nine of November'. Crookhaven is the first secure port when coming in off the Atlantic. Harcourt proudly writes that during the voyage he had lost only one landsman in Guiana, and just one sailor and an Indian boy at sea on the return passage.

The 1604 Treaty of London, favourable to Spain, was regarded in the American tropics as just another scrap of paper. The enmity continued. As the privateer captain Christopher Newport landed colonists in the James River in 1607, to the south there was considerable activity in Guiana, with much talk from Charles Leigh and Robert Harcourt of profitable commodities; all this while Ralegh was locked away in the Tower.

eleven

MAIDENHEADS LOST, 1611–18

Give me luck, and cast me into the sea.

Seventeenth-century proverb

In two letters written from the Tower in 1611 to Robert Cecil, Earl of Salisbury, Ralegh notes that his 1607 offer to send a ship to Guiana had been rejected, and that now he has lost his Sherborne estate, his fortune is less by £20,000.[1] Nevertheless, Guiana is still important, and it was still of interest to Cecil. The year before, Cecil had invested £600 in Sir Thomas Roe's voyage. Information sent to England by Roe may have sparked things between Cecil and Ralegh. Ralegh's letter to Cecil points out that Guiana could yet be the king's 'for the hazard of a reed, for the adventuring of an old and sorrow-worn man whom death would shortly have delivered *invito domino*, and who, if he had done well, it had been for the King'. Ralegh writes that as for his health, he finds 'little cause to hope to outlive another winter'. In the second letter from Ralegh to Cecil and the Privy Council, written before July 1611, Ralegh notes that Keymis will be leading an expedition of two armed ships to Guiana to find the San Thomé mine. Captain Moore, servant to Sir John Watts and a mariner who had sailed to Trinidad in 1609, 1610 and 1611 for tobacco, would command the vessels. Ralegh hopes that Keymis can find the mine, but if he cannot, Ralegh writes that his 'poor estate is utterly overthrown and my wife and children as utterly beggared'. He ends his letter by reminding Cecil that if the voyage brings back half a ton of ore, then by agreement Ralegh is to have his liberty, and that in the meantime, his free pardon is to be left in the hands of Anne, wife of King James, until the expedition returns. Vain hope.

Though it was to be another six years before Ralegh's situation altered, the years 1611–17 saw much political change. King James was strapped for money, and in February 1611, when Parliament was not forthcoming, he simply dissolved it. Apart from a brief period in 1614, Parliament was not to meet again until 1620.

Sir Thomas Roe and the *Lion's Claw* returned from the tropics in July 1611. Roe had explored 300 miles up the River Amazon, planted a colony near its mouth, and had visited Harcourt's settlers on the Wiapoco. By canoe, in Guiana he had negotiated thirty-two rapids but could not find the long sought after Manoa. He reported in a letter to Robert Cecil, dated 28 February 1611, that he had heard Spaniards at the Port of Spain speak of gold mines along the Orinoco, of a stronger fort at San Thomé and more colonies along the Orinoco.

At home, Ralegh's old enemy the Lord Treasurer, Sir Robert Cecil, who was not yet 50, died of dropsy on 24 May 1612. Another death was that of Prince Henry, who had got his father James I to agree to free Ralegh by Christmas 1612. In October the 18-year-old youth had contracted 'putrid fever' (typhoid) while in the polluted Thames, and despite being treated with Ralegh's elixir, died on 6 November 1612.

Worse still for Ralegh, the new Spanish ambassador arrived in London in 1613. Diego Sarmiento de Acuña, later 1st Conde de Gondomar, was a skilful and experienced diplomat whose chief aim was to stop the ongoing English attacks on Spain's colonies in the West Indies. Across the ocean, the 1604 treaty was merely paper. Gondomar and his agents set to work to see that Ralegh's plan would fail.[2] On the matter of containing Ralegh, Gondomar had James' willing ear. Politics aside, Gondomar told James that there was more than a grain of truth in Ralegh's claim of gold in Guiana. Some eight or nine years before, says Gondomar, Ralegh had demonstrated that his samples of sandy soil contained 'very fine gold at the rate of sixteen percent of weight'. Though true, the tests may have been bogus. Gondomar writes that Ralegh had petitioned for 500 men, asking the king only for ships. He would underwrite the voyage himself. Ralegh writes that if he fails, let him be beheaded aboard his ship.

The ambassador notes further that Ralegh's problem is that even with Cecil dead, there were still those of Cecil's party who would thwart Ralegh's plans, as they 'know and are guilty of the injustice and unreasonable way he [Ralegh] has been treated. All the more because they know him to be a man of great spirit and haughty aspirations such that having done such a signal service for the crown his authority and greatness would continue to increase as one who is known as the greatest seaman of this kingdom as his deeds in the Indies attest.' His deeds as vice-admiral in all Elizabeth's fleets were well known, and no seaman was greater in matters of the sea, 'not even the famous Captain Draque'. The English king, says the Spanish ambassador, might very much want to give him his freedom from the Tower, reminding him that he knows well that:

[Ralegh] never undertook anything against his person or state, his Council having condemned him in its arbitrariness and caprice and without the appearance of one single direct witness, other than those who they said they had heard it and those with presumptions and suspicions, nor had evidence against him been investigated. Thus his condition is solely [due to] the power and greatness of his enemies who, having much influence with the king, still detain him, the king not wishing to offend them, considering the fear they have of [Ralegh].

The ambassador shrewdly points out that given the poor state of the treasury, James might well find Ralegh's plan attractive. Gondomar writes he has learned one supporter alone had promised Ralegh 100,000 ducats for the voyage, 'nor will there be a gentleman or merchant in all of England who would not be delighted to advance him money on account for such an enterprise, because of the great confidence which they have in the personal good fortune and courage of the said Ralegh'.

Ralegh, aging in the Tower year by year while ever campaigning for his Guiana enterprise, was busy conducting tests in mineralogy, mixing elixirs from tropical herbs and writing his magnum opus, the *History of the World*. His manuscript was entered in the Stationers' Register in April 1611, though publication was delayed until March 1614. When it at last appeared on the stalls, its title page showed no author, but all knew who had written it. The king was not pleased and, in January 1615, had the popular book suppressed for two years.

Meanwhile, John Rolfe in 1614 had planted his first crop of tobacco in Virginia, the crop that was to save the moribund colony. The same year, Pocahontas accepted an invitation to dine at the Banqueting Hall. By 1616 the anti-Spanish sentiment in England had returned. Ralegh's star was at last in the ascendant. Guianian gold might buy Ralegh his freedom and could potentially pay off the king's financial problems.

Ralegh's *Destiny*

On 19 March 1616 Ralegh was released on parole from the Tower to pursue his Guiana project. He was still unpardoned, still under sentence of death, and accompanied by a keeper, but at least he was outside his prison walls. Ralegh went straight to shipwright Phineas Pett at Deptford and ordered a new ship built. She was to be named the *Destiny*, 440 tons, and would be admiral of a fleet of six to sail for Guiana. Ralegh spent £10,000 of his own money on the venture, virtually everything he owned. Another £20,000 came from other sources. On 26 August Ralegh received his commission from the Privy Council, with Ambassador Gondomar's provision that Ralegh was not to do any injury to Spaniards.

The *Destiny*, heavily armed with thirty-six cannon, was launched on 16 December 1616. Two weeks later, in January 1617, Ralegh was freed from his keeper. He could now pursue Guiana unhampered. Besides the *Destiny*, Ralegh's fleet included the *Encounter*, 160 tons, seventeen cannon; the *John and Francis*, 150 tons, twenty cannon; the *Flying Joan*, 120 tons, fourteen cannon; the *Husband*, 80 tons, six cannon; and the pinnace *Page*, 25 tons, three cannon. In all, it was a powerful fleet of nearly 1,400 tons, with around 140 cannon. With despatch, Gondomar sent the details to Spain. On 3 May Ralegh issued orders to his commanders: divine service twice daily, no stealing or gambling, no smoking between decks, no swimming unless authorised, no sleeping on the ground.

Ralegh's fleet of thirteen (others had joined him) set out from Plymouth on 19 June. Bad weather forced the fleet into Kinsale and Cork. Only at six on the morning of 19 August, with light winds north-easterly, then south-westerly, did the fleet finally set out from Cork for the tropics. Ralegh's own journal of the voyage tells the tale.[3]

Navigation by dead reckoning aboard the prophetically named *Destiny* is shown in Ralegh's careful daily records of the ship's heading, wind direction, and time and distance run for each heading. On 18 September he reached Gomera, in the Canaries. The Spanish opened fire and Ralegh replied by firing on their houses with some twenty shot from his demiculverin. He sent word to the governor that he needed only water. The two came to an understanding. There would be no hostilities, but just in case, the English ships would moor six ships broadside to the town, gun ports open, ready to fire. With a touch of his old gallantry, Ralegh sweetened the negotiations. 'By the Spaniard which carried my letter to the Count, I sent his lady six exceeding fine handkerchiefs and six pair of gloves.' She replied in a letter that she was sorry the island was barren, but please would Ralegh accept these tokens: 'Four very great loaves of sugar, a basket of lemons which I much desired to comfort and refresh our many sick men, a basket of oranges, a basket of most delicate grapes, another of pomegranates and figs.' He gave the lady's servants two crowns each and sent back 2oz of ambergris, 1oz of extract of amber, a great glass of rose water, 'a very excellent picture of Mary Magdalen, and a cutwork ruff'. The lady replied with breads, hens and more fruit: 'a basket of delicate white manchett, and two dozen of fat hens with diverse fruits'. Meanwhile, for three very hot days the crew filled 240 pipes of water.

On the evening of 5 September the fleet made for the Cabo Verdes, course south-south-westerly. Men began falling sick, and by the time Ralegh arrived there, two crew had died and another fifty were ill. By Monday 28 September, Michaelmas Day, there were sixty sick. The weather was deteriorating, and on 1 October Ralegh records that a 'hurecano fell upon us with most violent rain, and broke both our cables'. He was, he writes, 'so wet as the water ran in at my neck, and out at my knees, as if it had been poured on me with pails'. The rest of the fleet lost cables and anchors, including the *Confidence*, a flyboat and a pinnace, and the vessels of the fleet scattered during the storm.

On 4 October the *Destiny* set her course westward for the Americas. 'We filled our sails at twelve and stood away athwart the ocean steering away towards the coast of Guiana southwest by west.' During the passage, officers and crew died. One was the principal ore refiner Mr Fowler, a serious loss. At first the days' runs were about 30 leagues.[4] On 8 October, at latitude 11° 39' N, Ralegh's servant Crabb died: 'I had not any one left to attend me but my pages.' The *Destiny* entered the doldrums. A day's run slowed to 4 or 5 leagues.[5]

Stewed Prunes for a Burning Fever

More men died. Ralegh's cousin, Mr Hews, 'a very honest and civil gentleman having laid sick but six days', passed away on Sunday 12 October. 'We were at this time in miserable estate', Ralegh says, 'not having in our ship above seven days water, sixty sick men and nearly four hundred leagues off the shore, and becalmed'. By 13 October the fleet had lost Captain John Pigott, Ralegh's lieutenant-general by land, and Ralegh's 'honest friend Mr John Talbot, one that had lived with me eleven years in the Tower, an excellent general scholar and a faithful true man as lived'. Lost too were Mr Gardner and Mr Mordent, 'two very fair conditioned gentlemen, and my own cook Francis'. Captain Jennings also died and many more fell sick.

The winds in the doldrums were variable. For the twenty-four-hour run from noon to noon, 16–17 October, 'we could make no reckoning, for the wind changed so often between the south and the west, as after the changing of the tack divers times we found it best to take in all our sails and lie at hull, for the wind that blew was horrible with violent rain'. By nightfall on 18 October, the wind was gone and the weather was calm. Ralegh estimated (correctly) that their position was about latitude 9° N.

It was hot and humid, more men were sick and Ralegh's cousin Payton, a lieutenant in Wat Ralegh's company, died. Sunday 19 October was 'stark calm and extreme hot' and progress was just one league, yet the next night, fierce winds again forced them to lie ahull – a pattern that continued. On 22 October the crew watched a 'cloud called a spout' spin 2 miles to windward of them, a rare occurrence in those waters. By 24 October, with water nearly all spent, Ralegh ordered half-rations for all. His interest in navigation remained unusually keen. The noon sight on 28 October put the *Destiny* off the Brazilian state of Pará and the mouth of the River Amazon, on the equator, at longitude 68° W, given the +3° E variation for that time. Finally, on 29 October it rained, and the crew could fill three hogsheads of water.

But then Ralegh fell ill:

> The last of October at night rising out of bed, being in a great sweat by reason
> of a sudden gust and much clamour in the ship before they could get down the
> sails, I took a violent cold which cast me into a burning fever than which never

man endured any more violent nor never man suffered a more furious heat and an unquenchable drouth [thirst], for the first twenty days I never received any sustenance but now and then a stewed prune but drank every hour day and night, and sweat so strongly as I changed my shirts thrice every day and thrice every night.

What was generally a fourteen-day Atlantic passage had turned into a troublesome one of thirty-eight days. On 11 November the *Destiny* and the other vessels at last made landfall at the River Wiapoco. Since Ralegh had been there in 1595, many had called, claimed the land for England, planted colonists and sent home some commodities.

Now, at last, in November 1617 Ralegh was back. But he was too sick to leave his berth and go ashore. He sent his skiff to enquire after his old servant Leonard Regapo, who had returned to England with Ralegh in 1595 but was now living along the River Conawini. This man was 'the Indian who had been with me in England three or four years, the same man that took Mr Harcourt's brother and fifty of his men when they came upon that coast and were in extreme distress, having neither meat to carry them home nor means to live there but by the help of this Indian'. But Leonard had moved some 30 miles inland. Ralegh could not wait.

He weighed anchor and stood away for Caliana, the River Cayenne, where the *cassique* Harry, Ralegh's servant in the Tower for two years, now lived. Anchoring past some islands on 14 November, Ralegh sent his barge ashore to enquire after the *cassique*. Harry sent his brother to Ralegh with two other *cassiques*, promising provisions for the English. Ralegh writes: 'Mine own weakness which still continued, and the desire I had to be carried ashore to change the air, and out of an unsavoury ship, pestered with many sick men which being unable to move, poisoned us with a most filthy stench, persuaded me to adventure my ship over a bar where never any vessel of burden had passed.'

Ralegh's barge had also attracted the attention of 'one Janson of Flushing', a merchant mariner who had been trading there for about a dozen years. Having local knowledge of the waters, he offered to help bring the *Destiny* and the rest of the fleet over the bar. The *Destiny* drew 17ft, but Janson told Ralegh that at high tide, the 3 fathoms of water would be just enough to enter. It worked. On 17 November the English vessels all crossed the bar and anchored inside in 4 and 5 fathoms. Ralegh's old servant Harry arrived, having 'almost forgotten his English'. He brought great store of cassava bread, roasted mullets, a great store of plantains and pistachios. Ralegh was so ill he did not dare eat. After a day or so he was carried ashore to sit under a tent, where pork and armadillo helped him regain his strength. The other sick were brought ashore and the *Destiny* was fumigated. Captain Hastings, who had died ten days earlier, was buried ashore next to Sergeant Major Hart and Captain Henry Snedall. From 17 November until

4 December, while the remaining sick recuperated, the healthy crew assembled the barges for river travel, cleaned the ships, and trimmed and filled the water casks. The blacksmith set up his forge.

Leaving the *Chudley* there, the *Destiny* and the rest of the fleet set out on 10 December for the River Orinoco; there were 400 soldiers and sailors. Among those commanding the land companies was Ralegh's son, Wat Ralegh. In overall command was Ralegh's trusted and faithful lieutenant, Lawrence Keymis. The landing party set out on the 10th carrying a month's victuals. The ships remaining behind first anchored at Punto Gallo until the end of December and then, on 31 December, weighed and turned north for Port of Spain, anchoring 10 leagues away from the town. Ralegh sent Vice-Admiral Captain Penington to Punto Gallo to await Keymis' return. Ralegh crossed to the mainland on the last day of January 1618, where he heard from captured Indians that the English had taken San Thomé, killed the Spanish governor and others, and that the survivors had fled into the hills. Two of the English captains had been killed, they said. It is here that Ralegh's journal abruptly ends.

Wat Ralegh Leads Attack

What had happened? Schomburgk speculates that on 14 February Ralegh got the letter from Keymis, written on 8 January from the Orinoco, with the news that Ralegh's son Wat had died in attacking the town. Ralegh's letter to Sir Ralph Winwood says of Wat's death, 'with whom, to say truth, all the respects of this world have taken end in me'.

Spanish accounts show that James I had betrayed Ralegh to the Spanish. A Spanish royal *cedula* dated 19 March 1617 had warned Trinidad, Guiana and El Dorado that 'Gualtero Reali' was preparing a fleet to invade Guiana, and gave details. Since Keymis' voyage to Guiana in 1596, the Spanish had moved the town of San Thomé upstream from the mouth of the Río Caroní. It now had 140 houses and stronger defences. On the night of 1 January, according to the Spanish, 500 English had disembarked from a caravel and five launches and attacked the town. The Spanish at first retreated, but then counterattacked. The English fired the town. In the raid, Wat Ralegh and four others were killed.

In his *Apologie*, Ralegh writes that Keymis and his men, on finding not a village but a town, had set up camp a couple of leagues west of a mine, where that night they were surprised by a Spanish attack. The English, Keymis writes, had counterattacked and entered the town, when the Spanish attacked again. Wat Ralegh, notoriously hot-headed and not waiting for the musketeers, had led a company of pikes forward and had been fatally shot. He had come onto a Captain Erinetta with his sword, who took the small end of his musket and struck Ralegh on the head with the stock and felled him. The Spanish had retreated into a house adjoining the marketplace and fired on the English through loopholes. The Spanish then retreated into the woods. Once in possession of the town, Keymis set out to discover the mine, writes Ralegh. He had received Keymis' 8 January letter on 14 February 1618. In it, Keymis writes about attacking the Spanish and that, after much searching, he could not find the mine. These were just excuses, as Ralegh saw it.

After the skirmish, Keymis sent three vessels upriver 110 leagues to the River Guarico on a twenty-day expedition to find the mine. At a cost of some 250 men to disease or enemy fire, the English had only 600 reales, 150 quintals of tobacco, church bells and other items to show for their efforts. Spanish records value the destruction and plunder taken by the English when they left San Thomé on 29 January 1618 at 40,000 reales.

From the mouth of the river, Keymis sailed across to Trinidad. He now had to face Ralegh with the details of how his son Wat had been killed, that it was the English who had attacked the Spanish, and that they had found no gold. Ralegh was furious. He blamed Keymis. As Ralegh wrote in a letter to his wife Bess, 'he [Keymis] had undone me, and that my credit was lost forever'. Keymis replied to Ralegh that he then knew what to do. He went to his cabin and shot himself in the chest with his pistol. Hearing the shot, Ralegh called out. Keymis replied that as the piece had been long charged, he had only shot it off to discharge it. Ralegh was satisfied with the answer. The bullet had only glanced off Keymis' rib, but when Keymis' cabin boy came in half an hour later, he found Keymis on his bunk, dead, 'having a long knife thrust under his left pap through his heart, and the pistol lying by him'.

The crew of the *Destiny* mutinied, but Ralegh brought them back under his command with a golden hope of capturing the *flota* from Nueva España. From Saint Christopher's, Ralegh wrote to Bess on 21 March 1618: 'I protest before the majesty of God, that as Sir Francis Drake and Sir John Hawkyns died heartbroken when they failed of their enterprise, I could willingly do the like … My brains are broken.' Ralegh's *Destiny* and the others made landfall back at Kinsale, Ireland. Ralegh reached Plymouth that July.

Spanish News of Ralegh

A Spanish account, written after Ralegh's first Guiana voyage in 1595 but before his 1617 sailing, reports that in 1595 Ralegh, Keymis, the *cassique* Topiawari and another had reached a mountain in Guiana, and that the *cassique* had taken a pick-axe and dug down through the turf to sand yellow like gold.[6] And did Ralegh's sand contain gold? For more than three years he had been using the sand, with its high lustre, to blot the ink of his many letters written from the Tower. One day, being in conversation with a certain goldsmith he told him that he understood that a ship [Newport's return to England in 1607] had returned from the Indias with a sample of certain soil from which, it was said, a quantity of gold was extracted, and Raley said to him, apropos of this, that he should look at the sand which was on the table in which he had been assured there was gold. The goldsmith asked him to give him a little of that sand and, giving it to him, Raley said that he promised to give him one hundred ducats for the first grain of gold that he extracted from it. The goldsmith returned the following day laughing and requested that he give him the promised one hundred ducats because he had separated twelve percent of fine gold from the sand. Raley was astonished and delighted, and immediately paid him the hundred ducats. Raley then made three or four different trials and even better, was able to extract sixteen percent gold ore from the sand.

Gondomar notes the opinion of Antoine de la Fevre de la Boderie, French ambassador in England from 1605 to 1609 and ambassador extraordinary in 1610, who felt it was a great loss that Ralegh was kept prisoner, since he could 'do more good and service to this crown than all the English put together, but that if he were released and given his freedom he would immediately take revenge upon his enemies and would be intolerable just as he used to be when he was the favourite of the queen Lady Elizabeth'. Gondomar felt the pulse of the English nation, 'which for the most part holds to neither law, God or conscience', and of Ralegh: 'This Raley is continuing his pretensions in this business and he trusts that in the end he will make the voyage, chiefly because the necessity and stringency to which the affairs of this crown are reduced will oblige them to go as far as to try and test this business.'

Gondomar (almost certainly the author of the letter) urges that the 'surest and safest thing to do in this business is to find out when his ship will leave here for that place, which will be next Spring, and to ascertain likewise approximately when it will return, about which I will be able to give notice in due time, and, this being known, to give orders to have it seized on its return'.

The diplomatic spies did their work well: 'It is important that nothing of this matter comes to the ears of the English ambassador in Spain because, if he gives account of it in his letters to Raley and the latter suspects how news of his enterprise came to be divulged, those who wish to disrupt this undertaking would be deprived of the power to do it.' Gondomar had tried his best to prevent Ralegh's departure from England the previous June, 1617:

And even though I protested against it and tried to stop the voyage of this gentleman, his sworn promises to return with great treasures without injury to anybody and the many friends and influence which he had in England, advanced so that it was impossible to stop the voyage, even though the king much wished it, and all that it was possible to extract was that he gave warranty and sureties before he left not to do injury to the vassals or the territories of our lord king and that the king of England gave me his hand and word, as he told me, that if the [said] Walter Rale should do harm to the territory or the vassals of our lord king he would hand over him, with his ships and men so that our lord king could order punishment of them in Madrid.

The ambassador advised his king about Ralegh that 'there could be no trust in his promise nor his word telling him also in much detail and exactitude the ships men artillery and munitions which he carried and the site where the mine was which he had revealed to the [English] king with great secrecy which was in Guiana up the river Arenoco near to San Thomé'. He then gave his ambassadorial advice: 'I represented to His Majesty how necessary it was to forewarn [San Thomé] and have an armada in Trinidad to defeat and punish the English.'

Given all this, it is no surprise that the attack on San Thomé failed and that on Ralegh's return to England in July, he was quickly arrested. By August 1618 he was back in the Tower. When he entered it on 15 August 1618, among the personal effects taken from him were 'a Guiana idol of gold and copper', a map of Guiana, another of New Granada, one of the River Orinoco and one of Panamá, as well as samples of Guianian silver and gold. In a hasty trial, the sentence of death passed on Ralegh in 1604 was reaffirmed. Ralegh, then about 66, was led to the scaffold on the morning of 29 October 1618. It took two blows for the headsman to sever his head from his body.

Ralegh was gone, but his dream of an English tropical paradise did not die with him. The colonies along the Amazon and Orinoco rivers – more than a dozen of them – were to linger on into the 1640s, dying off largely because of the Spanish to the west and the Portuguese to the east. But by 1618, thanks to sea power, England had the weather gauge in pursuing what was to be her course: commerce, colonisation and empire. If not Guiana, then perhaps elsewhere under the tropic sun.

The years 1611–18 had brought great changes: first, Robert Cecil and Prince Henry died in 1612; the Conde Gondomar became ambasssador in 1613; and in 1617 Ralegh was paroled and sailed in the *Destiny* for Guiana, his last hope. There, his son Wat died, Ralegh's chances for pardon died, and that autumn, the last of the great Elizabethans was beheaded, his own tropical endeavour quite dead.

twelve

EPILOGUE: AFTER 1619

A star to every wandering bark,
Whose worth's unknown, although his height be taken.
William Shakespeare, Sonnet 116, published 1609

'In spite of King and Council, in spite of courtiers and of scaffolds', Ralegh had written in his *Apologie*, 'Englishmen shall know all about Guiana'. English interest in Guiana, and Irish interest as well, did in fact continue to grow.[1] When Ralegh was first there in 1595, the lands along the Amazon and Orinoco, an area nearly half the size of Europe, had hardly been exploited by Portugal or Spain. For the next fifty years, from 1596 to 1646, the Portuguese began only four settlements along the Amazon.[2] The English and Irish started fifteen. Four of these flourished for some years. From 1612 to 1623 they grew to six. From 1624 to 1646 there were five new ones. Between 1638 and 1642, the English planned a further large settlement on the Río Tapajós (500 miles above Pará, where it flows into the Amazon). And between 1642 and 1646 the Irish intended to colonise the entire Ilha Joannes at the mouth of the Amazon. Such was the allure of the tropics in England and Ireland well into the seventeenth century.

The Virginia Company established an elected legislative House of Burgesses in 1619. It was an act of optimism but also a desperate attempt to bring order to a poorly run settlement. Jamestown's site was a bad one, subject to typhus and typhoid, and it was populated, as Captain John Smith had early on complained, by too many gentlemen caterpillars of the Commonwealth who were unwilling to work. So poor were its prospects that six years after Ralegh's beheading, James I was to revoke the company's charter in 1624 and make it a Crown colony.

In 1619, the year following Ralegh's *annus horribilis*, English Puritan dissidents from Holland had not yet embarked. But in 1620 a small group of English

Separatists sailed from Plymouth for the New World in the *Mayflower*. They anchored in New England and began what was to become the third permanent English settlement in North America, after St John's and Jamestown.

Four years later, in 1624, the English first moved offshore from the coast of the Spanish Main into the Caribbean, and on Saint Christopher's set up the first of many English-speaking colonies.

Plague in England

The plague in England was particularly severe in 1625. In the last week of June the weekly death toll in London was 593, but by the second week of August it was 4,463. In the matter of diseases, England seemed no better than the tropics.[3] Captain Nathaniel Butler in 1625 compared the return of the English fleet from Spain, racked with the plague, to the disaster of the Armada: 'I will only say in brief that since '88 there was never the like expedition frustrated, and so frustrated.' A merchant sea captain, Butler recommended the familiar ratio of one man per 2 tons of shipload on long voyages, and, as had others including Ralegh before him, he advised washing decks with vinegar and water, burning tar between decks and locating the galley on the forecastle. It wasn't enough. Despite the recommendations, sailors were again dying in great numbers. The standards aboard ship had slipped.

Much had changed in 1625 when the Reverend Samuel Purchas published *Purchas His Pilgrimes*, the successor to Hakluyt's *Principal Navigations* a quarter of a century earlier. With Ralegh's death an era had passed. Now, early in 1625, King James I died and his son Charles assumed the English throne, fervently believing he had been divinely appointed. Some thought otherwise.

To educate urban Londoners to the realities of life in colonial America, Captain John Smith, that rough soldier of fortune, sometime governor of Virginia and admiral of New England, published his manuscript *An Accidence … for All Young Sea-men* in 1626, with other books and editions to follow: *An Accidence for the Sea* in 1636; *A Sea Grammar* in 1653, 1691 and 1699. Though William Borough had published his *Variation of the Compass* in 1581, John Smith's 1626 book is the first English manual of practical seamanship. It was followed in 1644 by lawyer and pirate Sir Henry Mainwaring's *Seaman's Dictionary*.

English Islands Under Tropic Sun

As early as 1605, the English had attempted to settle on the Caribbean island of St Lucia, but only in 1638 did they succeed with the first permanent settlement there.[4] In 1609 the English had unsuccessfully tried to colonise Granada, and it was only in 1763 in the Treaty of Paris that Britain gained the island. Bermuda, 1615, known as part of the Somers Isles, fits the period, though those islands lie outside the latitudes of the American tropics. Six years after Ralegh's death, Saint Christopher's in 1624 was successfully colonised by the English. Nine years after that, Lord Willoughby founded a settlement in Suriname.

In 1627 the English found Barbados abandoned by the Amerindians and set-tled on the uninhabited island, establishing its House of Assembly in 1639. English Puritans settled on the islands of San Andrés and Providencia off Colombia in 1629. Englishman William Claibourn was granted a patent for Roatán, in the Bay Islands of Honduras, in 1638, a claim challenged by the Spanish for the next 150 years, until the English lost it in 1782 and in 1859 ceded it and other islands to Honduras.

Antigua, Barbuda and Redonda became English in 1632, followed by Montserrat in the 1640s. In 1638 English buccaneers and black slaves from Jamaica began to arrive in the cays off Belize to cut wood for textile dyes, and though the 1763 Treaty of Paris gave England the right to cut wood there, it recognised Spanish dominion over the area. It was not until 1862, in response to the Americans' Monroe Doctrine, that Belize became a British colony as British Honduras. The name Belize came in 1973, and in 1980 a United Nations resolu-tion recognised Belizean independence, restated in the Belize Act the following year. Guatemala to date, however, still claims sovereignty over all or part of Belize. Eleuthera was a Separatist colony (and the first in the Bahamas) started in 1648 (or 1647) by seventy settlers and twenty-eight slaves from Bermuda. Anguilla became British in 1650.

Suriname saw sixty English settlers arrive under Captain Marshall, followed by an expedition in 1651. It grew to a colony with more than 500 plantations when the sugar boom of the 1650s made it rich, and after a complex history, that land became British Guiana in 1814, more than 200 years after Ralegh claimed it for England.

Admiral William Penn (Royalist father of the Quaker William Penn, the son who was given Pennsylvania by the king for his father's accomplishments) and General Robert Venables took Jamaica, the Caribbean's third largest island (after Cuba and Hispaniola), from the Spanish for England in 1655. In 1666 the Virgin Islands became British. In 1722 the British first attempted to colonise St Vincent, but only in 1796 were they successful.

The British occupied Guadeloupe in 1759, and in 1762 Martinique as well. But at the Treaty of Paris in 1763, Louis XV ceded Canada, Senegal, the Grenadines, St Vincent and Tobago to Britain in exchange for Guadeloupe, Martinique and some other West Indian islands. Such was the power of sugar.

That same year Dominica became British. The British took Trinidad from the Spanish in 1797, formally ceded to Britain in the Treaty of Amiens in 1802. Most of Spain's former colonies in the American tropics became independent after 1821, and over the years, most of Britain's colonies were granted independence. Political, economic and fiscal alliances in the Caribbean continue to cluster and then fracture. The area from the Amazon to the Orinoco, roughly Ralegh's Guiana, is now Brazil, Suriname, French Guiana and Guyana. English Guiana was overtaken by the Dutch, then regained by Britain in 1796; lost, then officially won by treaty in 1814. Ralegh's River Orinoco is now part of Venezuela, which to date still lays claim to part of Guyana, independent from Great Britain since 1966.

Since James Monroe promulgated his doctrine in 1823, warning Europeans not to meddle in American affairs, the Americans have more recently taken up the English-speaking cause in the tropical Americas. Panamá gained her independence from Spain in 1821; then in 1856 in the Watermelon War was put down by US marines. In 1903 US control of the canal was set by treaty 'in perpetuity' (but was rescinded in 1999). A final place among the English-speaking American tropics is Puerto Rico, early sought by Hawkyns, Drake, and briefly held by Cumberland in the 1590s. In 1898, at the conclusion of the Spanish-American War, the island became a US territory, and in 1917 Puerto Ricans became American citizens.

The politics of the region at the present time are still changing. From the start, change has always been the constant in the Caribbean, and so it will continue, as long as there are imperial palms and beaches of fine sand, as long as there is a thirst for gold, minerals, oil, brazilwood and sugar.

Paradise Lost, Regained

Why, then, did the English not succeed in establishing a greater presence – through trade, warfare or settlement – in the American tropics? Clearly, the Spanish and Portuguese prevented them from doing so. Their long-established political and military power in both Europe and the New World, especially naval power, was overwhelming. During the critical years 1580–1640, when the fleets of Portugal and Spain were under Spanish command, English ships faced the combined firepower of the two greatest navies of Europe, as Hawkyns, Ralegh, Drake and Grenville repeatedly discovered in the English Channel, but especially in the Azores, the Caribbean and along the Spanish Main.

The English enterprise in the tropics was hindered for other reasons as well. From the start, it was an area that was nominally Portuguese and Spanish as a result of the Pope's division of the New World at the Treaty of Tordesillas (1494, 1506), whereby any newly discovered lands went to the Portuguese and Spanish. All other countries, including England, were excluded. Throughout the sixteenth century, England, as a marginal power, did not want to antagonise Spain, the most powerful country in Europe.

Despite Spanish fears, with only a few celebrated exceptions, English ships throughout the sixteenth century were not at all successful in attacking the Spanish treasure fleets, nor could the English establish any permanent naval bases in the Caribbean until the 1620s. The tropical heat overwhelmed the English, who functioned better in a cooler climate more similar to that of England. Because of the climate and the northern Europeans' vulnerable immune systems (unlike those of the Africans), disease and sickness spread quickly and killed off many of the ships' crews, soldiers and colonists.

The Indians of Latin America were better organised politically than their counterparts in North America so there was no political vacuum into which the English could move. Next, whereas the Portuguese and Spanish conquests had strong royal backing, the English ventures, for fear of Spanish reprisal, were mostly private ones. Though there might be royal money invested in an English voyage, it was not an official undertaking by the Crown but rather an individual or corporate effort. To Spanish eyes it was piratical. As for money, unlike Portugal and Spain, Elizabethan England simply did not have enough for large-scale ventures until late in this period, too late to stop the flow of gold and silver. When Hawkyns and Drake finally did lead an English armada to the Caribbean in 1595, the two commanders and hundreds of the men were fatally struck down by disease, and those left were too few to attack the Spanish. Too weak, too little, too late.

Despite such impediments, an English tropical paradise was no mere flight of fancy for a land where citrus trees bloom. Driven first by trade, the period between 1516 and 1618 found England hotly contesting Portuguese and Spanish claims to the area. Off Cabo San António, in the harbours of Cartagena and San Juan, along the banks of the Amazon and Orinoco, and at negotiations at Somerset House in 1604, England did what she could to challenge Iberian power. She lost.

From those voyages of Cabot and Pert in the Spanish West Indies in the early 1500s to Ralegh's Guiana in 1618, English ships sought command of the seas from Spain for a full 100 years in the Caribbean. Elizabeth's Protestant seadogs were fierce in their faith and strong in their lust for gold. They were tropics-bound in leaky ships. They suffered ague, the bloody flux, storm and starvation. They were a determined lot, who against the overwhelming odds of Spanish cannon, musket and sword, challenged Portuguese and Spanish hegemony with English blood, sweat and sea brine. Here was no cloistered virtue of principle so much as a pragmatic mercantilism that drove heavily armed English merchantmen to the tropics to put money in the purse, gold and silver in the coffers, nutmeg, flax, cochineal and brazilwood into the warehouses of Bristol, Southampton and London. Trade, not flag, was then and still is the true matter of Britain.

For a full century the Hawkyns, Drakes, Raleghs and scores of others in the American tropics sought to enter Spanish ports to traffique, and where they could, settle, or where they could not, make war. Five hundred years later, the seismic tremors of their efforts are still felt in the heat of trade and politics. The English mariner who sails under the tropic Caribbean sun must inevitably follow in the wakes plowed first by Elizabeth's seadogs.

NOTES

1. Brave New World, 1516–68

1. Richard Hakluyt (ed.), *The Principal navigations, voyages, traffiques & discoveries of the English nation … Richard Hakluyt … 1598–1600*, 12 vols. Extra Ser. 1–12. For the Hakluyt Society (Glasgow: James MacLehose & Sons, 1903–05), 10:5. Abbr. *PN*.
2. *PN*, 10:2–3.
3. Samuel Purchas (ed.), *Hakluytus Posthumus or Purchas his pilgrimes, contayining a history of the world in sea voyages and lande travells by Englishmen and others, by Samuel Purchas … 1625*, 20 vols. Extra Ser. 12–33. For the Hakluyt Society (Glasgow: James MacLehose & Sons, 1905–07), 16:106. Abbr. *PP*.
4. James A. Williamson, *Hawkins of Plymouth*, 1949, 2nd edn (London: Adam & Charles Black, 1969), 20.
5. *PN*, 11:23–5.
6. James McDermott, *Martin Frobisher, Elizabethan Privateer* (New Haven: Yale University Press, 2001), 191.
7. Quoted in Michael Lewis, *The Hawkins Dynasty: Three Generations of a Tudor Family* (London: George Allen and Unwin Ltd, 1969), 46–7.
8. Ibid., 47.
9. *PN*, 9:338–58.
10. Williamson, *Hawkins of Plymouth*, 38–9.
11. Ibid., 46.
12. *PN*, 10:7–8.
13. Harry Kelsey, *Sir John Hawkins: Queen Elizabeth's Slave Trader* (New Haven and London: Yale University Press, 2003), 15.
14. *PN*, 10:8.

15. Anthony's Roll, Pepysian MSS, Magdalene College, Cambridge.

16. *PN*, 10:9–63.

17. Clarke, *Atlantic Pilot Atlas*, 9. At that latitude, winds throughout the year are a generally reliable Northeasterly Force Four. But just there, sailing in January, Hawkyns had to contend with the northern edge of the Intertropical Convergence Zone, the ITCZ, where the north-east and south-east trade winds converge in a 120-mile band (2° of latitude) running WSW to Brazil.

18. The normal ratio at the time for crew to a ship's tonnage was about one man to 2 tons' displacement. At 910 tons, his ships could support about 455 men. Though his crew numbered 150, the additional 600 slaves put the number of mouths to feed at 750 – well over the limit.

19. Williamson, *Hawkins of Plymouth*, 91–2.

20. Ibid., 87.

21. *PN*, 10:64–74.

22. Kelsey, *Sir John Hawkins*, 56.

23. 'Florida' then meant most of southern North America, from the Atlantic coast below the Chesapeake to New Spain. See Ortelius, *Theatrum Orbis Terrarum*, 1584 edn, and Wytfiet, *Descriptionis*, 'Florida et Apalche', 1597.

24. James Clarke, *Atlantic Pilot Atlas*, 4th edn (London: Adlard Coles Nautical, 2006), 58–61.

25. Wright, *Spanish Documents concerning English voyages to the Caribbean, 1527–1568. Selected from the archives of the Indies at Seville*, Ser. 2, No 62 (London: Hakluyt Society, 1929), 131–52. Abbr. *SD*.

26. *PN*, 10:71.

27. *SD*, 134.

28. *PN*, 10:71–3.

29. *SD*, 152.

30. Clarke, *Atlantic Pilot Atlas*, 60–1; Rear Admiral William J. Kotsch, *Weather for the Mariner*, 2nd edn (Annapolis: Naval Institute Press, 1977), 167–8.

31. *PN*, 10:73–4.

32. Ibid., 10:74.

2. Storm Swell, 1569–76

1. *PN*, 9:378–97.

2. Irene A. Wright (ed.), *Documents concerning English voyages to the Spanish Main 1569–1580 I: Spanish documents selected from the archives of the Indies at Seville II: English accounts 'Sir Francis Drake revived'; and others, reprinted*, Ser. 2, No 71 (London: Hakluyt Society, 1932), 1–9. Abbr. *DE*.

3. *DE*, 9–10.

4. Ibid., 11.

5. Ibid., 12–5.

6. Ibid., 31–5.

7. Ibid., 245–326.

8. *PN*, 11:227–90.

9. In this earlier period a cable = 720ft or 120 fathoms (1 fathom = 6 ft). Now, a cable = 0.10 nautical mile or 608ft, or more roughly, eight shackles = 100 fathoms or one cable.

10. *DE*, 300.

11. Ibid., 302.

12. Ibid., 40–1.

13. Ibid., 44–5.

14. Ibid., 54–9.

15. Ibid., 68–70.

16. *PN*, 10:82–8; rpt. ed. *DE*, 334–8.

17. Wright's edition in *DE* takes as exemplar the text in *PN*, 10:77–81. Much of Oxnam's story, in telling detail, is found in an account by the Portuguese Lopez Vaz, written in 1586 from the River Plate. See also *DE*, ix, xlii, xlvii and Doc. 29, 327 ff. Sir Richard Hawkyns' account of Oxnam's voyage is found in Hawkyns' telling of his own unsuccessful 1593 voyage to the Pacific, published 1622, and found edited by Wright in *DE*, 339 ff. Williamson, Wright, Andrews, Parry and Kelsey are among the best authorities on Oxnam and Drake. Some other historians, for instance, have Oxnam setting out from Plymouth in 1574, 1575 or 1576, all on the same voyage.

18. James A. Williamson, *The Age of Drake*, 1938 (London: A. & C. Black, 1965), 133–44; *Dictionary of National Biography* (2007), s.v. 'Oxenham'.

19. One league is 3.18 nautical miles. The nautical mile (1 min. of latitude) is averaged as 6,080ft.

20. Vaz, in *DE*, 327–33.

21. Hawkyns, in *DE*, 339–41.

22. *DE*, 169–77.

23. Ibid., 115.

24. Vaz, in *DE*, 328, 230.

25. *DE*, 100–1.

26. Hawkyns, in *DE*, 340–1.

27. Vaz, in *DE*, 328–33.

28. *DE*, 132–5.

29. Ibid., 144–8.

30. Ibid., 149–52.

31. Ibid., 154–7.

32. Hawkyns, in *DE*, 330, 341.

33. *DE*, 232–4.

3. Near Gale, 1577–81

1. Several early authors narrate Drake's circumnavigation: Hakluyt (includes Vaz), 1598–1600, rpt. *PN*, 11:101–33, 148–62; Purchas, 1626, Hakluyt text 'reviewed and corrected', rpt. *PP*, 2:119–49; Nichols, *Drake Revived*, 1628, rpt. *DE*; John Wynter, commander of the *Elizabeth*, author, 'Edward Cliffe, Mariner', rpt. *PP*, 11:148–62; survivor Peter Carder, rpt. *PP*, 16:136–46. Among secondary accounts is the recent excellent Harry Kelsey, *Sir Francis Drake: The Queen's Pirate* (New Haven: Yale University Press, 1998). For Drake's circumnavigation, quotations from *PN*, *PP* and *DE*, the source is given contextually and cited, as necessary, in the notes.
2. *PN*, 11:133–47.
3. *DE*, 200–2.
4. *PN*, 11:153.
5. Ibid., 11:105–8.
6. *DE*, 223–31.
7. *PN*, 11:26–32.
8. *DE*, 232–4.
9. *PN*, 11:135.
10. *PP*, 2:129.
11. Ibid.
12. *PN*, 11:159–60.
13. Ibid., 11:264–87.
14. Ibid., 11:159–60.
15. *PP*, 16:136–46; Amilcar d'Avila de Mello, 'Peter Carder's Strange Adventures Revealed', *Mariner's Mirror*, 93, No 3 (August 2007), 261–8.
16. *PN*, 3:753.
17. Ibid., 11:118–23. Also 9:319–26.
18. Ibid., 11:118–9.
19. *DE*, 235.
20. Ibid., 236–7.
21. *PN*, 11:125–32.
22. Ibid., 11:34–9.
23. Ibid., 11:31–3.
24. See E.G.R. Taylor, *The Original Writings and Correspondence of the Two Richard Hakluyts* (London: Hakluyt Society, 1935), I: 139–46; George B. Parks, *Richard Hakluyt and the English Voyages* (New York: American Geographical Society, 1928).
25. Louis B. Wright, *Gold, Glory, and the Gospel*, 344.

4. Severe Gale, 1582–88

1. *PN*, 11:164–71.
2. Ibid., 11:172–202.
3. Ibid., 11:92–5.
4. Irene A. Wright (ed. and trans.), *Further English voyages to Spanish America 1583–1594. Documents from the archives of the Indies at Seville illustrating English voyages to the Caribbean, the Spanish main, Florida, and Virginia*, Ser. 2, No 99 (London: Hakluyt Society, 1951, issued for 1949), 1–3. Abbr. *FE*.
5. Taylor, *Original Writings*, II, 211–326; also Wright, *Gold*, 345.
6. *PN*, 10:88–97.
7. *FE*, 11–5.
8. Ibid., 15–6.
9. *PN*, 10:97–134; Mary Frear Keeler (ed.), *Sir Francis Drake's West Indian Voyage, 1585–86*, Ser. 2, No 148 (London: Hakluyt Society, 1981). Abbr. *DWIV* and used as the primary source for this voyage; Julian S. Corbett, *Papers Relating to the Navy During the Spanish War, 1585–1587* (London: Navy Records Society, 1898, rpt. 1987), containing the *Primrose* journal (in Keeler as Doc. 10). Keeler and Kelsey, *Drake*, 240–79, provide the fullest recent accounts of the voyage.
10. Kelsey, *Drake*, 256–7.
11. *FE*, 16–9.
12. Ibid., 20–2.
13. Ibid., 22–3.
14. Ibid., 25–7.
15. Ibid., 32–7.
16. *PP*, 2:149–85; *FE*, 46–52.
17. *FE*, 52–7.
18. Kelsey, *Drake*, 263–72.
19. *DWIV*, 202.
20. *PP*, 2:167–74.
21. Kelsey, *Drake*, 271.
22. *DWIV*, 105–6.
23. Ibid., 106, 202–5.
24. Ibid., 66–8.
25. *FE*, 60–1.
26. Ibid., 32–7.
27. Ibid., 64–129.
28. Ibid., 129–36.
29. Ibid., 161–3.
30. Kelsey, *Drake*, 274, has 27 May; Keeler, *DWIV*, 205, has 28 May in transcribing the *Primrose* journal. The difference may be because traditionally, the nautical day began at 1200 hours, the time of the noon sight.

31. St Augustine, Florida, is at latitude 29° 54' N; the Elizabethan printer wrongly has 36° N.

32. *DWIV*, 266. Keeler credits Quinn for this information.

33. Ibid., 69, 270–5.

34. Quoted in *DWIV*, 59–62.

35. Kelsey, *Drake*, 280–1.

36. *PN*, 11:202–27; *PP*, 16:5–106. Unless noted, *PN* followed in text.

37. *PN*, 11:290–347; *PP*, 2:149–85; Keevil, *Medicine and the Navy, 1200–1900*. Vol. 1: 1200–1649 (Edinburgh and London: E. & S. Livingstone Ltd, 1957), 95.

38. Keevil, *Medicine and the Navy*, 1:66–7.

39. *FE*, 163–4.

40. Ibid., 171–3.

41. Ibid., 178–80.

42. Ibid., 189–90.

43. Ibid., 192–5.

44. Ibid., 195–8.

45. Ibid., 220–5. As Wright notes in one of her early books, 1916 (quoted here 220, note 2): 'A Dominican, I think – a fellow of fine phrases (the first example I have found of true tropical eloquence)!' Indeed this is so.

46. *EPWI*, 40–9.

5. Profit in Piracy, 1589–91

1. Kenneth R. Andrews (ed.), *English Privateering Voyages to the West Indies, 1588–1595*, Ser. 2, No 111, Hakluyt Society (Cambridge: Cambridge University Press, 1959). Abbr. *EPWI*. Andrews' text, rather than *PN* or *PP*, generally followed. Portions of this chapter rely heavily on Andrews' painstaking work.

2. *EPWI*, 7.

3. Ibid., 31.

4. Andrews found that of the twenty-five voyages examined, fifteen made some profit, and three or four an extraordinary amount. Five lost money, and for the rest there is insufficient evidence, *EPWI*, 33.

5. Quoted in *EPWI*, 37.

6. G.C. Williamson, *George, Third Earl of Cumberland (1558–1605) His Life and His Voyages, A Study from Original Documents* (Cambridge: Cambridge University Press, 1920), 36–40.

7. *PN*, 10:156–7; *EPWI*, 53–5, prints Robert Abraham's deposition, more accurate than Hakluyt, as Abraham was aboard. Hakluyt gets the date of departure and various details wrong.

8. David Beers Quinn, Raleigh Aslin Skelton and Alison Quinn (eds), Richard Hakluyt, *Principall Navigations*, 1589 (Cambridge: Hakluyt Society, 1965). Abbr. *PLN*.

9. *PP*, 16:8–12.

10. Given the high-pressure weather system generally centred at the Azores (and the low-pressure cell over Iceland), these islands some 930 miles west of Lisbon have always been a key to both westward and eastward passage-making for sailing vessels in the Atlantic. In sailing west from England, the clockwise flow of wind to the east of the Azores high is southerly, hence favourable for reaching the Canaries and Cabo Verdes, where vessels joined the easterly trade winds. In sailing east from the Caribbean, the navigator seeks the two westerly trades generated by the bottom of the anti-clockwise Icelandic low and the top of the clockwise Azorean high. It is as if the ship eastbound is squirted through as these two contrary gears mesh. The Azores are thus central to the story of the American tropics. Many critical sea battles were fought off those nine islands.

11. *PN*, 11:381–4; *EPWI*, 59–85; *FE*, 244 ff.

12. Ibid., 10:166–7.

13. Ibid., 10:164–6.

14. *FE*, 244–5.

15. *PN*, 10:173–4.

16. *FE*, 246–9.

17. *PN*, 10:176–8.

18. *FE*, 258–9.

19. *PN*, 10:163–4.

20. Ibid., 10:158–9.

21. *PN*, 10:159–61.

22. Ibid., 10:161–3.

23. *PP*, 16:12–3.

24. *PN*, 10:194–203.

25. *PN*, 35:65–7; *PN*, 10:178–83; *EPWI*, 107–12.

26. In addition to Ralegh, and later Tennyson and many historians, see Peter Earle, *The Last Fight of the Revenge* (London: Methuen, 2004).

27. *FE*, 263.

28. Ibid., 264.

29. Ibid., 264–5.

30. Ibid., 266–7.

6. Indigo, Sugar, Penguins, 1591–93

1. *PN*, 11:389–416.

2. Keevil, *Medicine and the Navy*, 1:107.

3. *PP*, 16:146–77.

4. Ibid., 16:13–7.

5. *EPWI*, 173–4.

6. *PN*, 10:184–90; *EPWI*, 184–208.
7. Ibid., 10:190–3; *EPWI*, 209–18.
8. *EPWI*, 219–24. Andrews writes about just these two voyages.
9. *PP*, 16:18.
10. *EPWI*, 236–83.
11. Ibid., 298–307.
12. Ibid., 300–2.
13. Ibid., 308–25.
14. Ibid., 330–7.
15. Ibid., 338–76.
16. *PP*, 16:18–26.

7. A *Daintie* at Dear Cost, 1593–95

1. *PP*, 17:57–198.
2. Ibid., 17:199–204.
3. *PN*, 11:43–64.
4. *PP*, 16:22.
5. See Williamson, *Cumberland*, 126 ff.
6. *PN*, 10:203–12.
7. *PP*, 16:25–6.

8. Committed to the Deep, 1595–96

1. *PN*, 10:338–433; Robert H. Schomburgk (ed.), *The discovery of the large, rich, and beautiful empire of Guiana*, Ser. 1, No 3 (London: Hakluyt Society, 1848). Abbr. *DEG*; V.T. Harlow (ed.), *Colonising Expeditions to the West Indies and Guiana, 1623–1667*, Ser. 2, No 56 (London: Hakluyt Society, 1925); and Harlow, *The Discoverie of the large, and bewtiful Empire of Guiana, by Sir Walter Raleigh* (London: Argonaut Press, 1928); Joyce Lorimer (ed.), *Sir Walter Ralegh's 'Discoverie of Guiana'*, Ser. 3, No 15, Hakluyt Society (Cambridge: Cambridge University Press, 2006). Abbr. *DG*. Among the many recent studies are Robert Lacey, *Sir Walter Ralegh* (London: Phoenix Press, 1973); Stephen Greenblatt, *Sir Walter Ralegh: The Renaisssance Man and His Roles* (New Haven: Yale University Press, 1973); Stephen Coote, *A Play of Passion: The Life of Sir Walter Ralegh* (London: Macmillan, 1993). English voyages to the Orinoco and the Amazon rivers have since the 1840s been extensively edited by the Hakluyt Society.
2. Joyce Lorimer (ed.), *English and Irish Settlement on the River Amazon 1550–1646*, Ser. 2, No 171 (London: Hakluyt Society, 1989), 67.
3. *PN*, 10:213–26; *EPWI*, 377–98.
4. Keevil, *Medicine and the Navy*, 1:107.

5. For over forty years English navigators had been using (along with the astrolabe) the cross-staff, introduced to England by John Dee in the 1550s. The navigator must simultaneously fix in his sight the height (elevation or altitude) of the heavenly body and the horizon without shifting the instrument. In measuring the sun, he had to look directly at it and determine the angle (height) made from sea level to its centre and the horizon. Given the instrument and conditions at sea, it was easy to be wrong. Error can easily enter the calculations. In 1594, just a year before Ralegh sailed, John Davis invented the back-staff from a design made by Thomas Hariot, scientist and friend of Ralegh. This back-staff or quadrant staff was a better instrument, but by no means perfect. Its accuracy was to be improved over the next fifty years. The Davis quadrant staff could measure altitudes to 45° and, given its design, the navigator no longer had to look directly at the sun.

6. Schomburgk estimates that Ralegh sailed at most 250 miles and that he rowed up the River Orinoco as far as the River Caroní.

7. Quoted in Keevil, *Medicine and the Navy*, 1:105.

8. Coote, *A Play of Passion*, 52.

9. *EPWI*, 395–6.

10. Lorimer (ed.), *Ralegh's 'Discoverie of Guiana'*, contrasts the manuscript with the printed version.

11. BL, Sloane MS 1133 ff. 45r–52v, printed by Schomburgk and Harlow.

12. *LVDH*, 85–107.

13. Keevil, *Medicine and the Navy*, 1:107, diagnoses amoebic dysentery as the cause of death for both Hawkyns and Drake; J.B. Black, *Reign of Elizabeth, 1558–1603*, 2nd edn, Oxford History of England (Oxford: Clarendon Press, 1969), 341–2, dysentery for both; Lewis, *Hawkins Dynasty*, 16, that Hawkyns died of overwork and worry; Williamson, *Hawkins of Plymouth*, 341–2, Hawkyns' cause of death unrecorded; Kelsey, *Drake*, dysentery.

14. *PP*, 16:77–8.

9. Taken at the Flood, 1596–1603

1. *PP*, 16:301–9.

2. *PN*, 10:266–76.

3. Ibid., 10:441–501.

4. Ibid., 11:1–15.

5. The Wiapoco, now the Oyopok, latitude 4° N, at Brazil's border with French Guiana.

6. River Coritime or Courontyne, the border between Suriname and Guyana.

7. Guyana lies between latitude 2° N and latitude 8° N.

8. Lorimer, *Ralegh*, 307, n.1.

9. *PP*, 16:27–106; Williamson, *Cumberland*; Richard T. Spence, *The Privateering Earl* (Stroud: Sutton Publishing, 1995).

10. Lorimer, *Ralegh*, 311–24.

11. Ibid., 313–5.

12. *PP*, 16:292–7.

13. Quoted in Coote, *A Play of Passion*, 297.

14. Raleigh Trevelyan, *Sir Walter Raleigh* (London: Allen Lane, 2002), 354.

15. John Aubrey, *Brief Lives*, ed. Oliver Lawson Dick (London: Secker and Warburg, 1949).

10. No Scallop Shell of Quiet, 1604–10

1. *PP*, 16:309–23.

2. Ibid., 16:324–37.

3. Ibid., 16:338–51.

4. Ibid., 16:352–7.

5. Ibid., 19:284–97.

6. Lorimer, *Sir Walter Ralegh's Discoverie of Guiana*, 289–90. Abbr. *DG*.

7. *DG*, 290–1.

8. *PP*, 16:413–6.

9. Ibid., 16:358–402.

11. Maidenheads Lost, 1611–18

1. *DG*, 292–5.

2. Ibid., 299–300.

3. Schomburgk (ed.), *Discovery of Guiana*.

4. One league, as noted above, is 3.18 nautical miles, and one nautical mile is averaged as 6,080ft. Ralegh carefully records the ship's course, wind direction, time and distance run for each board; that is, he employed dead reckoning. The board was the traverse board, used each watch to determine course made good. It was a round piece of wood marked with the points of the compass, eight holes per point. Every half an hour (when the glass was turned) one of the pegs tied to the centre of the board was put in the hole on the ship's compass heading. At the end of each watch, course made good was figured from the pegs. Ralegh's journal shows the usual twenty-four-hour course run, calculated from noon to noon, when the sun's height was taken at its zenith. As longitude could not then be accurately determined at sea, it was only rarely recorded.

5. The doldrums near the equator, where the trade winds neutralise each other, are now called the Intertropical Convergence Zone (ITCZ).

6. *DG*, 300–5.

12. Epilogue: After 1619

1. British Guiana. With independence in 1966 the name changed to Guyana.
2. Lorimer, *English and Irish Settlement on the River Amazon 1550–1646*, xiv–xxv.
3. Keevil, *Medicine and the Navy*, 1:162–73.
4. Sarah Cameron and Ben Box (eds), *Caribbean Islands Handbook with the Bahamas* (Bath: Trade & Travel Publications Ltd, 1995), passim.

BIBLIOGRAPHY

Abbreviations

(Full entry given in sources below)

DE   Wright, Irene A. (ed.), *Documents concerning English voyages to the Spanish Main 1569–1580*

DEG   Schomburgk, Robert H. (ed.), *The discovery of the large, rich, and beautiful empire of Guiana*

DG   Lorimer, Joyce (ed.), *Sir Walter Ralegh's 'Discoverie of Guiana'*

DV   Jones, John Winter (ed.), *Divers voyages touching the discovery of America*

DWIV   Keeler, Mary Frear (ed.), *Sir Francis Drake's West Indian voyage 1585–86*

EI   Lorimer, Joyce (ed.), *English and Irish settlement on the River Amazon 1550–1646*

EP   Andrews, Kenneth R. (ed.), *English privateering voyages to the West Indies 1588–1595*

FE   Wright, Irene A. (ed.), *Further English voyages to Spanish America 1583–1594*

LVDH   Andrews, Kenneth R. (ed.), *The Last Voyage of Drake and Hawkins*

PLN   Quinn, David Beers, Raleigh Ashlin Skelton and Alison Quinn (eds), *Principall navigations, voiages and discoveries ... 1589*, 1965

PN   Hakluyt, Richard (ed.), *Principal Navigations Voyages Traffiques & Discoveries ... 1598–1600.* Rpt. 1903–05

PP   Purchas, Samuel (ed.), *Hakluytus Posthumus, or Purchas His Pilgrimes – 1625.* Rpt. 1905–07

SD   Wright, Irene A. (ed.), *Spanish documents concerning English voyages to the Caribbean 1527–1568*

Primary Sources

Andrews, Kenneth R. (ed.), *English privateering voyages to the West Indies, 1588–1595. Documents relating to English voyages to the West Indies from the defeat of the Armada to the last voyage of Sir Francis Drake, including Spanish documents contributed by Irene A. Wright*, Ser. 2, No 111, Hakluyt Society (Cambridge: Cambridge University Press, 1959). Abbr. *EPVWI*

——— (ed.), *The Last Voyage of Drake & Hawkins*, Ser. 2, No 142, Hakluyt Society (Cambridge: Cambridge University Press, 1972). Abbr. *LVDH*

Barbour, Philip L. (ed.), *The Complete Works of Captain John Smith (1580–1631)*, 3 vols, The Institute of Early American History and Culture, Williamsburg (Chapel Hill: University of North Carolina Press, 1986)

Corbett, Julian S. (ed.), *Papers Relating to the Navy During the Spanish War, 1585–1587* (London: Navy Records Society, 1898). Rpt. 1987

———, *Drake and the Tudor Navy* (London: Longmans, Green & Co., 1898). Facs. rpt. (Aldershot: Temple Smith, Gower Publishing Co. Ltd, 1988)

Hakluyt, Richard (ed.), *The principal navigations, voyages, traffiques & discoveries of the English nation ... 1598–1600*, rpt. 12 vols, Extra Ser. 1–12, Hakluyt Society (Glasgow: James MacLehose and Sons, 1903–05). Facs. rpt. of 1903–05 edn (New York: Augustus M. Kelley Publishers, 1969). Abbr. *PN*

Harlow, V.T. (ed.), *Colonising expeditions to the West Indies and Guiana, 1623–1667*, Ser. 2, No 56 (London: Hakluyt Society, 1925)

———, *The Discoverie of the large, and bewtiful Empire of Guiana, by Sir Walter Raleigh* (London: Argonaut Press, 1928)

Keeler, Mary Frear (ed.), *Sir Francis Drake's West Indian voyage 1585–86*, Ser. 2, No 148 (London: Hakluyt Society, 1981). Abbr. *DWIV*

Latham, Agnes and Joyce Youings (eds), *The Letters of Sir Walter Ralegh* (Exeter: Exeter University Press, 1999)

Lorimer, Joyce (ed.), *English and Irish settlement on the River Amazon 1550–1646*, Ser. 2, No 171 (London: Hakluyt Society, 1989)

——— (ed.), *Sir Walter Ralegh's 'Discoverie of Guiana'*, Ser. 3, No 15, Hakluyt Society (Cambridge: Cambridge University Press, 2006). Abbr. *DG*

Purchas, Samuel (ed.), *Hakluytus Posthumus or Purchas his pilgrimes, contayning a history of the world in sea voyages and lande travells by Englishmen and others, by Samuel Purchas ... 1625*, rpt. 20 vols, Hakluyt Society, Extra Ser., Nos 12–33, Hakluyt Society (Glasgow: James MacLehose & Sons, 1905–07). Abbr. *PP*

Quinn, David Beers, Raleigh Ashlin Skelton and Alison Quinn, (eds), *The principall navigations, voiages and discoveries of the English nation, by Richard Hakluyt Imprinted at London, 1589*, 2 vols, Extra Ser., No 39 (London: Hakluyt Society, 1965). Abbr. *PLN*

Quinn, David Beers (ed.), *The voyages and colonising enterprises of Sir Humphrey Gilbert*, 2 vols, Ser. 2, Nos 83–4 (London: Hakluyt Society, 1940)

Schomburgk, Robert H. (ed.), *The discovery of the large, rich, and beautiful empire of Guiana*, Ser. 1, No 3 (London: Hakluyt Society, 1848). Abbr. *DEG*

Whitehead, Neil L. (ed.), *The Discoverie of the Large, Rich, and Bewtiful Empyre of Guiana* (Manchester: Manchester University Press, 1997)

Wright, Irene A. (ed.), *Documents concerning English voyages to the Spanish main, 1569–1580 I: Spanish documents selected from the archives of the Indies at Seville II: English accounts 'Sir Francis Drake revived', and others, reprinted*, Ser. 2, No 71 (London: Hakluyt Society, 1932). Abbr. *DE*

—— (ed. and trans.), *Further English Voyages to Spanish America 1583–1594. Documents from the archives of the Indies at Seville illustrating English voyages to the Caribbean, the Spanish Main, Florida, and Virginia*, Ser. 2, No 99 (London: Hakluyt Society, 1951 – issued for 1949). Abbr. *FE*

—— (ed.), *Spanish documents concerning English voyages to the Caribbean, 1527–1568, Selected from the archives of the Indies at Seville*, Ser. 2, No 62 (London: Hakluyt Society, 1929). Abbr. *SD*

Secondary Sources

Andrews, Kenneth R., *Drake's Voyages: A Re-Assessment of Their Place in Elizabethan Maritime Expansion* (London: Weidenfeld and Nicolson, 1967)

——, *Elizabethan Privateering: English Privateering during the Spanish War 1585–1603* (Cambridge: Cambridge University Press, 1964)

——, 'The Elizabethan Seaman', *Mariner's Mirror*, 68 (1982): 245–2

——, *Ships, Money and Politics: Seafaring and Naval Enterprise in the Reign of Charles I* (Cambridge: Cambridge University Press, 1991)

——, *The Spanish Caribbean: Trade and Plunder 1530–1630* (New Haven: Yale University Press, 1978)

——, *Trade, plunder and settlement: Maritime enterprise and the genesis of the British Empire, 1480–1630* (Cambridge: Cambridge University Press, 1984)

Appleby, John C., *Under the Bloody Flag: Pirates of the Tudor Age* (Stroud: The History Press, 2009)

Arróniz, Othón, *La batalla naval de San Juan de Ulúa 1568* (Xalapa, México: Biblioteca Universidad Veracruzana, 1982)

Aubrey, John, *Brief Lives*, ed. Oliver Lawson Dick (London: Secker and Warburg, 1949)

Black, J.B., *The Reign of Elizabeth, 1558–1603*, 1936, 2nd edn, Oxford History of England series (Oxford: Clarendon Press, 1969)

Cameron, Sarah and Ben Box (eds), *Caribbean Islands Handbook with the Bahamas* (Bath: Trade & Travel Publications Ltd, 1995)

Clarke, James, *Atlantic Pilot Atlas*, 4th edn (London: Adlard Coles Nautical, 2006)

Coote, Stephen, *A Play of Passion: The Life of Sir Walter Ralegh* (London: Macmillan, 1993)

Davies, Godfrey, *The Early Stuarts, 1603–1660*, 1937, 2nd edn, Oxford History of England series (Oxford: Clarendon Press, 1967)

Dean, J.S., 'Bearding the Spaniard: Captain John Oxnam in the Pacific', *The Northern Mariner/Le marin du nord*, 19, No 4 (October 2009): 379–92

Earle, Peter, *The Last Fight of the Revenge*, 1992 (London: Methuen, 2004)

Froude, James Anthony, *English Seamen in the Sixteenth Century* (New York: Charles Scribner's Sons, 1895)

Greenblatt, Stephen, *Sir Walter Ralegh: The Renaissance Man and His Roles* (New Haven: Yale University Press, 1973)

Hoffman, Paul E., *The Spanish Crown and the Defense of the Caribbean, 1535–1585: Precedent, Patrimonialism, and Royal Parsimony* (Baton Rouge: Louisiana State University Press, 1980)

Keevil, J.J., *Medicine and the Navy 1200–1900*, Vol. 1: 1200–1649 (Edinburgh and London: E. & S. Livingstone Ltd, 1957)

Kelsey, Harry, *Sir Francis Drake, The Queen's Pirate* (New Haven: Yale University Press, 1998)

———, *Sir John Hawkins, Queen Elizabeth's Slave Trader* (New Haven and London: Yale University Press, 2003)

Knight, R.J.B., *Guide to the Manuscripts in the National Maritime Museum*, Vol. 1, The Personal Collections, National Maritime Museum (London: Mansell Information/ Publishing Ltd, 1977)

Kotsch, Rear Admiral William J., *Weather for the Mariner*, 2nd edn (Annapolis: Naval Institute Press, 1977)

Lacey, Robert, *Sir Walter Ralegh* (London: Phoenix Press, 1973)

Lewis, Michael, *The Hawkins Dynasty, Three Generations of a Tudor Family* (London: George Allen and Unwin Ltd, 1969)

Lindsay-MacDougall, K.F., *A Guide to the Manuscripts at the National Maritime Museum* (London: National Maritime Museum, 1960)

Loades, David, *England's Maritime Empire: Seapower, Commerce and Policy, 1490–1690* (Harrow: Longman, 2000)

———, *The Tudor Navy, An administrative, political and military history* (Aldershot: Scolar Press, 1992)

Mackie, J.D., *The Earlier Tudors, 1485–1558*, 1952, Oxford History of England series (Oxford: Clarendon Press, 1972)

Mancall, Peter, *Hakluyt's Promise: An Elizabethan's Obsession for an English America* (New Haven: Yale University Press, 2007)

Marcus, G.J., *A Naval History of England*, Vol. 1: *The Formative Centuries* (London: Longmans, 1961)

McDermott, James, *Martin Frobisher, Elizabethan Privateer* (New Haven: Yale University Press, 2001)

Mello, Amilcar d'Avila de, 'Peter Carder's Strange Adventures Revealed', *The Mariner's Mirror*, 93, No 3 (August 2007): 261–8

Moorhouse, Geoffrey, *Great Harry's Navy, How Henry VIII Gave England Seapower* (London: Weidenfeld & Nicolson, 2005)

Naish, F.C. Prideaux, 'The Mystery of the Tonnage and Dimensions of the *Pelican–Golden Hind*', *The Mariner's Mirror*, 34, No 1 (January 1948): 42–5

Nelson, Arthur, *The Tudor Navy: The Ships, Men and Organisation 1485–1603* (London: Conway Maritime Press, division of Chrysalis Books Ltd, 2001)

Parry, J.H., *The Age of Reconaisssance* (London: Weidenfeld and Nicolson, Ltd, 1968)

——, *The Spanish Seaborne Empire*, 1966 (Berkeley: University of California Press, 1990)

Pennington, L.E. (ed.), *The Purchas Handbook*, 2 vols, Ser. 2, Nos 185, 186 (London: Hakluyt Society, 1997)

Parks, George Bruner, *Richard Hakluyt and the English Voyages* (New York: American Geographical Society, 1928)

Quinn, David Beers (ed.), *The Hakluyt Handbook*, 2 vols, Ser. 2, Nos 144–5 (London: Hakluyt Society, 1974)

——, *Raleigh and the British Empire*, 1947, new edn (London: The English Universities Press Ltd, 1962)

——, 'Sailors and the sea' in Allardyce Nicoll (ed.), *Shakespeare in his own Age* (Cambridge: Cambridge University Press, 1964), pp. 21–36

——, *Sir Francis Drake as Seen by His Contemporaries* (Providence: The John Carter Brown Library, 1966)

——, 'Some Spanish Reactions to Elizabethan Colonial Enterprises' in *Transactions of the Royal Historical Society*, Ser. 5, Vol. 1 (London: Office of the Royal Historical Society, 1951), pp. 1–23

Richmond, Admiral Sir Herbert, *The Navy as an Instrument of Policy, 1558–1727* (Cambridge: Cambridge University Press, 1952)

Robinson, Gregory, 'The Evidence about the *Golden Hind*', *The Mariner's Mirror*, Vol. 35, No 1 (January 1949): 62–3

Rodger, N.A.M., *The Command of the Ocean: A Naval History of Britain: 1649–1815*, Vol. 2, 2004 (London: Penguin, 2006)

——, *The Safeguard of the Sea: A Naval History of Britain. Vol. I: 660–1649*, 1997 (London: Penguin, 2004)

Rowse, A.L., *The Expansion of Elizabethan England* (London: Macmillan & Co. Ltd, 1955)

——, *Sir Richard Grenville of the Revenge: An Elizabethan Hero* (London: Jonathan Cape, 1937)

Rumeu de Armas, Antonio, *Los Viajes de John Hawkins a America (1562–1595)*, Publicaciones de la Escuela de Estudios Hispano-Americanos de Sevilla, 35, No 9 (Sevilla: Editorial Católica Española, S.A., 1947)

Spence, Richard T., *The Privateering Earl* (Stroud: Sutton Publishing, 1995)

Taylor, E.G.R., *The Original Writings and Correspondence of the Two Richard Hakluyts*, 2 vols (London: Hakluyt Society, 1935)

——, *Tudor Geography 1485–1583* (London: Methuen & Co. Ltd, 1930)

Trevelyan, Raleigh, *Sir Walter Raleigh* (London: Allen Lane, 2002)

Waters, David W., *The Art of Navigation in England in Elizabethan and Early Stuart Times*, 1958, 2nd edn, rev. Modern Maritime Classics, Reprint No 2 (Greenwich: National Maritime Museum, 1978)

——, *The Elizabethan Navy and the Armada of Spain*, Maritime Monographs and Reports No 17 (Greenwich: National Maritime Museum, 1975)

Williamson, G.C., *George, Third Earl of Cumberland (1558–1605) His Life and His Voyages, A Study from Original Documents* (Cambridge: Cambridge University Press, 1920)

Williamson, James A., *The Age of Drake*, 1938 (London: A. & C. Black, 1965)

——, *Hawkins of Plymouth*, 1949, 2nd edn (London: Adam & Charles Black, 1969)

——, *The Observations of Sir Richard Hawkins* (London: Argonaut Press, 1933)

Woodman, Richard, *Neptune's Trident: Spices and Slaves, 1500–1807, A* History of the British Merchant Navy, Vol. 1 (Stroud: The History Press, 2008)

Wright, Louis B. (ed.), *The Elizabethans' America: A Collection of Early Reports by Englishmen on the New World* (Cambridge, MA: Harvard University Press, 1966)

——, *Gold, Glory, and the Gospel* (New York: Atheneum, 1970)

Youings, Joyce, 'Did Raleigh's England Need Colonies?' in Joyce Youings (ed.), *Raleigh in Exeter 1985: Privateering and Colonisation in the reign of Elizabeth I*, Exeter Studies in History No 10 (Exeter: Exeter University Press, 1985)

ABOUT THE AUTHOR

James Seay Dean is emeritus professor, University of Wisconsin-Parkside, where he was Director of International Studies, Professor of English and Humanities and Adjunct Professor of Modern Languages (Portuguese) and Music, and where he taught maritime history and literature. He has been awarded a Senior Fulbright Fellowship to Brazil, numerous National Endowment for the Humanities grants and research fellowships in England at Harris Manchester College, Oxford; at Exeter and East Anglia universities; and in the United States at Wisconsin, Vanderbilt, Chicago, Illinois and Brown universities. He has served on the editorial board of *The American Neptune*, published numerous articles in nautical, literary and historical journals, and is the author of *Sailing a Square-Rigger* (1995) and two other books. He has crewed on the *Corwith Cramer* (Woods Hole, Massachusetts), a 140ft brigantine engaged in oceanographic research throughout the Caribbean. For twelve years he served as Sailing Master, teaching navigation, weather and ship-handling aboard barquentines in the Atlantic, Mediterranean and Caribbean. He has made several transatlantic passages, recently as first mate and navigator on a 43ft sloop from the Caribbean to England. In the same capacity, he has sailed from England to Gibraltar and in the Mediterranean and Adriatic seas. As captain of a 37ft cutter, he has sailed the Pacific coast of Canada. His own yacht is a small 40-year-old Westerly sloop.

INDEX